HEMINGWAY'S NICK ADAMS

HEMINGWAY'S NICK ADAMS

Joseph M. Flora

Louisiana State University Press

Baton Rouge and London

Copyright © 1982 by Louisiana State University Press
All rights reserved
Manufactured in the United States of America
Design: Patricia Douglas Crowder
Typeface: Palatino
Composition: G&S Typesetters, Inc.
Printing and binding: Thomson Shore, Inc.

Library of Congress Cataloging in Publication Data
Flora, Joseph M.
   Hemingway's Nick Adams.
   Includes index.
   1. Hemingway, Ernest, 1899–1961—Criticism and interpreta-
tion.   2. Hemingway, Ernest, 1899–1961—Characters—Nick
Adams. I. Title.
PS3515.E37Z594   813'.52   81-14284
ISBN 0-8071-0993-2   AACR2

for my sons
Ronald, Stephen, Peter, David

Contents

Maps

Acknowledgments

I am grateful to many of my colleagues at the University of North Carolina at Chapel Hill for much good talk about Hemingway. For the present study, I wish to acknowledge the encouragement of C. Hugh Holman, to whom I first described my plan. As chairman of the Department of English, James R. Gaskin gave valued support. C. Townsend Ludington shared with me the Hemingway–Dos Passos correspondence, a correspondence written largely during the years Hemingway was writing of Nick. Weldon Thornton, Louis D. Rubin, Jr., Joseph Blotner, and Christine Lape Flora gave careful readings of the manuscript and made valuable suggestions. Alan Clugston, Rebekah F. Kirby, Melissa Marion, and Thomas Warburton, Jr., provided spirited assistance when I sought their help on special problems. Jo Gibson has ably and cheerfully provided excellent secretarial assistance, for this project and for others. For all I feel a deep sense of appreciation.

I am indebted to Professor James Shaw of the University of Michigan, with whom I explored much of the Hemingway country near Little Traverse Bay. And I remember my own initiation into the study of Hemingway with able and inspiring teachers at the University of Michigan; I have, in part, relived those good hours in further exploration of Hemingway with my own students. I am also grateful for advice and encouragement from the staff at Louisiana State University Press; I especially wish to thank Martha L. Hall, my editor, for her cooperation and assistance.

A Kenan Research Leave enabled me to complete the bulk of the writing, and I am happy to acknowledge that favor.

A Nick Adams Chronology

The stories and fragments in the righthand column do not have the authority of the stories in the lefthand column since Hemingway never gave his approval to their publication. But the reader can usually tell about where they would have come in Nick's life.

"Three Shots"

"Indian Camp"
"The Doctor and the Doctor's Wife"

"The Indians Moved Away"

"Ten Indians"
"The End of Something"
"The Three Day Blow"
"The Light of the World"
"The Battler"
"The Killers"

"The Last Good Country"
"Crossing the Mississippi"
"Night Before Landing"

Chapter VI of *In Our Time*: "Nick sat against the wall . . ."
"Now I Lay Me"
"A Way You'll Never Be"
"In Another Country"

"Summer People"
"Wedding Day"

"Cross-Country Snow"
"Big Two-Hearted River"

"On Writing"

"An Alpine Idyll"
"A Day's Wait"
"Wine of Wyoming"
"Fathers and Sons"

I was not a hawk although I might seem a hawk to those who had never hunted . . .

"In Another Country"

You should have been an Indian, he thought. It would have saved you a lot of trouble.

"The Last Good Country"

HEMINGWAY'S NICK ADAMS

Introduction

In the years since Hemingway's death in 1961 there have been many attempts to adjust the critical evaluation of his work, to place him where he more precisely belongs— sometimes, it seems, to place as low an evaluation on him as the critics dare.[1] Hemingway will survive any number of posthumous devaluations: his talent is major. It is and will be impossible to describe twentieth-century American fiction without giving him extended coverage.

The Hemingway character most secure during the devaluation of Hemingway was Nick Adams. Nick is the central character of *In Our Time* (1925), the first major Hemingway publication, fifteen short stories with vignettes serving as interchapters. Nick stories also appear in two of Hemingway's short story collections, *Men Without Women* (1927) and *Winner Take Nothing* (1933). As if to prove Nick's importance, in 1962 Hollywood made a film based on the Nick Adams stories, *Hemingway's Adventures of a Young Man*. The only other work by Hemingway to be made into a movie in the 1960s was a 1964 remake of "The Killers," perhaps the most famous of all Nick stories. Philip Young had stressed the importance of Nick Adams to Hemingway's work several years before Hemingway's death in his *Ernest Hemingway*

1. As reported in the August, 1977, issue of *Esquire*, LXXXVIII, 71–81, selected living writers were asked to identify those twentieth-century writers whose reputations were most inflated. The piece was called "American Writers: Who's Up, Who's Down?" It was obvious that Hemingway was down.

(1952), and Young found no reason to change that position in *Ernest Hemingway: A Reconsideration* (1962). Hemingway gave us other memorable portraits, but it is safe to say that no other character in his fiction is as important as Nick. And none has more consistently caught the imagination of Hemingway's readers.

One reason for the original attraction to Nick was fascination with the life of Ernest Hemingway, for Nick Adams was obviously autobiographical. So were most of Hemingway's other protagonists, but Nick was special in several ways. He had a precise origin and a precise background, usually given only obliquely to such heroes as Jake Barnes and Frederic Henry. Hemingway discovered Nick early in his career and kept returning to him. Although Nick seemed to be a means for Hemingway to deal with a part of his experience, perhaps to get rid of it—one function of writing as Nick would eventually explain—beyond that he was a means to create a work of art, something to be judged as art and distinct from his life.

Hemingway's attitude toward the autobiographical was curious. Although he depended in his fiction on the events of his life as much as did any writer of his time, Hemingway did not ever feel the need for writing an autobiography. He was hardly inclined towards writing a factual analysis of his life such as H. G. Wells's *Experiment in Autobiography*. When Hemingway's friend F. Scott Fitzgerald became confessional in such essays as "The Crack-up," Hemingway was embarrassed for him. Nor was biography a genre he much liked—least of all for himself. He wanted no biography of himself while he was alive and preferred that there be none until he had been dead a hundred years.[2] He did not cooperate with Charles Fenton when Fenton started his pioneering work, *The Apprenticeship of Ernest Hemingway* (1954), nor with Philip Young when he began to explore his work and life. Hemingway wanted no editions of his letters. Even though as a public figure Hemingway had given interviews and had

2. Carlos Baker, *Ernest Hemingway: A Life Story* (New York: Charles Scribner's Sons, 1969), vii.

written in his own voice about certain aspects of his life and values, he wanted to be kept from the curious. Usually he regretted surrendering to the autobiographical impulse. And the spare and moving recollections of the posthumous *A Moveable Feast* (1964) led many readers to conclude that Hemingway was wise to harbor no large ambitions for autobiography, for they found his portraits of his associates not only marred by malice but misleading in their analysis of literary debts. Hemingway's declared purpose in *Green Hills of Africa* (1935) was to test whether accurate presentation of his own experience as his own experience could "compete with a work of the imagination."[3] The negative verdict was not long in coming. Critics of Hemingway were, and are, in general agreement with Edmund Wilson that the public Hemingway "is certainly the worst-invented character to be found in the author's work."[4]

Although Hemingway was not as discreet as Nathaniel Hawthorne, his instinct was close to that which Hawthorne espoused in "The Custom-House" preface to *The Scarlet Letter*. Hawthorne found it permissible to "prate of the circumstances that lie around us, and even of ourselves" as long as the writer "keep the inmost Me behind its veil."[5] Hawthorne recognized that the close reader of his fiction would come closer to understanding him than would most of his schoolmates and lifemates.

What was best in Ernest Hemingway emerged not in his pronouncements about himself but in the character of Nick Adams, a character who shared with his creator a background and a history to a greater extent that any other character in his fiction. Although Hemingway often protested

3. Ernest Hemingway, "Foreword," *Green Hills of Africa* (New York: Charles Scribner's Sons, 1935).
4. Edmund Wilson, "Hemingway: Gauge of Morale," *The Wound and the Bow: Seven Studies in Literature* (New York: Farrar Straus Giroux, 1978), 184. Wilson's essay first appeared as "Ernest Hemingway: Bourdon Gauge of Morale," *Atlantic*, CLXIV (July, 1939), 36–46. *The Wound and the Bow* was first published in 1941 by Houghton Mifflin.
5. Nathaniel Hawthorne, "The Custom-House," *The Scarlet Letter* (Boston: Houghton Mifflin, 1960), 5–6.

biographical readings of the Nick Adams stories, he also acknowledged in various ways the intimate connection: it is not surprising that one of Nick's most private sobriquets, Wemedge, was Hemingway's nickname before it was Nick's. In the Nick Adams stories Hemingway defined key aspects of his personality more revealingly than he ever did in direct statements about his own life.

Nick Adams is special not only among Hemingway's heroes, but in American literature. Our interest in Nick transcends our interest in Hemingway's life. Nick is a character of short stories but nevertheless excites the imagination as do the heroes and heroines of our greatest novels. He lives with the likes of Huck Finn (there was great aptness in Young's associating the two) and only a few others. E. M. Forster in *Aspects of the Novel* declares that the successful rendering of people is the most important requisite for the novelist, and the general reader and a good many novelists would agree with Forster. Furthermore, Forster says that the great character in a novel has the tendency to bounce into life and will not stay put between the covers of a book. Nick Adams has that capacity to bounce into life. Readers familiar with Hemingway's life and works and who visit his Michigan country will probably be imagining Nick's adventures rather than Hemingway's. The stories will come to the memory as one half-expects to see Nick on a summer's day emerge from the water of Walloon Lake. Although the Hemingway cottage on Walloon Lake is a designated national historic site, one does not visit it as a shrine. One sees instead a spot that recalls a place in a story, and the story is allowed to play again in the imagination. It is not academics only who go seeking out Nick's places—although to be sure the academics have. Thousands of nonacademics have responded to Hemingway's vivid rendering of place and the rendering of Nick's adventures. According to *Michigan Living: Motor News*, the official publication of the Automobile Club of Michigan, a handful of the Hemingway faithful shows up each summer in the upper peninsula of Michigan

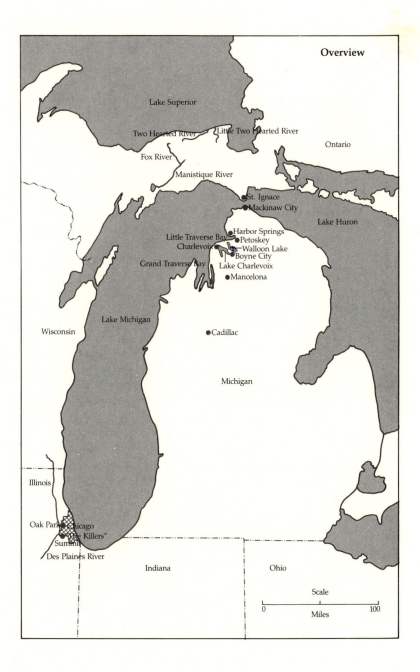

Overview

Lake Superior

Two Hearted River   Little Two Hearted River

Ontario

Fox River

Manistique River

St. Ignace

Mackinaw City

Lake Huron

Harbor Springs

Little Traverse Bay   Petoskey

Charlevoix   Walloon Lake

Boyne City

Grand Traverse Bay   Lake Charlevoix

Mancelona

Lake Michigan

Wisconsin

Cadillac

Michigan

Illinois

Oak Park   Chicago
"The Killers"
Summit
Des Plaines River

Indiana   Ohio

Scale

0   100

Miles

looking for the Big Two-Hearted River.[6] Although there is a Two-Hearted River and a Little Two-Hearted River in upper Michigan, there is no Big Two-Hearted River. As Sheridan Baker, an academic who made the trip, has demonstrated, Hemingway's river is based on the Fox, one of the upper peninsula's best brook trout streams.[7] It is still there, and so is Seney. It is possible to go walking, camping, and fishing where Nick Adams once did, and that campers and fishers still seek to trace Nick's steps is evidence of the especially vivid quality of the fictional personality.

An important literary ancestor for Nick Adams is Sherwood Anderson's George Willard—the young man who grows up in Winesburg, Ohio, learns what is important about Winesburg and then leaves the town, eventually, the reader is certain, to write about it. *Winesburg, Ohio* (1919) is a collection of short fiction that is more than a collection, suggesting in its cumulative force the novel. However, the reality of George is not the most engrossing aspect of the book. Anderson, and the reader after him, is more interested in the citizens of Winesburg who shaped George than in George himself. Winesburg, rather than George, emerges clearest and stays longest in the reader's memory. The reading of *Winesburg, Ohio* was doubtless one of the most significant explorations of Hemingway's apprenticeship period. He could sense the possibilities for shaping stories on a character, particularly an autobiographical character, into something like a novel. But he wanted a hero who would be more important than Anderson's and who would help give the book he envisioned a more definite shape than *Winesburg* had. Although *In Our Time* reached out in more directions than did *Winesburg*, the reappearing character was unforgettable. And Hemingway put greater demands on the reader

6. Leland Day, "Meanwhile, Back at the 'Big Two-Hearted River,'" *Michigan Living: Motor News*, LX (August, 1977), 19, 35, 38.

7. Sheridan Baker, "Hemingway's Two-Hearted River," *Michigan Alumni Quarterly Review*, LXV (Winter, 1959), 142–49. Baker's essay, the best essay on this famous Nick story, has been reprinted in Jackson J. Benson (ed.), *The Short Stories of Ernest Hemingway: Critical Essays* (Durham: Duke University Press, 1975), 150–59.

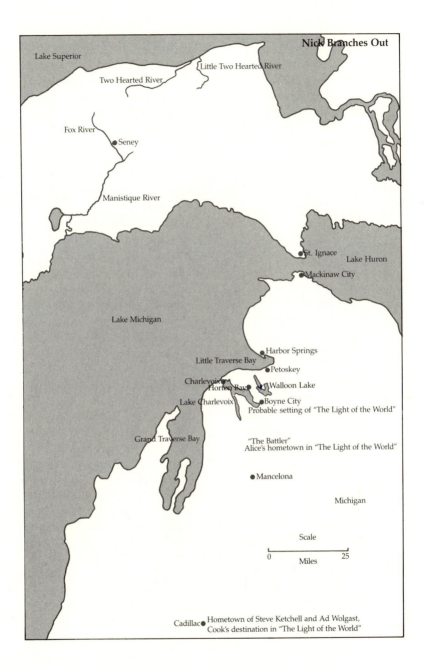

Lake Superior

Little Two Hearted River

Two Hearted River

Fox River

●Seney

Manistique River

●St. Ignace

Lake Huron

●Mackinaw City

Lake Michigan

●Harbor Springs

Little Traverse Bay

●Petoskey

Charlevoix●

Horton Bay● ●Walloon Lake

Lake Charlevoix

●Boyne City

Probable setting of "The Light of the World"

"The Battler"

Alice's hometown in "The Light of the World"

Grand Traverse Bay

●Mancelona

Michigan

Scale

0   25

Miles

Cadillac● Hometown of Steve Ketchell and Ad Wolgast,

Cook's destination in "The Light of the World"

of *In Our Time* than Anderson had on the reader of *Winesburg*. Hemingway's suggestion of the fragmentary through his interchapters challenged his reader to seek for connections between the stories, to see how Nick was changing and where those changes would lead him.

In a review of *In Our Time* D. H. Lawrence called the book "a fragmentary novel," declaring that it is really about one man. He concluded that the pieces of *In Our Time* are "enough to create the man and all his history: we need know no more."[8] Lawrence had said some important things about the book, and about Nick's importance to it, but Hemingway did not see Nick's story as finished in the way that Lawrence did. It is true that with "Big Two-Hearted River" Hemingway had brought Nick to a significant moment, to a turning point—as I will later explore. But that turning point was significant for Ernest Hemingway, too; he would find Nick useful in the future for defining issues for himself—ideally the exploration would lead to publication. But apparently a story might serve a function for him—as the first (in all probability) Nick story, "Summer People," did—and Hemingway would feel no compulsion to publish. When *In Our Time* was first published, Hemingway had written more about Nick than was between the covers of the book. That he might write of Nick again would seem likely to anyone who could know the whole of Hemingway's apprenticeship. Nick, for Hemingway, was more than a type— as Lawrence described him—and the need to fill in the picture of Nick's career became something of a constant for Hemingway. He had many stories he wanted to tell about Nick, and he later did so. *In Our Time* contains fewer than half of the Nick stories eventually published.

Sherwood Anderson had invented a new form in creating through linking short stories a *Bildungsroman* (or a novel about a young man's education). F. Scott Fitzgerald had An-

8. D. H. Lawrence, review of *In Our Time*, in Robert P. Weeks (ed.), *Hemingway: A Collection of Critical Essays* (Englewood Cliffs, N.J.: Prentice-Hall, 1962), 93–94. The review first appeared in *Calendar of Modern Letters*, IV (April, 1927).

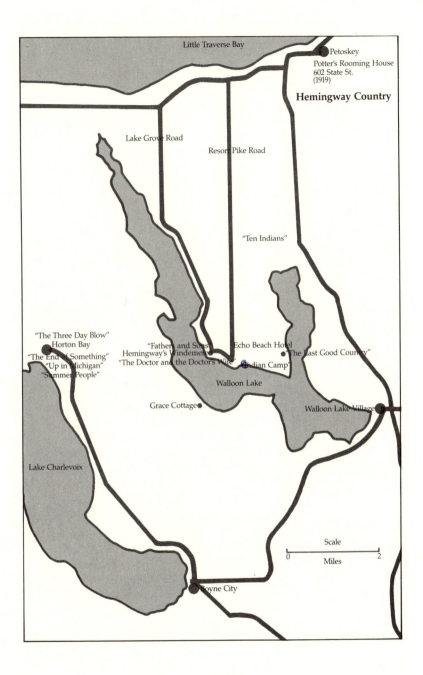

Little Traverse Bay

Petoskey
Potter's Rooming House
602 State St.
(1919)

Hemingway Country

Lake Grove Road

Resort Pike Road

"Ten Indians"

"The Three Day Blow"
Horton Bay
"The End of Something"
"Up in Michigan"
"Summer People"

"Fathers and Sons"
Hemingway's Windemere
"The Doctor and the Doctor's Wife"

Echo Beach Hotel

"The Last Good Country"

Indian Camp

Walloon Lake

Grace Cottage

Walloon Lake Village

Lake Charlevoix

Scale
0   2
Miles

Boyne City

derson's lead as well as the example of *In Our Time* when in 1928 he started writing a series of short stories based on his boyhood and young manhood. (Hemingway's debt to Fitzgerald was considerable, but Fitzgerald also benefited from Hemingway's work). By April 27, 1929, he had published in the *Saturday Evening Post* eight such stories about one Basil Duke Lee. Fitzgerald told Maxwell Perkins that he had thought of them as a "light" novel, and Perkins, who liked the stories, encouraged Fitzgerald to think in those terms. Part of the "novel" would concentrate on Basil's female counterpart, Josephine Perry. Fitzgerald planned to write a story bringing Basil and Josephine together. But despite the encouragement from Perkins, Fitzgerald never did so, and he abandoned plans for a Basil and Josephine "novel."[9] Many years later two academicians felt that Fitzgerald's reasons for objecting to the publication of the stories as a novel no longer obtained and so convinced Charles Scribner's Sons. Now all of the stories are conveniently together as *The Basil and Josephine Stories* (1973). Editors Jackson R. Bryer and John Kuehl went sensibly about their business and arranged the stories chronologically, Basil first and Josephine second.

The history is of interest here because of its place in the history of the new genre of linking stories, but for other reasons as well. Basil, though an interesting character, has never captured the popular imagination in the way Gatsby has, or even approached Nick Adams for vitality. Of course, Fitzgerald had more modest goals for him. Basil is a piece of nostalgia that Fitzgerald saw as representative of a class in a clearly defined period. As he intended, there was a great deal of Tarkington about the scheme.

The year before Scribner's published *The Basil and Josephine Stories* they had brought out *The Nick Adams Stories*, but with considerably more fanfare and excitement. So far as we know, Hemingway had never envisioned a book of Nick

9. See Introduction, F. Scott Fitzgerald, *The Basil and Josephine Stories*, ed. Jackson Bryer and John Kuehl (New York: Charles Scribner's Son's, 1973), vii–xxvi.

Adams stories. It could not be, like the Fitzgerald book, a modest scholarly addition to an established writer's claims on our attention. In the first place, Nick Adams was one of Hemingway's characters most fascinating to his readers. Basil Duke Lee was not nearly as well known, nor was he as essential a character to Fitzgerald's entire work as Nick was to Hemingway's. Fitzgerald had studied Basil in a well-defined era for a restricted period; arranging the stories chronologically gave Bryer and Kuehl no great difficulties. Hemingway, on the other hand, had written about his protagonist's life from early boyhood into middle age. Even though many of the stories share a locale in Michigan's northern lower peninsula, Nick became a wanderer, went to war, and lived in Europe before making his adult way back to a base somewhere on his native side of the Atlantic. The chronology of the Nick stories, as they had come to Hemingway's readers through three volumes, was no neat progression.

Moreover, there was sometimes doubt about whether a given story actually was about Nick. Critics had more or less agreed that the young narrator of "The Light of the World" is Nick Adams, but there are other Hemingway stories with an unnamed narrator whom some critics have thought Nick Adams, but other critics have not.[10] The latter critics have wanted to see each story only in its own terms. If Nick is not named, they argue, why bring him in? Such critics underplay the fact that Hemingway, with more than a touch of the poet, had labored mightily to make his first major book, *In Our Time*, function as a complex unity. They ignore his careful placement of the short stories in his other books. Since there was not even agreement about which were Nick

10. Many Hemingway scholars were probably surprised to have Barbara Sanders fault critics of "Cross-Country Snow" for assuming that the Nick of the story is Nick Adams. Sanders says that the Nick of the story "may or may not be the same Nick" found in the "so-called Nick Adams Stories." She asks, "Couldn't different people in different stories share the same name?" See her "Linguistic Analysis of 'Cross-Country Snow,'" *Hemingway's Experiments in Structure and Style, Linguistics in Literature*, I (Spring, 1976), 43–52.

Adams stories, any editor or critic who might attempt to do
with the Nick Adams stories what Bryer and Kuehl had
done with Fitzgerald's Basil and Josephine stories was bound
to run into some difficulty.

As early as 1947 Philip Young (who subsequently became
one of the most influential Hemingway critics) suggested to
Scribner's that readers would benefit from a single volume of
all the Nick Adams stories arranged chronologically, although when Young first conceived of such a book, Hemingway had not finished writing about Nick (to be sure, Young
could not know this). Scribner's replied that Hemingway
would probably not like the project, and it lay dormant for
many years. After Hemingway's death, a surprising amount
of unpublished Nick material was discovered. There was a
completed short story, fragments of other works, and a long
part of a Nick novel—an abundance that indicates how profoundly useful Nick had been to Hemingway both as he
developed his craft and as he dealt with difficult aspects of
existence. The consensus at Scribner's was that the public
should have all of the Nick material. Appropriately, the publisher looked to Philip Young for assistance in the formation
of a book. Young would now have additional problems as
well as those he would have encountered had his original
proposal been accepted. He may even have wondered if it
was really wise to publish unfinished work along with some
of the best American short stories.

The actual editing of the new material (mainly, Young
says, judicious cutting of the novel) was done at Scribner's.
Young wrote a long preface for the book but then set it aside
and replaced it with a brief preface as perhaps more appropriate for the general reader.[11] Young arranged the stories
chronologically, as he saw the chronology. But, curiously,
even by his own reckoning, Young did not include all the
Nick stories. He does not believe Nick is an important char-

11. The longer introduction was published as " 'Big World Out There':
The Nick Adams Stories" in *Novel: A Forum for Fiction*, VI (Fall, 1972), 5–19. It
was reprinted in Benson (ed.), *The Short Stories of Ernest Hemingway*, 29–45.

acter in "A Day's Wait" and so omits the story. There were at least 107 reviews of the book, only one pleasing to Young.[12] At a 1973 conference on Hemingway, Young reported on his own wounds that resulted from the experience.[13] Hemingway probably would not care much for the reviews either—and most certainly he would not care for the book, for it rearranged the Nick stories and put more emphasis on Hemingway's life than on his artistry.

Young's guiding principle of arranging the stories according to the chronology of Ernest Hemingway was unsettling for some readers. The Nick that came across to me in Young's book was not entirely the Nick that I had thought Hemingway had created. In Hemingway's arrangement of *In Our Time* I read "The End of Something" and "The Three Day Blow" well before I read "Big Two-Hearted River." Young reversed the order indicating that the two Marjorie stories were postwar and should thus follow "Big Two-Hearted River." I had to think about that. I granted the autobiographical aspects of Nick, but I could not equate him entirely with Hemingway. Some critics claimed it was profitable to read the stories as Young had arranged them, for they could then be read as a psychological biography of Hemingway. But I think that the stories can be read in another order, closer to Nick's own biography, and still as a psychological biography of Hemingway. I had to reaffirm my prime obligation to Nick. He *is* a character with a fictional life that is his, distinct from Hemingway's, and I feel obligated to trust Hemingway's directions for seeing Nick. Flannery O'Connor's statement about use of autobiography puts the emphasis where it belongs: "Anyway, you have to look at a novel or a story as a novel or a story; as saying something

12. The review pleasing to Young was that of Louis D. Rubin, Jr., published in the Washington *Star*, April 23, 1972, Sec. C, p. 6. Rubin's piece is in Robert O. Stephens (ed.), *Ernest Hemingway: The Critical Reception* (New York: Burt Franklin, 1977), 482–84.

13. Philip Young, "Posthumous Hemingway, and Nicholas Adams," in Richard Astro and Jackson J. Benson (eds.), *Hemingway in Our Time* (Corvallis: Oregon State University Press, 1974), 13–23.

about life colored by the writer, not about the writer colored by life."[14]

My idea for this study grew out of my response to *The Nick Adams Stories*, although my goal is far from being mere repudiation of Young's work. Indeed, I have benefited greatly from his work. I conceived of this study, rather, as giving assent to Young's claim that Nick Adams is the most important single character in Hemingway. To that end my study treats *all* of the Nick stories; it examines them as stories, but in the light of Hemingway's placement of them and in their relationship to each other. It seemed to me useful to have a critical book concerned with all of the stories, including "A Day's Wait" and one other first person story that strongly suggests Nick, "Wine of Wyoming." There has been much able criticism (and some less able) on many of these stories, but others of them have received only slight attention. Often the criticism is brief since the authors have the whole body of Hemingway's work to cover, and they must get to the novels. These critics do not agree, of course. I have sought to identify areas of disagreement without turning my study into an encyclopedia of criticism. It has been my intention to keep the focus on Nick Adams and his experience and the artistry of the work that reveals him.

Even though Young attempted to arrange the Nick stories following Hemingway's chronology (at the end of his "Preface" to *The Nick Adams Stories*, Young sends the reader to four "Biographical Studies" but suggests no criticism), he had also to follow the sense of the fiction, for some of the stories are not based on an event in Hemingway's life—"Indian Camp," for one example, "The Killers" for another.[15] My discussion also depends on a chronological sense of

14. Flannery O'Connor, *The Habit of Being*. Letters edited and with an Introduction by Sally Fitzgerald. (New York: Farrar, Straus, Giroux, 1979), 158.

15. The four studies Young recommends are Carlos Baker, *Ernest Hemingway: A Life Story*; Leicester Hemingway, *My Brother, Ernest Hemingway* (New York: World, 1962); Constance Cappel Montgomery, *Hemingway in Michigan* (New York: Fleet Press Corporation, 1966); and Marcelline Hemingway Sanford, *At the Hemingways: A Family Portrait* (Boston: Little, Brown,

Nick's life, although for thematic reasons I depart somewhat from the chronological pattern, most obviously by considering "The Last Good Country" in my final chapter. I first consider Nick as a young boy, then as an adolescent, then as a soldier in war, and then as a soldier recently returned from war. In Chapter Five I study Nick as a married writer, then view him as a writer and father. I consider "The Last Good Country" by itself in my final chapter, for it presents special problems. It was Hemingway's last piece of writing on Nick (for that reason, we may get a greater feeling for Hemingway's emotional life by considering it last) and also his longest. It is accomplished enough, although unfinished, to deserve more than passing reference. But the Nick of that work in progress does not fit easily into a chronological reading of the stories because he is not sufficiently consistent with the Nick of the other stories. He is too brooding, too victimized. Furthermore, it should be kept in mind that Hemingway was viewing this Nick differently—he was portraying him as a character in a novel, and no reader need have any previous knowledge about Nick. With the short stories, Hemingway expected that his readers would remember Nick from previous units, and he built upon what he had achieved in the earlier work. Throughout my study, I have found the other fragments of most interest as they relate to the themes of the finished stories, but they are sometimes also of interest as they reveal Hemingway in the struggles of composition.[16]

1962). Since the publication of these studies, another Hemingway sister, Ernest's favorite, has also written a book about her brother. See Madeline Hemingway Miller, *Ernie: Hemingway's Sister Remembers* (New York: Crown, 1975). Madeline (known as Sunny) is the biographical counterpart to the Littless of "The Last Good Country."

16. John R. Cooley's 1980 essay on Nick Adams shows both the danger of treating the fragmentary material as finished stories and the danger of reading Young's book as a Nick novel. Attempting to trace the notion of the "good place" in Young's chronology as Nick's and climaxes his charting of Nick's progress by treating "On Writing" as a finished story rather than as material deleted from "Big Two-Hearted River." See Cooley's "Nick Adams and 'The Good Place,'" *Southern Humanities Review*, XIV (Winter, 1980), 57–68.

Most of the Nick Adams stories are fairly short. The average reader could read through them all—including the eight new pieces in *The Nick Adams Stories*—in a few hours, but he would miss a lot. Hemingway meant to engage his reader deeply with these stories; he sought active reading. The reader is challenged to probe, to discover how the stories relate to each other—and to other units of the books in which Hemingway placed the stories. The reader of this book will want to refer to both *The Nick Adams Stories*, the only place to find the new Nick material, and to *In Our Time, Men Without Women,* and *Winner Take Nothing.*[17] To assist the reader, I have given a page reference in the body of the text for quoted passages, first to the stories in the volume by Hemingway (*IOT, MWW, WTN*) and then to *The Nick Adams Stories* (*NAS*). Since Young did not inlcude "A Day's Wait" or "Wine of Wyoming" in *The Nick Adams Stories*, there will be only the single reference—to *Winner Take Nothing*—for those stories.

Although geographical names appear frequently in the Nick Adams stories, most readers will be unfamiliar with this geography. I have provided the reader with several

17. *In Our Time* (New York: Charles Scribner's Sons, 1925; rev., 1930); *Men Without Women* (New York: Charles Scribner's Sons, 1927, 1955); *Winner Take Nothing* (New York: Charles Scribner's Sons, 1933, 1961). Readers using *The Fifth Column and the First Forty-Nine Stories* (New York: Charles Scribner's Sons, 1938) or *The Short Stories of Ernest Hemingway* (New York: Charles Scribner's Sons, 1954) will find that both collections retain the ordering of the original volumes, and they will have little difficulty finding the quoted passages. Hemingway's retention of the order in *In Our Time, Men Without Women,* and *Winner Take Nothing* emphasizes the importance of the ordering to him. As a young writer, Hemingway had to fight vigorously to retain his ordering of the stories for *In Our Time.* Neither *Men Without Women* nor *Winner Take Nothing* is the "near novel" that *In Our Time* is, and in comparison, Hemingway's approach to the ordering seems more casual. But finally arrangement of the stories was his. After having taken a somewhat indifferent approach to the ordering of *Men Without Women,* Hemingway made clear to Maxwell Perkins that the author would be assuming this responsibility. On May 27, 1927, he wrote Perkins: "I can arrange their order in the galleys." See *Ernest Hemingway: Selected Letters, 1917–1961,* ed. Carlos Baker (New York: Charles Scribner's Sons, 1981), 252. The final arrangement is quite different from the tentative order Hemingway had presented Perkins on May 4, 1927. See *Selected Letters,* 250.

maps that will help familiarize him with the geography. Most of the stories are set in a small area off Michigan's Little Traverse Bay; only one story takes place in the upper peninsula. I have also included a map locating the Summit of "The Killers" and Oak Park, Hemingway's birthplace. This map will also give readers a sense of the considerable effort it took in the early years of the century to get from Oak Park to Walloon Lake. As Carlos Baker describes the journey, the Hemingways typically traveled from Oak Park to Chicago by train, then by steamer up Lake Michigan to Harbor Springs on Little Traverse Bay, then by train to Petoskey, and then by another train to Walloon Lake (called Bear Lake when the Hemingways first made the trip), finally by rowboat across to Windemere, the Hemingway cottage. So it must have been with the Adamses.

Chapter One
The Boy

The chronicle of Nick Adams is the account of a sensitive boy's learning to accept his own and the world's limitations. Eventually, he becomes a writer who then makes the process of definition the ultimate subject of his art.

Nick Adams grew up with many advantages in the early years of the twentieth century. His father was a doctor who practiced near Chicago, but a medical practice and the role of respected citizen were not enough to satisfy him. A hunter and a fisherman, and wanting to share the pleasures of the outdoors with his son, he provided his family with a summer cottage on a beautiful lake near Little Traverse Bay in northern Michigan. The doctor himself spent as much time in this removed country as he could. Nick, his mother, and his siblings were able to spend their entire summers in the north, which Nick, like his father, preferred to the life of the city or suburb.

Eventually the call of the twentieth century took Nick away from the more elemental experiences of the northern woods—and from a respectable surburbia that Hemingway never even bothered to portray. World War I changed many things and many lives, including Nick's. He was seriously wounded in the war, and his close brush with death put a sharp focus on all of the self-doubts he had ever had. Shocked by what he had seen and what had happened to him, he wondered if he would ever function in "normal" life. In a hard-fought struggle he came to accept himself. His

ability to accept complexity was especially tested in his
views toward women and marriage. He married and had a
son, and through that son, Hemingway takes the reader
close to the themes Nick had pondered as a young boy in
the Michigan woods.

The stories that reveal Nick Adams to us are the opposite
of a case study. To know Nick Adams is to explore with him,
and there is more poetry than naturalism in Hemingway's
treatment. For instance, it is only in the fifth Nick Adams
story of *In Our Time* that the reader learns Nick's last name.
The revelation comes appropriately there, for "The Battler"
is the first story to show Nick out on his own. Hemingway
had given Nick the name *Adams* in the "first" Nick story he
ever wrote, "Summer People," but the story remained unpublished during Hemingway's life. Only belatedly did
Adams get into *In Our Time*, for "The Battler" was the last
story of that book to be written, and it is the only story of
the book to use *Adams*. The revelation of Nick's last name
comes in dialogue when a hobo asks him to identify himself.
In a sense one's last name is more essentially one's own than
the first name. It ties one up with a tradition, with one's
roots. A first name is more accidental. It might be a parent's
whim, a popular name at the moment, or an attempt by the
parent to mold the child's destiny—as the name *Ernest* was
for the Pontifexes of Samuel Butler's *The Way of All Flesh*. As
Nick goes out on his own, he goes as an Adams. As the
young man moves toward greater control of his own life, his
family name takes on increasing importance and becomes
more his label.

Hemingway could not have given Nick a last name that
would be more resonant. *Adams* is one of the most significant of American family names. To be an Adams was a very
complex fate, as *The Education of Henry Adams*, published in
1907, had demonstrated. Henry Adams' autobiography emphasized the burden of the inheritance and struck a hauntingly modern note in its description of Henry's struggle to fit
into the nineteenth century. Nick Adam's problem is not

very different. Like Henry Adams, he often seems to be caught between two centuries. The reader of "The Battler," upon learning Nick's last name, might be struck that Henry Adams is also the name of Nick's father. There is an immense appropriateness about that, too, for Dr. Adams also wavers between two worlds. Whereas the whole of Chapter I of *The Education of Henry Adams* might be a good prologue to the Nick stories, one paragraph from that chapter could also describe the tension that belongs to both Nick and his father as it had to the earlier Henry Adams:

> Winter and summer, then, were two hostile lives, and bred two separate natures. Winter was always the effort to live; summer was tropical license. Whether the children rolled in the grass, or waded in the brook, or swam in the salt ocean, or sailed in the bay, or fished for smelts in the creeks, or netted minnows in the salt-marshes, or took to the pine-woods and the granite quarries, or chased muskrats and hunted snapping-turtles in the swamps, or mushrooms or nuts on the autumn hills, summer and country were always sensual living, while winter was always compulsory learning. Summer was the multiplicity of nature; winter was school.[1]

Of course, *Adams* is also close to *Adam*, the primal man. To be sure we often think of Hemingway's Nick in this way. We feel his innocence— and we anticipate his fall. *Nick* is an appropriate name for a boy of the woods and the world. It conveys a certain adventurous spirit, especially since it is a common designation for the devil, usually as Old Nick. The name had been used for its satanic dimension in a popular novel of the nineteenth century, Robert M. Bird's *Nick of the Woods* (1837). Bird's novel sought to create a sense of terror as it showed a civilized man being transformed into a savage in the course of living in the forest. By naming his hero Nick, Hemingway prepares us for future complexity, for *Nick* is also a diminuitive of *Nicholas*, the name of a saint and five popes. (The complexities of the name Nick were

---

1. Henry Adams, *The Education of Henry Adams* (Boston and New York: Houghton Mifflin, 1927), 9.

useful to F. Scott Fitzgerald when he named the narrator of *The Great Gatsby* Nick Carraway. The two Nicks came into being almost simultaneously, although Nick Adams appeared in print before Fitzgerald's novel was published.)

Hemingway portrays aspects of experience that Henry Adams does not evoke in his depiction of sensuous summers. The elemental quality of Nick's summers in Michigan is unquestionably stronger than those Massachusetts summers of Henry Adams. Hemingway's high school stories aside, the first published story using his Michigan material is "Up in Michigan." The story is autobiographical no less than many of the Nick stories—more certainly than "Indian Camp," the initial Nick story of *In Our Time*. "Up in Michigan" recounts the seduction of a young waitress in Hortons Bay by a young blacksmith. According to Carlos Baker, the incident is based on Hemingway's first sexual intercourse—an event Baker thinks occurred *after* Hemingway's return from World War I.[2] Jim Gilmore, the blacksmith, elicits no sympathy from the reader; our sympathy is for the waitress who suffers the loss of her romantic illusions as well as her virginity. For Jim, the girl is merely an object. Nick Adams would never behave with such insensitivity. Yet the story is a useful prelude for defining the reality of northern Michigan where Nick will be tested. Sexual and other elemental emotions are more to the fore in Nick's Michigan summers than they were in his winter environment.

Gertrude Stein found "Up in Michigan" objectionable because of its explicit sexual treatment, but Hemingway stood by the story. He would have liked to include it in *In Our Time*, but he had to give way to the accepted standards of the period.[3] Had the story made its way into *In Our Time*, however, it would obviously have colored our interpretations of the Nick stories and of the world of *In Our Time*. Hemingway had planned that the story would come imme-

2. Carlos Baker, *Ernest Hemingway: A Life Story* (New York: Charles Scribner's Sons, 1969), 64.
3. *Ibid.*, 182.

diately after "Indian Camp," and its very title would be useful for defining the backdrop of the Nick stories.[4] For all
practical purposes, Hemingway managed to put the story
into *In Our Time* years later when he arranged *The Fifth
Column and the First Forty-Nine Stories* (1938). That collection
keeps the order of the three major collections intact, but
Hemingway placed "Up in Michigan" immediately preceding the opening piece of *In Our Time*. To be "up in Michigan" is to be removed from the civilization of pleasant
suburbs. The world of northern Michigan provided Nick
during his summers with a beautiful but elemental place.
There Nick could know something of the frontier experience
that had been an essential part of American history. Since
we later see Nick as a young man returning to Michigan on
his own, we may also conclude that what Michigan symbolizes came to be his preferred world. Although Nick increasingly rejects his parents, it should be emphasized that
in giving him northern Michigan they gave him a great deal.

In the rerevised *In Our Time* of 1938, then, the reader
carries into his reading of "Indian Camp"—the story showing Nick at his youngest—the aura of a tale of broken illusions and a lost innocence.[5] "Up in Michigan" reveals that
human sexuality can be brutally selfish—and the woman its
chief victim. "Indian Camp" also makes sexuality a serious
and frightening business, for even when sexuality is not
selfish it can lead to fearsome consequences. But, more important, "Indian Camp" has a strong undercurrent intimat-
ing that Nick Adams will soon experience the shattering of
comforting illusions. The pain of lost innocence is at the
very core of human experience. Hemingway's treatment of
these themes is more complex in "Indian Camp," which was
not only the first Nick story to appear in print, but also

4. Hemingway made clear the planned placement of "Up in Michigan"
in a letter to Dos Passos, April 22, 1925. See *Ernest Hemingway: Selected
Letters, 1917–1961*, ed. Carlos Baker (New York: Charles Scribner's Sons,
1981), 157.
5. The other revision of *In Our Time* took place in 1930 when Hemingway
added "On the Quai at Smyrna" as the book's opening.

ranks among Hemingway's best.[6] It touches keys that haunt
the reader in ways Hemingway could not have anticipated
when he completed it: in the beginning, suicide receives a
kind of justification. But personal implications of Hemingway's life and death aside, it is clear that Nick is Adamic in
the story, thereby raising some of the most basic questions
that man has always pondered. From that perspective, too,
the title "Work in Progress," under which it was first published, seems apt.

In "Indian Camp" Nick, roused from his tent for a night
ride across the lake to the Indian camp, is the archetypal
innocent. Hemingway tells us nothing about Nick that
would make us qualify our sympathetic feeling for his
youthful entry into a complex world. Throughout the Nick
stories, journey (psychological and spiritual more than
physical) usually helps define meaning. The first words of
the story and the first we hear from Nick are natural, but
also symbolic: "Where are we going, Dad?" (*IOT*, 15; *NAS*,
16). The story suggests that Nick is too young to realize the
real answer to his question, for it is larger than he knows. (It
turns out that his father does not fully know either.)

Nick is very young during the time of "Indian Camp." Not
only is he the questioner of the story, but he receives answers that make his extreme youth clear. "There is an Indian
lady very sick," says his father (*IOT*, 15; *NAS*, 16). A teenager or adult would have received more exact information in
syntax less formal. But the answer satisfies the doctor's son,
who is leaning back "with his father's arm around him."
Hemingway's technique in the story may be described in
large part as catechetic. The questions are profound, beyond
the comprehension of the questioner ultimately, and so are
the answers. Yet the answers, if uncomprehended, carry
authority and assurance.

Nick seems to sense that the night's journey is to take him

6. "Indian Camp" appeared in *Transatlantic Review*, 1 (April, 1924) under
the heading "Work in Progress," a title that reveals Hemingway's perception
of Nick in a larger context, of Nick as protagonist in something like a novel.

into totally new experiences. It is dark and there is mist over the lake. The opening sentences of the story immediately signal the sense of action to come—and action in a world far beyond the secure one Nick has known as a doctor's son: "At the lake shore there was another rowboat drawn up. The two Indians stood waiting" (*IOT*, 15; *NAS*, 16).

The reader may wonder why Nick, so obviously young, is going on this night journey. It is clear that he is already in surroundings at least once removed from the normal life of a doctor's son. There is a "camp" rowboat—so Nick with his father and Uncle George have already taken a journey to the more primitive, the more basic. By design, theirs is a group of men without women.

When the doctor's party gets into the boats for the row across the lake, no one gives instructions about who should get into which boat. Nick and his father quite naturally get into one boat, Uncle George into the other. From the beginning of the story, George's presence sets off an ideal obligation in the relationship between father and son. Furthermore, the narrative evokes something of an aura from the tradition of Indian culture: fathers give instructions to sons as they are initiated into manhood. The doctor is the important man of the hour—for the Indian lady and for Nick. Nick has a guide who is assured—or seems to be—and can give him answers that are reassuring. One's father—and not one's uncle—should be, and here is, that reassuring voice.

But almost as soon as Hemingway has set the stage for the important father-son focus, he indicates that Uncle George will have a symbolic role. (George and Nick never speak to each other in the story—further creating the sense of the doctor's primacy for the initiate.) "Functionless" on the journey across the lake, Uncle George smokes a cigar "in the dark" (*IOT*, 15; *NAS*, 16). When his boat is beached, he gives the Indians cigars. The gesture, as a remnant of Indian rituals, reinforces the sense of the white man's arrival into the Indian world. The fact that there are cigars offered by the white man rather than a pipe by the Indian hints at the changed position of the Indian in the white world. The Indi-

ans of the story have lost much of their power and pride.
They live in shanties and make their livelihood through an
enterprise (logging) of the white man. Indians had become
associated with cigars mainly in the phenomenon of the
wooden Indian statue commonly placed outside tobacco
shops: tobacco had been their gift.

But as Nick enters this Indian world, he will discover that
the life of the more primitive people can teach him a great
deal, for the primitive contains values that the doctor's son
needs to discover. A journey to "Indian Camp" may be far
more useful to the young boy than a camping trip with his
father and uncle, however good that might be. For there is
light in the Indian camp. As the doctor, Nick, and Uncle
George make their way through a meadow, they follow the
young Indian "who carried a lantern." Ahead it is "much
lighter" on the logging road, and the Indian is able to blow
out his lantern. Light comes from the shanties, and in the
shanty nearest the road there is "a light in the window" and
an old woman stands in the doorway "holding a lamp"
(*IOT*, 16; *NAS*, 17).

Even though the white visitors will get jarred from some
of their assumptions before the story ends, it is also clear
that the Indian has had to reach out to the technology of the
whites. A young Indian woman has been in labor for two
days. The old women in the camp have been assisting her,
but they must finally admit they can be of no further use.
The theme of the separation between men and women with
which the story mutedly began is made more important.
The Indian men, helpless to aid the woman, have moved up
the road where they cannot hear her screams, where they sit
to smoke "in the dark" (*IOT*, 16; *NAS*, 17). In this story, as
in many of the Nick stories, and in much of Hemingway's
work, there is the stark sense that the world is a hospital. A
common response to the pain of the world is to sit "in the
dark" far from the screams.

We typically characterize the Indian as possessing an
admirable stoicism. Hemingway emphasizes the pain involved in merely getting into the world by making the In-

dian woman no passive sufferer. Everything in "Indian
Camp" is complex and tends towards ambiguity; the stereo-
types will not hold. The woman is screaming as the doctor
arrives, and she continues screaming, quite unsettling Nick.
The doctor tries to assure Nick that the screams "are not
important" (*IOT*, 17; *NAS*, 18). If the woman is to be helped,
someone has to discipline himself and not hear the screams.
That is what doctors commonly do. Nick has to admire his
father as he goes about his business—certainly a part of him
takes consolation from the explanations that his father gives.
Probably the doctor's professional stance gives Nick the
courage not to buckle during the primitive Caesarian operation he partly watches and assists.

Nick can also observe how those not trained to work in a
hospital react. Since the doctor has no anaesthesia in his
camp, he needs Uncle George and the three Indians (not
privileged to join the other men) to hold the woman down.
When the woman's pain becomes so great that she bites
Uncle George, he instinctively curses, "Damn squaw bitch!"
(*IOT*, 18; *NAS*, 18), and the young Indian who had rowed
him over laughs. The event is useful for guarding against
reading too much into George's later indictment of the doctor. George is quite human in his reaction, and the young
Indian's response to George is further instructive on human
behavior. Only the implied narrator (to use the distinction of
Wayne C. Booth's *The Rhetoric of Fiction*) outside the story
has demonstrated the compassion that the woman's suffering demands.

However traumatic the event of birth can sometimes be
(the doctor later reassures Nick that the case has been exceptional), getting out of life can also be a gruesome event. The
overriding irony of "Indian Camp" is that the doctor, who
has thought to educate his son on the ways of birth, has
brought him also to witness death. For although the Indian
men have removed themselves from the sound of the woman's screams (save for the three who assist the doctor), one
has been unable to do so because of bad luck. The Indian's
woman's husband is in the bunk above her because he had

cut his foot badly with an ax three day before. While the woman screams and the doctor instructs Nick and then operates, the husband does act the part of the stoical Indian. Hemingway makes his lesson in stoicism forcefully. Just after the doctor has told Nick that he does not hear the woman's screams "because they are not important" a one-sentence paragraph makes a stark contrast: "The husband in the upper bunk rolled against the wall" (*IOT*, 17; *NAS*, 18). Obviously to him the screams are important, and he does hear them. The Indian male is taught to endure pain. In part, he measures his manhood by his ability to demonstrate an indifference to excruciating pain. The husband has been enduring his own pain, but finally his wife's pain is more than he can bear, and he cuts his throat—quietly but efficiently.

Doctor Adams understandably takes satisfaction from the fact that he is able to deliver the woman's baby, saving her life and the baby's. But he increasingly loses the reader's approval—and Uncle George's—as he talks about his achievement. Hemingway tells us that the doctor "was feeling exalted and talkative as football players are in the dressing room after a game" (*IOT*, 19; *NAS*, 19). This has not been a football game, however. Uncle George is the average, fallible man in the story, and although he respects the doctor's knowledge, he finds the doctor's self-esteem distasteful. He defines for us the vast difference between the way a child regards the superior wisdom of the parent and the way the rest of humanity regards the wise one. The time after this birth should be a time to refrain from talking, but the doctor talks on, using the clichés of the approved bedside manner: "Ought to have a look at the proud father. They're usually the worst sufferers in these little affairs" (*IOT*, 20; *NAS*, 20).

The man of words is then brought down hard when he discovers how the husband "took it." Nick, too, has seen something he will never forget, and the doctor is left to repent.

Hemingway restores the doctor to favor as he and Nick make the journey back across the lake together. The dia-

logue contrasts markedly with the professional tone the doctor has been using in the shanty. He is here father, not
doctor; and Nick is glad to get back to that relationship. The
doctor shows that he is also glad to return to this level of
experience as he addresses his son with the diminutive: "I'm
terribly sorry I brought you along, Nickie" (*IOT*, 20; *NAS*,
20). Nick seems eager to be reassured: he uses *Daddy* four
times in addressing his father. Nick is still the questioner,
and his father still has the answers. We note that only the
first question has to do with the birth, however, for the
suicide has obviously impressed Nick more profoundly. Finally he asks the climactic question that relates all of the
events of the experience to his own life: "Is dying hard,
Daddy?" (*IOT*, 21; *NAS*, 21).

The question and the answer ("No, I think it's pretty easy,
Nick. It all depends") produce a marked resonance in the
story since the Indian has been a major element in it. Traditionally the value of the good death was one instilled in the
Indian boy from earliest years. Dying was not something to
be feared; rather, to die ignobly would be the disaster. In the
white culture death seems to be more fearful, but for the
time being, Nick is reassured by his father's answer. Nick
has returned from the night experience to the comforting
day world: "The sun was coming up over the hills. A bass
jumped, making a circle in the water. Nick trailed his hand
in the water. It felt warm in the sharp chill of the morning"
(*IOT*, 21; *NAS*, 21).

Hemingway indicates how much of the night's experience
is beyond the boy in the famous end line of the story: "with
his father rowing, he felt quite sure that he would never die"
(*IOT*, 21; *NAS*, 21). A major theme of the Nick stories is
Nick's coming to grips with the idea of death, especially
his own death—something Nick briefly in "Indian Camp"
catches a glimpse of, but then dismisses. The Indian's death,
while vivid, does not touch Nick personally, nor is Nick
unusual in this ability to dismiss death. This ability of the
young is not necessarily soon outgrown, or the change necessarily welcomed. Conrad's Marlow touches on the same

experience in "Youth": "I remember my youth and the feeling that will never come back any more—the feeling that I could last forever, outlast the sea, the earth, and all men; the deceitful feeling that lures us on to joys, to perils, to love, to vain efforts—to death; the triumphant conviction of strength, the heat of life in the handful of dust, the glow in the heart that with every year grows dim, grows cold, grows small, and expires—and expires, too soon, too soon—before life itself."[7] But Nick, after his Indian camp visit, would not ever be as carefree about death as Conrad's Marlow could be. Nick's strange journey to the Indian camp will haunt him on other nights, and his later recollections of his father's superficial explanations will make him doubt his tutor's wisdom even as Uncle George has.

Sherwood Anderson defined the line into manhood in the penultimate story of *Winesburg, Ohio*; it comes when the boy "for the first time takes the backward view of life."[8] Anderson's George Willard has been led to this position through his mother's death when he was eighteen. The point here is not to suggest an influence but to define a problem for Nick's progress, to see where Nick has to go. Nick's coming to terms with death will be decidedly more difficult than it was for George Willard. Nick's premature initiation in "Indian Camp" has not led him to take "the backward view of life."

The grimness of death and the questions about the meaning of death—not to mention the strong sense of the universe as an arena of pain—come so forcefully to Nick and to the reader that it is possible to miss the positive implications of "Indian Camp." There is, of course, the upbeat at the end of the story that comes with the doctor's recognition that he has taken Nick into waters way over his head, his apology to Nick, and the image of their love as they row back together.

---

7. Joseph Conrad, "Youth," in *Youth and Two Other Stories* (Garden City: Doubleday, Doran, 1933), 36–37. *Youth and Two Other Stories* first appeared in 1903.

8. Sherwood Anderson, "Sophistication," *Winesburg, Ohio* (New York: B. W. Huebsch, 1919), 286.

That Nick will later reflect on the mistakes of his father-guide is clear from his question about Uncle George's whereabouts, for George—overwhelmed by the events of the night including his disgust for the doctor but probably some disgust at his own inadequacies in the face of them—has remained behind. Nick has not missed the challenge to his father in George's ironical line: "Oh, you're a great man, all right" (*IOT*, 20; *NAS*, 20). But there is a bond of love between Nick and his father that gives the boy something he needs and will never forget.

The bond between father and son is an important dimension of the light that ends the story. And the doctor, who has witnessed birth and death many times before, is frank and truthful as he answers Nick's questions. Although some critics have dwelt on the doctor's weaknesses, the doctor has some real wisdom and convincing humanity. His humanity is much in evidence at the story's end. He empathizes with the Indian husband: "He couldn't stand things, I guess," he explains to Nick. The doctor's last speech of the story is the admission to Nick that under certain circumstances dying can be easier than living. That is a lesson that Nick cannot totally comprehend, but it helps dissipate the horror that he had earlier felt in his first confrontation with a violent human death.

In addition to this light—literal, emotional, and symbolic—that ends "Indian Camp," there are other lights in the story, the lights of the Indian camp itself. Other stories reveal that the most shocking of the visits to the Indian camp was not the only one Nick made. Presumably the later visits would cause him to reflect on matters of dying and birth, but they would also clarify other dimensions of Indian experience. The Indians were a vanishing race and for that reason often judged inferior, but "Indian Camp" conveys a great sense of their humanity, of their suffering and ability to love, and of their solidarity. The need of the Indian wife has mobilized the entire camp, although there are specialized roles.

But although Nick would come to sense a good deal about

the value in Indian culture and although he could understand that under certain conditions suicide was understand-
able and that sometimes birth is very hard, the story raises
hard questions about the relationship between men and
women who love, questions about obligations that the Nick
of "Indian Camp" could hardly begin to verbalize. What sort
of bond is marriage if it would lead a husband to kill himself
because his wife suffered? The risk seems high indeed if, in
Frederic Henry's terms, "This was what people got for loving each other."[9] Although "Up in Michigan" reveals how
someone who gives herself to someone who does not gen-
uinely care for her can be crushed and discarded, "Indian
Camp" indicates that even if two people love each other, the
penalty for loving may be too great. By aligning his destiny
with that of a woman, the Indian husband has accepted her
pain. The husband has been able to bear his own pain, but
her pain in addition is too much for him. His suicide suggests that he was dying in his wife's place. Loving between
man and woman and between father and son are matters
that Nick will pause over, time and time again.

Hemingway had originally started "Indian Camp" with a
direction much simpler than the vast issues the story ultimately raises, as we can tell from reading the fragment
"Three Shots." In a sense, of course, as soon as we have
read the fragment we realize we should not have, for it is
rejected material and not part of the night's events. Hemingway's reasons for rejecting the prelude are not difficult to
ascertain. He was not yet ready to raise the issue of Nick's
bravery—that would come later. With the fragment, Nick's
archetypal value is lessened. Nick should be an attractive
character, and Hemingway, rightly, chose to emphasize
Nick's innocence rather than his cowardice. To have father
say "I know he's an awful coward" and to have George respond "I can't stand him . . . He's such an awful liar" (*NAS*,
14, 15) gives the reader a mistaken image of Nick, and the
exchange needlessly makes us suspicious of George. The

9. Ernest Hemingway, *A Farewell to Arms* (New York: Charles Scribner's
Sons, 1929), 320.

accusations suggest an older boy than we have in "Indian Camp." The action of the fragment indicates a young boy. Nick is old enough for his father and uncle to take on their camping trip, but too young for the night's fishing. Furthermore, the talk does not take place in Nick's presence. In "Indian Camp" nothing occurs that we do not experience with the young boy. In the fragment, Nick's fears of the night seem too exceptional—the singing in church of the hymn "Some day the silver cord will break" is not adequate motivation for the night fears that will later plague Nick, but the experience at the Indian camp is. Nick seems slightly comic in the fragment, a nuisance as Uncle George has it. The business of "Indian Camp" is altogether too serious for so amusing a frame. "Three Shots" does, then, sound several uncertain notes.

The fragment is perhaps most revealing because of what it suggests about Hemingway's approach to the doctor's character, and the portrayal of the doctor is quite consistent (as Nick's is not) with the portrayal in "Indian Camp." The doctor shows great patience and tact in dealing with his son. "What was it, Nickie?" said his father after a frightened Nick had called him and George back the previous night (*NAS*, 15). The doctor displays a gentle authority—and we are glad that Uncle George, who is not very patient, does not take it upon himself to instruct Nick. Everything in the fragment is to the doctor's credit. Before the trio leaves for the Indian camp the doctor rummages through the duffel bags, looking for the best surgical instruments he can find—he knows the summoning emergency may be severe. Furthermore, taking Nick along is completely justified. A reader of "Indian Camp" may at first wonder about the doctor's bringing Nick, but the story does not need attention to the detail, for it implies that Nick has been camping with his father. The doctor's miscalculation was in having Nick assist, in assuming that he could use the experience to instruct Nick.

The other fragment that touches on Nick's boyhood, titled by Young "The Indians Moved Away," also provides some hints about Dr. Adams' character; it also emphasizes the

importance of the Indians to the formation of Nick's character. Stories and fragments that deal with Nick's boyhood all
touch the Indian world. Because Nick spent his summers in
Michigan close to Indians, he has been made aware of values and aspects of his American heritage that would be
mere book knowledge if he had never lived in the North
near the Indians. "The Indians Moved Away" is a mood
piece wherein an older Nick is remembering the plight of
the Indians ("There were no successful Indians" *NAS*, 35) in
the land that the whites have taken over. Nick remembers
that he could smell the Indians before they arrived at the
cottage door to sell the summer berries they had picked: "It
was a sweetish smell that all Indians had" (*NAS*, 34). He
knew, too, that the Ojibways were being destroyed by drink,
the white man's gift to them. He recalls the incident of the
death of the Indian who had lived on a neighboring farm.
The Indian had gotten drunk in Petoskey on the Fourth of
July, lain down on the railway tracks on the way home, and
been run over by a train—a heavily symbolic event.

Apparently Nick's predisposition to comprehend Indians
and Indian ways comes to him from his father. We know
from "Now I Lay Me" that the doctor treasured Indian ar-
tifacts, and we know from "Indian Camp" that the Indians
sought his assistance in time of need. Critics of the Nick
stories have not, however, looked very favorably on the doctor. One has attacked him for racism and even found him
culpable in the emergency at the Indian camp for practicing
such professional procedures as the careful washing of his
hands and asking George to lift the blanket so that his
hands would remain clean while he operates.[10] The vilifica-
tion is excessive. "The Indians Moved Away" confirms that
both the doctor and his son knew many of the Indians by
name and had their affection. In the fragment Nick recalls a
homely incident about an Indian named Simon Green, an

---

10. Linda Welshimer Wagner, *Hemingway and Faulkner: inventors/masters*
(Metuchen, N.J.: Scarecrow Press, 1975), 60–61. Wagner's analysis first ap-
peared as part of "Juxtaposition in *In Our Time*" in *Studies in Short Fiction*,
XII (Summer, 1975), 243–52.

incident that reveals Indian feeling for Nick *and* his father. In
thinking about the incident, the reader should recall the
tradition of the silent Indians and bear in mind that Simon
owned his farm. He did not need to pay obeisance to the
Adamses, and indeed none of the Indians of the Nick stories is particularly obeisant. While Simon's horse was being
shod at the blacksmith's one day, Nick was gathering worms
under the eaves of the shed. Green sat outside in the sun.

> "Hello, Nick," he said as Nick came out.
> "Hello, Mr. Green."
> "Going fishing?"
> "Yes."
> "Pretty hot day," Simon smiled. "Tell your dad we're going to
> have lots of birds this fall." (*NAS*, 35)

The commerce between the Indians and the Adamses is no
slight thing. The Indians respected the white man's medicine and the man, just as the doctor cared about his pa-
tients. After the Caesarian operation in "Indian Camp," the
doctor says, "I'll be back in the morning." In "The Doctor
and the Doctor's Wife" we learn that Dr. Adams has nursed
Dick Boulton's wife through pneumonia—hence Boulton is
now obligated to make some payment. A late Nick story,
"Fathers and Sons," also underscores that the doctor had a
strong interest in things Indian; Nick tells his son "he had
many friends among them" (*WTN*, 161; *NAS*, 267). We assume that the doctor, like Nick, had made many trips to the
Indian camp.

In each of the stories of Nick's boyhood, the doctor's character is major. The title of the second *In Our Time* story, "The
Doctor and the Doctor's Wife," emphasizes the importance.
Although that story is also a Michigan story, Dr. Adams is
in a strikingly different setting for it than he was in "Indian
Camp." No longer engaged in the adventure of night fishing
and camping, he is in a more domestic arena. He is in front
of his cottage (a sort of midway station between the world of
"Indian Camp" and the Chicago area where he practices)
making provisions for domestic comfort and necessities. The
title "The Doctor and the Doctor's Wife" also indicates that

the disturbing aspects of marriage that Nick sensed in "Indian Camp" will be dramatized on a more "civilized" level. However, Nick is being made more conscious of other dangers in marriage, of traps that are more insidious than the biological trap of birth and death. His experiences in his home have suggested to him that the husband can easily be a victim. Such powerful connections with "Indian Camp" are made all the more forceful since the Indian culture evoked in the first story carries into the second—although it is now viewed in the light of day rather than the shadows of dark and of night.

Whereas "Indian Camp" portrayed the white man's entrance into an Indian world, "The Doctor and the Doctor's Wife" shows the Indian coming into the white world. The process of decay that the fragment "The Indians Moved Away" describes is here made dramatic through the portrayal of Dick Boulton. Dick's name does not even sound Indian (as Billy Tabeshaw's does). Hemingway says: "Dick was a half-breed and many of the farmers around the lake believed he was really a white man" (*IOT*, 26; *NAS*, 23). But Dick can speak Ojibway—necessary for communication with Billy Tabeshaw, who does not understand English. As a half-breed, Dick knows the ways of whites and Indians. In "The Doctor and the Doctor's Wife" he takes an Indian revenge on the white man, using white man's tactics.

The American past has many chapters in which the white man outmaneuvers the Indian over possession rights. Hemingway plays on that tradition in the story as Dick Boulton uses the tricks of language to break the treaty—to keep from having to honor his word to the doctor. He and Billy and Eddy Tabeshaw are here to cut driftwood lying along the shore from the logging booms. The lumbermen might or might not come for them, the economic advantage being questionable.

If they do not come, the logs would only rot on the beach. There is a subtle ethical distinction here, an ambiguity that belongs to the white man rather than to the Indian. In "Indian Camp" the doctor was in command, the great man.

Here he is being tested; his measure is being taken. In the earlier story he was "Daddy," the guide to a young son. Now he is "Doc," an address that is too familiar and which Dick keeps repeating as he keeps up the attack: "Well, Doc . . . that's a nice lot of timber you've stolen" (*IOT*, 26; *NAS*, 23). The doctor falls into Dick's trap and does exactly what Dick wants—he dismisses Dick. In the heat of anger, the doctor even threatens to beat Dick up. Aware that his threat is ridiculous, the doctor retreats: "he turned away and walked up the hill to the cottage. They could see from his back how angry he was. They all watched him walk up the hill and go inside the cottage" (*IOT*, 28; *NAS*, 24). To mark his triumph, Dick gloats to the Tabeshaws; Eddy laughs; but the older Billy—in tune with the Indian honor of the past and of the debt owed the doctor—does not. When Dick leaves the gate open as they leave, Billy closes it. Even in the reactions of the Indians, Hemingway cautions us against too simple an evaluation of the doctor.

The doctor's defeat has not been pleasant for the reader to observe, and Billy's gesture underscores the compassion the narrator creates for him as Dr. Adams takes his lonely walk up the hill to nurse his wounds. The repetition that describes the doctor's walking up the hill not only creates sympathy for him, but it emphasizes the distance between the lakeshore and the cottage. The doctor's defeat has at least been private.

Many readers have failed to see that the defeat is private. Hemingway himself blurred the distinction between art and life when he said that the story was about the time that he discovered that his father was a coward, a comment that may be useful for the student of Hemingway's biography, but not for the story. Perhaps F. Scott Fitzgerald had heard this biographical interpretation from Hemingway, for in his 1926 essay "How to Waste Material" he inaugurated a critical reading that many later critics accepted. Pointing out that in "The Doctor and the Doctor's Wife" and certain other of the *In Our Time* stories Hemingway had created something "tempermentally new," Fitzgerald says: "In the first of these a man is backed down by a half breed Indian after committing himself to a fight. The quality of humiliation in the story is so intense that it immediately calls up every such incident in the reader's past. Without the aid of a comment or pointing a finger one knows exactly the sharp emotion of young Nick who watches the scene."[11]

In Hemingway's story, however, at the time of the confrontation with Dick, there has been no mention of Nick's presence at all, although Hemingway indicates that the story will be Nick's by immediately identifying the doctor as "Nick's father" (*IOT*, 25; *NAS*, 22). We see only the Indians and the forlorn figure of the doctor as he makes his way up the hill. There is still emotion aplenty for the reader, but Nick's feelings have not yet entered the story. The doctor will find Nick a short while later, in the woods, a distance further than the cottage from the scene of the doctor's humiliation. We soon learn, too, that the doctor's wife inside the cottage has heard nothing of the row outside.

His manhood smarting, the doctor enters the cottage in need of solace. Instead, he meets a new confrontation, one the reader finds more embarrassing than the first, especially as we realize that this scene does not seem unique, as the beach episode did. Nick will enter the story only *after* the second confrontation, as the second plays on the first.

The battle is again waged on the verbal level. Nick's father is no longer "Doc" but a nauseating "dear"—which Mrs. Adams repeats as insistently as Dick repeated "Doc." When she wants to emphasize a demand or to rebuke her husband, she changes the form of address to "Henry." And the doctor's response is to give her what she wants. The contrast between the doctor here and the authoritative professional of "Indian Camp" is astounding. To be sure, there are comic touches to the exchange between the doctor and his wife— as there is a perverse comedy in the doctor's being manipulated by the half-breed. The doctor's wife is a Christian Sci-

11. F. Scott Fitzgerald, "How to Waste Material: A Note on My Generation," *Afternoon of an Author* (New York: Charles Scribner's Sons, 1957), 117. Fitzgerald's essay first appeared in *Bookman*, May, 1926.

entist—itself a suggestion that he does not have his house in order. The religion is not particularly efficacious for Mrs. Adams—she is in bed with a sick headache. Her Bible is really a weapon rather than something that gives her spiritual direction. She can quote scripture, but very selectively. For her the Bible is essentially a closed book, and she cannot be reading it in her darkened room.

The scene between the doctor and his wife is a scene of symbolic castration. The gulf between husband and wife could not be greater; they have not only separate beds but separate rooms. Mrs. Adams lies in a darkened room, cut off from the realities (and complexities) of the outside world such as the reader has just witnessed. Having obtained from the doctor an account of the beach episode, she says: "Dear, I don't think, I really don't think that anyone would really do a thing like that" (*IOT*, 30; *NAS*, 26). The unhappy doctor, meanwhile, sits on his bed cleaning his shotgun, readying it in case Dick Boulton returns. Although the doctor's first consious thought was probably revenge (the Indians could see "how angry he was"), the reader is more aware of the speed with which any desire for revenge dissipates and is replaced with a larger sense of frustration than of intent to murder. As he cleans the gun, the doctor notices a pile of unopened medical journals, still in their wrappers, on the floor by the bureau. The doctor is irritated since the journals are an affront to his self-image of competence; the reader, of course, senses the conflict between the elemental man quick to seek his own revenge and the civilized man, committed to solutions to problems through the rational and the dissemination of results through the printed word. Furthermore, a doctor is especially committed to the preservation, not the taking of life.

However, the civilized method is not without its own price, its own dangers. It can undermine the very values it claims to preserve and can easily become self-obsessed and destructive of the life-force it should celebrate, as the scene inside the cottage illustrates. As soon as she is informed of the altercation with Boulton, Mrs. Adams puts the doctor on the defensive: "I hope you didn't lose your temper, Henry" (*IOT*, 29; *NAS*, 25). The doctor must surrender the smouldering desire for revenge. The gun he is cleaning becomes a symbol of his tarnished masculinity. Bested again in a difference of opinion, he dutifully places the gun in the corner behind the dresser.

The event symbolizes the larger surrender to his wife. The doctor will not fight her any more than he would fight Dick Boulton. But Dick Boulton goes away; Mrs. Adams remains. There is no doubt about where the reader's sympathy is intended to be between the opposition posed by the doctor and the doctor's wife. An imperfect man, the doctor is aware of his failings; he is annoyed by his unread journals. His wife, on the other hand, seems fully satisfied with herself. The reader, however, notes the correspondence between the doctor's unread journals and the wife's unread Bible.

The doctor's surrender complete, Mrs. Adams is ready to take on her son. "If you see Nick, dear, will you tell him his mother wants to see him?" (*IOT*, 30; *NAS*, 26) she says.[12] The "his mother" is more than quaint nineteenth-century formality. It is ominous that Mrs. Adams does not specify a reason, some task or the like. Having reasserted her power over her husband, she moves to bring Nick into her orbit. The doctor's frustrated response to her request is to slam the door behind him, a counterpoint to Dick Boulton's leaving

12. Some readers, like F. Scott Fitzgerald, have tried to make Nick present at the doctor's first humiliation. Others, most notably Philip Young, would have him at the second. See Young's *Ernest Hemingway: A Reconsideration* (University Park: Pennsylvania State University Press, 1966), 33. Clinton S. Burhans, Jr., says whether or not Nick saw the quarrel and retreat is uncertain. See his "The Complex Unity of *In Our Time*," in Jackson J. Benson (ed.), *The Short Stories of Ernest Hemingway: Critical Essays* (Durham: Duke University Press, 1975), 21. It is difficult to make a case for Nick's being present. The very structure of the story argues against even calling Nick's presence uncertain. Hemingway has been careful to parallel the successive humiliations of the doctor—and to place Nick far from them. For further comment on these critics and the story see my "A Closer Look at the Young Nick Adams and His Father," *Studies in Short Fiction*, XIV (Winter, 1977), 75–78.

the gate open when he departed. But the doctor quickly makes his own amends: "'Sorry,' he said, outside her window with the blinds drawn" (*IOT*, 31; *NAS*, 26).

One of the reasons Doctor Adams has been frequently misunderstood by some of Hemingway's readers is that they fail to consider him in part as a product of nineteenth-century genteel values. There is more to him, or we would not have seen him as Hemingway intended that we first see him—camping in the woods and then assisting the all-but-forgotten Indians. He is a complex man. The reader's task is to understand him—not to condemn him for not mirroring widely held views of the latter part of the twentieth century. The doctor's problem anticipates what will become Nick's problem. The doctor is caught between the pull towards his own self-fulfillment and his obligations towards others, towards family and society.

The essential justice of Philip Young's comparison of Nick to Mark Twain's Huckleberry Finn is a commonly accepted tenet of Hemingway criticism. It needs to be seen, however, that Nick's plight is also parallel to his father's. And because Nick has the kind of father that he does, the meaning of "civilization" is more complex than it is in Mark Twain's masterpiece. Huck Finn is an archetypal orphan in a book that teems with orphans and the making of orphans. Huck's father evokes few loyalties. Indeed, as the action gets underway Huck is seeking to escape his father—mother he has not. Huck can slip in and out of a family context—at the widow's at the Grangerfords', at the Phelpses'. Family is something that he comprehends imperfectly, and it is not surprising that he would wish to light out for the territory at the end of the novel. It is far different with Nick (as we shall see) and with his father. Nick's father has promises to keep, and those promises have somehow frustrated his sense of fulfillment. In "Indian Camp" the doctor, after he performs the successful Caesarian delivery, could tell Uncle George, "That's one for the medical journal" (*IOT*, 19; *NAS*, 19). But in "The Doctor and the Doctor's Wife" we noted that his medical journals are unread. We need not be over-harsh in judging the doctor, for—as Hemingway makes clear—he is a man given to judging himself.

Hemingway's own too easy statement blurring the distinction between biography and fiction has doubtless contributed to the tendency towards harsh judgment. But Hemingway the artist made more subtle distinctions. His brilliant use of the "echo scene" in *A Farewell to Arms* utilized a technique that he had been developing in and between his earliest stories—as such details as reference to the medical journals in "Indian Camp" and "The Doctor and the Doctor's Wife" and the use of the gate and the bedroom door in the latter story reveal. Looking at the doctor's two retreats, we can clarify his alleged "cowardice." As destructive as we may feel the doctor's wife to be, no one could seriously argue that the proper response for the doctor would have been to shoot her, any more than shooting Boulton would have been an appropriate action. We might understand such an action, but it would not be a satisfactory answer. In civilization, men and women should find better ways to solve their problems. A man does not need to shoot his wife to prevent her from destroying his masculinity. Similarly, we would be disappointed if the doctor had tried to solve his differences with Dick Boulton by fighting. Every advantage would be Dick's, and the doctor would have been outsmarted in every way. The doctor's mistake was in letting Dick manipulate him into what turns out to be Dick's reneging on what was due the doctor for services rendered. Given that the doctor played into Dick's hand, the wise and right course was retreat. The two incidents together demonstrate that the doctor can be manipulated—too easily manipulated. Dick and Mrs. Adams are skilled manipulators who can use language to achieve their ends. For Dick, the fight would have been a bonus, but for the doctor retreat is not necessarily surrender.

In the two incidents, the doctor shows himself weaker in the second. Even as a man of his time and class, the doctor could have asserted himself. But we sense from the episode that retreat has been easier for him. He cannot speak authoritatively to his scripture-quoting wife. Here he has not retreated, he has unquestionably surrendered.

After that surrender, Nick becomes the issue. We have clear portraits of the doctor and his wife. The title of Hemingway's story puts the focus on the important choice (in a story full of choices) that Nick must make. It should be noted that although the first three times Hemingway refers to Doctor Adams in the story he calls him "Nick's father," during the episodes with Dick Boulton and Mrs. Adams, Hemingway always speaks of "the doctor." Nick has not witnessed his father's disgraces but has instinctively placed himself beyond the cottage where his mother holds sway. Hemingway makes unmistakable the distance that Nick has placed between himself and the cottage. The doctor "walked in the heat out the gate and along the path into the hemlock woods. It was cool in the woods even on such a hot day. He found Nick sitting with his back against a tree, reading" (*IOT*, 31; *NAS*, 26). The heat is not only of the day. Still it is often possible to escape various kinds of heat. One way to deal with the unpleasant is to go to the woods—as Nick already knows.

Nick's choice of his father at the story's end is one of the most touching moments in the Nick canon. The father has been severely beaten and needs something; he finds it in his son. To his father's announcement that Nick's mother wants to see him, Nick answers, "I want to go with you" (*IOT*, 31; *NAS* 26). The doctor's release is one in nature and with his son's companionship. Nick, still quite young, addresses his father with the "Daddy" that compensates the doctor ("Doc," "dear," "Henry") for his earlier disgraces. "I know where there's black squirrels, Daddy." The doctor, in a gesture of love (toward Nick) and defiance (toward his wife), ends the story in another choice: "All right . . . Let's go there." In the exchange with Nick, Hemingway brings us back to the opening of the story by labeling the doctor Nick's father. In very short space Hemingway uses the designation "his father" three times, creating a sense of benediction.

"The Doctor and the Doctor's Wife"—although masterful

in its rendering of crucial events on a particular day—creates the framework to enable the reader to understand better Nick's later choices. It has not been necessary to have Nick see those events. It is enough to create the sense of conflict at the Adamses, to create the issues that the child will gradually be able to formulate for himself. In "The Last Good Country" Nick's sister says, "Haven't we seen enough fights in families?" (*NAS*, 85). If "Indian Camp" suggests to the reader of *In Our Time* through the Indian couple the depths and the risks of love, it was in a matrix that Nick could hardly comprehend. But the vibrations of the institution of marriage are completely negative in "The Doctor and the Doctor's Wife," and Nick has to respond to them daily. His sympathies go easily to his father.

Nick's rejection of his mother (and to that extent his rejection of the family as a meaningful frame for his life) is quite total. It is significant that in no Nick story does Hemingway show us Nick in the presence of his mother. Not even in his late return to Nick for "The Last Good Country," the unfinished novel begun in 1952, does Hemingway put Nick and his mother together.

One story of *In Our Time* does bring a mother and son together, "Soldier's Home." In studying the returned soldier, Harold Krebs, Hemingway deals with concepts close to realities in the Nick stories. It may not be entirely reprehensible that Fitzgerald in reviewing *In Our Time* made it a Nick story: "Nick leaves home penniless; you have a glimpse of him lying wounded in the street of a battered Italian town, and later of a love affair with a nurse on a hospital roof in Milan. Then in one of the best stories he is home again. The last glimpse of him is when his mother asks him, with all the bitter world in his heart, to kneel down beside her in the dining room in Puritan prayer."[13] We can easily imagine Mrs. Adams making such a request, but Fitzgerald was working too hard to make a novel of *In Our Time*. Hemingway made Krebs very different from Nick. Krebs comes from

13. Fitzgerald, "How to Waste Material: A Note on My Generation," 117.

a stolid midwestern background without the perspective
that life "up in Michigan" provides Nick. If Hemingway ever
considered making the story a Nick story, he drew back;
Nick would not surrender to his mother as Krebs did to his.

The Nick story where we most expect to find Mrs. Adams
but do not is "Ten Indians," and Hemingway surely anticipated that we would be looking for her. He is certainly much
concerned with the realities of the Adams family life in the
story. His method, as usual, depends heavily upon what he
does not portray but implies.

In "Ten Indians" Nick is somewhat older than we found
him in "The Doctor and the Doctor's Wife," but not by much.
The title taken from the child's song "One little, two little,
three little Indians" carries through the Indian theme of the
other stories of Nick's boyhood, and it also implies that he is
still in the child's world, important for the ending of the
story. But, clearly, Nick has approached adolescence. He is
now consciously interested in sex, and the story is partly
about his sexual education. As a story of education, "Ten
Indians" again makes important use of journey to stress the
development of the protagonist.

Nick's journey has two parts, both—significantly—on the
Fourth of July. Although the journey takes Nick home, he is
moving closer to the time when he will claim his own independence. The Indians "celebrate" this holiday by going into Petoskey and getting drunk. Nick and his companions
count the bodies of collapsed Indians as they make their
way home late at night. They have counted nine as the
action of the story begins.

Nick is the guest of the Joe Garner family. Whereas the
American Indian has no special cause to rejoice over the
Fourth, for most Americans it is the important holiday of the
summer. In Nick's time in the early years of the century it
was, next to Christmas, the greatest holiday of community
goodwill and decidedly a family day. It is disturbing that
Nick is not with his own family, especially since we are not
told why, although Mrs. Adams would be unlikely to care to

see Petoskey's baseball team. For the Adamses, at any rate, this Fourth was not a family day.

A family outing does, of course, require effort—the bulk of it usually falling to the mother. In "Ten Indians" Hemingway suggests the effort of such an outing through portrayal of certain details of the journey. It is early in the century, and the route involves departure from the main highway. The boys have to get out at one place on the sandy road as the horses work hard to pull the wagon up the hill. For Nick—and the Garners—the effort of getting to Petoskey is well worth it. From the top of the hill by the schoolhouse, Nick sees "the lights of Petoskey and, off across Little Traverse Bay, the lights of Harbour Springs" (*MWW*, 169; *NAS*, 28). He can see where he has been, and he knows with whom. Mention of the schoolhouse is appropriate only because of the sexual education theme that is obviously important to the story, but also as a reminder of what Nick has been learning through the Garners about his own family. There is an important kind of education that does not take place in schoolhouses. Winter, as Henry Adams said, is school.

Nick is content enough with the Garners. They are glad to have him, and he feels very comfortable with the parents and their two sons. As the family banters, we sense the familial pleasures that Nick finds attractive. "Them Indians," Mrs. Garner says as the family makes its amused observations on the Indian behavior, counting the drunken Indians asleep by the side of the road.

Discussion about the spot on the road where Garner had once hit a skunk leads Nick to observe that he saw two last night, and his innocent remark finds suitable interest in the family. Boylike, young Carl challenges Nick's observation: "They were coons probably" (*MWW*, 170; *NAS*, 28). The challenge allows Nick to assert his authority, a stance that has no counterpart in "Indian Camp" or "The Doctor and the Doctor's Wife": "They were skunks. I guess I know skunks." Carl sees some easy fun: "You ought to . . . You got an Indian girl." Nick finds it pleasant to be teased about Prudence Mitchell, although he denies that Prudence is his girl. The easy talk amongst the Garners about girls anticipates the second half of the story, where Nick will again talk about Prudence—this time to his father.

Although Nick obviously feels comfortable with the Garners (they could hardly do more to make him feel at home—to both Mr. and Mrs. Garner he is Nickie), he is nevertheless aware that he belongs to another family. He thanks the Garners for taking him on their family outing, but he must decline their invitation to stay for some supper. He makes a telling remark: "I better go. I think Dad probably waited for me" (*MWW*, 172; *NAS*, 30). Nick's failure to mention his mother has to give the reader pause, especially since Mrs. Garner has been so relaxed (but not lax) in her roles as mother and as wife. She whispered her little sexual joke to her husband during the conversation about Prudence, leaving Joe to say that Nick could have Prudence: "I got a good girl" (*MWW*, 171; *NAS*, 29). There is a sickness at the Adamses', this story suggests. In contrast to Nick's mother, Mrs. Garner stands ready to cook for Nick as she will cook for the rest of the family.

"Ten Indians" made its first appearance in 1927 in *Men Without Women*, only two years after *In Our Time*. Hemingway plays on the ending of "The Doctor and the Doctor's Wife" as he has Mrs. Garner tell Nick as Nick is about to leave: "Send Carl up to the house, will you?" (*MWW*, 172; *NAS*, 30). She does not say why, but she doubtless needs Carl for some practical chore since it is now mealtime. There is nothing ominous here, as there was when Mrs. Adams requested that the doctor send Nick to her. Nick even comes close to his mother's language as he relays the message to Mr. Garner: "Will you tell Carl his mother wants him?" (*MWW*, 173; *NAS*, 30). Nick's "his mother" has a natural quality to it that Mrs. Adams lacked when she spoke to her husband. One could argue that the episode merely shows Nick as being dutiful, but we have seen enough of Mrs.

Garner to know that Carl would not find the message threatening or distasteful—as Nick did in the earlier story.

That there is a great gulf fixed between the Garners and the Adamses is emphasized in the paragraph describing Nick's journey home. Nick is barefoot and moves with ease along the path through the meadow and through the dry beech woods. Finally he sees the lights of the cottage. By calling our attention to the lights, Hemingway reminds us of Nick's earlier pause by the schoolhouse when he looked back towards the lights of Petoskey, the freedom of a bigger world. Then Hemingway gives us the first of two frozen moments of time: "Through the window he [Nick] saw his father sitting by the table, reading in the light from the big lamp" (*MWW*, 173; *NAS*, 30).

Doctor Adams is still a source of strength for Nick. Although Nick is growing away from his father and his family, "Ten Indians" nevertheless shows some of the positive aspects of the relationship between Nick and his father, as we would expect from both "Indian Camp" and "The Doctor and the Doctor's Wife." As Nick enters, his father is obviously pleased to see him and uses the familiar diminutive address: "Well, Nickie . . . was it a good day?" Nick responds in the enthusiasm of the day, using language appropriate to a boy about to enter adolescence: "I had a swell time, Dad. It was a swell Fourth of July" (*MWW*, 173; *NAS*, 30).

"Ten Indians," like "Indian Camp" and "The Doctor and the Doctor's Wife," has moved from scenes of action and movement involving several characters to quiet exchange between father and son. At the end of "Indian Camp" Nick was noticeably the questioner. The exchange at the end of "Ten Indians" starts with the father as questioner—itself a sign that Nick is nearing his own independence: was it a good day, are you hungry, where are your shoes, who won the ball game?

The doctor serves Nick supper—an event that conveys his great affection for Nick. (The scene contrasts with the eating

scene in "Soldier's Home" where Harold Krebs is nauseated
by his mother and the food she serves him.) "It's grand"
(*MWW*, 174; *NAS*, 31), Nick says of the food his father has
put before him.[14]

But the scene does more than accent the father's affection
for the son and the son's for the father, and it does more
than call attention to the absent mother. Hemingway signals
the new emphasis through a transitional paragraph, one
which presents the story's second frozen moment: "His father sat down in a chair beside the oil-cloth-covered table.
He made a big shadow on the wall" (*MWW*, 174; *NAS*, 31).
Thereafter the psychological dimensions of the scene get
more complex. The father asks his last question, and it becomes clear as he watches Nick that he has more on his
mind than sharing Nick's day—although the reader, like
Nick, takes his interest in Nick's day as genuine. As Nick
finished the supper with huckleberry pie, he becomes the
questioner. The average teenager shows little interest in his
parents' activities. Nick's questions are something of a *mi-
rabile dictu*: "What did you do, Dad?" (*MWW*, 174; *NAS*, 31)
he asks. And Nick learns of his father's morning of fishing.
The questions Nick asks are like those a parent might ask of
a son. "What did you do this afternoon?" Nick asks next. It
is worthy of notice that Nick started his questioning of his
father with sincere interest. Nick's questioning becomes a
quest for information about the missing tenth Indian of the
story only after he learned that his father had been walking
by the Indian camp. Because Nick persists, he learns that his
father saw Prudence Mitchell "having quite a time" with
Frank Washburn. Since Prudie is, in some sense, Nick's girl,
his happy Fourth of July is about to end on a sour note.
Bright things can quickly come to confusion.

14. Jackson J. Benson contrasts Mrs. Garner's warm supper with that
served Nick in order to emphasize the coldness of the doctor. Nick eats cold
chicken, cold milk, and cold pie. See Benson's *Hemingway: The Writer's Art of
Self-Defense* (Minneapolis: University of Minnesota Press, 1969), 12. But
Nick's "It's grand" is, I think, genuine. This hot Fourth of July is not a night
for hot chocolate, and those huckleberries come from the woods. It is not a
bad repast for a boy who has been away all day.

Nick's confusion as well as his passionate interest in Prudie is emphasized in the dialogue. Nick knows that Prudie
has not been in Petoskey; so when he hears that his father
has been walking near the Indian camp, he pursues the
point. But he does not ask directly about Prudie, rather
he moves by indirection: "Didn't you see anybody at all?"
(*MWW*, 175; *NAS*, 31). Nick does not want to believe the
truth he has feared. Hearing it, he looks for an out: "How
did you know it was them?" His father saw them. Grasping
at straws, Nick says, "I thought you said you didn't see
them." Of course, the doctor had said no such thing. Although Nick must ask again who was with Prudie, finally he
cannot ask the climactic question and manages only, "Were
they happy?" (*MWW*, 176; *NAS*, 32).

Having come to his own awareness of sexuality, Nick cannot speak directly to his father about it. His father finds the
topic equally difficult to discuss and takes his eyes away
from Nick, although he was consciously looking at Nick during the dark turn in the conversation.[15] Particularly since
Nick's father is a medical doctor, later twentieth-century
readers may be especially amused at his reticence and his
extreme embarrassment. Having answered Nick's question
concerning the happiness of Prudie and Frank, the doctor
goes outside for a few moments. But for the early years of

15. The doctor, to be sure, is inexpert on sexual instruction. His weaknesses do show through here, but he seeks what is best for Nick. I find it
difficult to see him playing a sadistic role here—as Philip Young suggests
that he is. The instance is another example of the tendency to use Hemingway's biography wrongly—something that has plagued Hemingway criticism. Of the episode in "Ten Indians" Young says: "The tenth Indian is
Prudence Mitchell. And now there are none: Prudie does not appear in the
story, but she was Nick's girl, and when he gets home the doctor tells him
he has seen her 'having quite a time' in the woods with another boy. What
we are not told is that in life this Indian girl, who sometimes worked for
Mrs. Hemingway, was Prudence Boulton, daughter of the man who perhaps humiliated the doctor—who in turn may take satisfaction in telling
Nick what he saw." See "'Big World Out There': *The Nick Adams Stories*," 33.
Clearly, Dr. Adams can hardly be getting a measure of vindication from his
son's turning from Prudence Mitchell because Prudence Boulton's father
had humiliated Dr. Hemingway. Furthermore, Dr. Adams' character does
not need this additional vilifying.

the century, the doctor's attitudes are not unusual, and probably most parents find sex a difficult thing to talk about with their children. In any case, we feel in the scene that despite Nick's affection for his father, he is about ready to seek other guides, other companions.

For Nick, the happy boyhood Fourth has ended. The tears have come, and he refuses the second piece of pie that the doctor offers in propitiation. So Nick goes off the bed. Hemingway's final look at Nick—alone at the end of this story— is detached and amused. Nick feels that his heart is broken. But as he lies abed, he gradually comes to feel that the world has not ended. Nature is again reassuring, the note that marks the end of all three stories dealing with Nick's boyhood. Nick "heard a wind come up in the trees outside and felt it come in cool through the screen" (*MWW*, 177; *NAS*, 33). When Nick awakens during the night, he hears "the wind in the hemlock trees outside the cottage and the waves of the lake coming in on the shore" and he goes back to sleep. In the morning there is a big wind blowing, the waves are running high, and Nick is awake a long time "before he remembered that his heart was broken" (*MWW*, 177; *NAS*, 33). Although Nick's experience here parallels the broken hearts of many a young boy and girl, the main point of the story is not merely amusement. Nick has entered into his sexual awareness, and with this sexual awakening, he will move away from the guidance of the doctor, even as he had previously separated himself from the guidance of the doctor's wife.

The three stories of Nick's boyhood, then, revolve around Nick's relationship with his father. Nick increasingly senses his father's inadequacies, but the stories also contain much evidence of Nick's deep feeling for his father. Nick shares many things with Dr. Adams; Hemingway associates their love for the outdoors most frequently with the life of the Indian, a simpler life in many ways and one that stressed continuity between father and son. But the pressures of the civilized world have weakened the Indian, and they also weaken the bond between Nick and his father. The stories of

Nick's boyhood also anticipate Nick's later struggle for meaningful union with a woman. The traumatic events of "Indian Camp" suggest to Nick that the risks of marriage—or any deep commitment—may be very great. "The Doctor and the Doctor's Wife" reveals that marriage might prove even more awful than the predicament of the wounded Indian husband who is trapped in the shanty with his suffering wife. But as Nick matures sexually, he is nevertheless pulled in the direction of outside commitments. Through the likes of the Garners of "Ten Indians" he realizes that there may be a more satisfying form of marriage than his parents exemplify. And finally his quick rebounding from his "heartbreak" over the faithless Prudence suggests that there is a healthy resilience in Hemingway's hero.

Chapter Two
The Adolescent

After the stories of Nick's Michigan boyhood, Philip
Young's collection presents a grouping under the
heading "On His Own." But if we give Hemingway's structure of *In Our Time* due consideration, we will find Young a
bit premature in placing Nick on his own.

Hemingway wrote Edmund Wilson, before *In Our Time*
was ever in print, that the book "has a pretty good unity."[1]
Several critics have written on those unities, assuming that
the chronology of Nick's life was one of Hemingway's principles of arrangement. Clinton S. Burhans, Jr. declares: "Hemingway arranges the stories—with one exception ["My Old
Man"] in a roughly chronological order," adding that the
first five stories are set in pre-World War I America.[2] Young
takes two of these stories and places them after Nick's return from the war to the States. However, the change does
strange things to the patterns of *In Our Time*, where Hemingway has Nick wounded in the middle vignette of the

1. Edmund Wilson, "Emergence of Ernest Hemingway, " *The Shore of
Light* (Farrar, Straus and Young, 1952), 123. Wilson's essay, which contains
letters from Hemingway to him, is reprinted in Carlos Baker (ed.), *Hemingway and His Critics* (New York: Hill and Wang, 1961), 55–61. In a letter of
April 22, 1925, to his friend John Dos Passos, Hemingway insisted on the
unity of *In Our Time* and expounded on his problem with the publisher,
whose proposed changes would mar that unity. See *Ernest Hemingway: Selected Letters, 1917–1961*, ed. by Carlos Baker (New York: Charles Scribner's
Sons, 1981), 157. Hemingway made the same point to other correspondents.
2. Clinton S. Burhans, Jr., "The Complex Unity of *In Our Time*," Jackson
J. Benson (ed.), in *The Short Stories of Ernest Hemingway: Critical Essays* (Durham: Duke University Press, 1975), 17. Burhans' article first appeared in
Modern Fiction Studies, XIV (1968), 313–28.

book—suggesting that Nick's wounding is central to the book, to be sure, but also indicating a chronological pattern. The stories after that vignette deal with the returned soldier.

To justify his departures from the arrangement of *In Our Time*, Young says that Hemingway was still adolescent after his return from the war, and he quotes Hemingway's sister Marcelline's judgment that after his return from war her brother was "more like a boy of sixteen than a man approaching his twenty-first birthday."[3] But the writer of *In Our Time* was not immature as a writer. He knew which of Nick's love experiences were adolescent, and he made them suit *Nick's* chronology. The logical place to view Nick after "Ten Indians" is "The End of Something" and "The Three Day Blow"—despite Young's also arguing from internal evidence that the stories are postwar: he notes rumrunners and the business about "not thinking." The reference to rumrunners comes, however, in "Summer People," and the "not thinking theme" is too constant a theme in Hemingway to justify departure from the chronology of *In Our Time* on that basis. The desire not to think about Marge may initiate Nick's later resolve not to think about many things. Besides, "Ten Indians" makes clear that Hemingway viewed his hero as sexually awakened, even experienced. The story anticipates Nick's complicated feelings about the women he loved in his later adolescent years. A very late piece of evidence that Nick was sexually experienced in the prewar years even if Hemingway was not is the unfinished "The Last Good Country." There Mr. Packard asks Nick about his girl, and the description of the relationship sounds very much like Nick's relationship with the Marge of "The End of Something" and "The Three Day Blow." Late in "The Three Day Blow" Nick's friend Bill feels that Nick "might get back into it [the relationship with Marge] again" (*IOT*, 59; *NAS*, 215). In "The Last Good Country," which is set before World War I, Nick confesses to Mr. Packard, "None of it was her fault. She's just built that way. If I ran into her again I guess I'd get

3. Philip Young, " 'Big World Out There': *The Nick Adams Stories*" in Benson (ed.) *The Short Stories of Ernest Hemingway*, 40.

mixed up with her again" (*NAS*, 100). If Marge's portrait in the late piece takes on dimensions not found in the earlier stories, it is nevertheless clear that Hemingway viewed Nick as rather experienced in those adolescent years.

The reference to Nick's girl in the late story is a tribute to a vibrant character who touched Nick more deeply than did the Prudie of "Ten Indians"; yet there are significant parallels between "Ten Indians" and "The End of Something." "Ten Indians" was also "the end of something"—something similar to but finally different in kind as well as degree from the experience of Nick in the latter story. Both stories progress towards meeting with a guide who desires that Nick end a relationship with a girl. Both stories show that love is difficult to talk about. However, in the second story it seems unlikely that Nick will get over his "broken heart" as quickly as he had in the first. We view him with his girl in the second story and so can test the quality of the relationship more precisely. In "Ten Indians" we only heard Nick's being kidded about "his girl"; then we heard about her afternoon with another boy. In "The End of Something" a friend rather than his father plays the part of guide. "The End of Something" is the first story to portray Nick away from the family context that has marked the three stories of his boyhood.

The story also moves us away from the locale of the lake where the Adamses have their cottage. We are at Hortons Bay (setting of "Up in Michigan") on near-by Lake Charlevoix. Hemingway begins "The End of Something" with a lengthy description of Hortons Bay and its history. The description is useful for marking Nick's entry into adventures in widened surroundings and into the complexities of history. The history of Hortons Bay is also a symbol for the relationship now about to end between Nick and Marjorie, and because the symbol is based on a massive change in what had appeared permanent, it indicates that the affair between Nick and Marjorie has been much more than the sexual games Nick played with Prudie: "The schooner moved out of the bay toward the open lake carrying the two great saws, the traveling carriage that hurled the logs against the revolving circular saws and all the rollers, wheels, belts and iron piled on a hull-deep load of lumber. Its open hold covered with canvas and lashed tight, the sails of the schooner filled and it moved out into the open lake, carrying with it everything that made the mill a mill and Hortons Bay, a town" (*IOT*, 35; *NAS*, 200). For Hortons Bay, the departure of the schooner is cataclysmic.

"The End of Something" is the only Nick story published during Hemingway's lifetime that portrays him for an extended scene with a female companion, and that uniqueness of method also stresses Marjorie's importance. Women will be important to his life—he will even marry—but Hemingway characteristically showed him as a man without a woman. Although we never see Marjorie again, she is unforgettable in this account of love among the ruins. She seems highly suitable to the life Nick chooses in rejecting his mother. There are no Victorian codes to keep Marjorie from accompanying Nick as they set out lines for a night of fishing.

If northern Michigan gives Marjorie a great deal of freedom for a girl, it is also worth pointing out that Nick has been allowed much freedom in the north. The internal evidence of this story would make Nick still a teenager. The mill has been gone for ten years, and Nick tells Marjorie that he can "just remember" it (*IOT*, 36; *NAS*, 201), suggesting that he is about sixteen or seventeen. Nick obviously is older than the Nick of "Ten Indians." There we first saw him in the beginnings of an authoritative role: "They were skunks. I guess I know skunks." Now he make greater claims, and he is clearly Marjorie's teacher. He will shortly confront her with "I taught you everything" (*IOT*, 40; *NAS*, 203). Indeed, we find him instructing Marjorie in the story. Nick knows a lot—about fishing; but he is inexpert in matters of the heart and is about to have a genuine experience in heartbreak.

As the evening's fishing begins, Marjorie goes happily about their business, expecting a repetition of the happiness she has known in the past with Nick. Hemingway conveys the quality of their past together simply but unmistakably:

"She loved to fish. She loved to fish with Nick," and he gives us a good many of the details of their fishing—it is made as real as the lumbering once was on Hortons Bay. But as the fishing goes on, we sense that Nick has more than fishing on his mind. He is old enough now for some calculated deception. Marjorie initiates most of the conversation, but Nick wants to talk only about the fishing. The negative signals become too obvious to Marjorie, and as they beach the boat, she must finally ask: "What's the matter, Nick?" The moment not yet ripe for Nick to tell her, he cheats: "I don't know" (*IOT*, 38; *NAS*, 202).

The night should be right for kissing and caresses around the firelight, but that they will not be forthcoming is clear. After Marjorie unpacks the basket of supper, Nick says, "I don't feel like eating" (*IOT*, 39; *NAS*, 203). Marjorie coaxes, but Nick's dark feelings (toward himself more than anything) are manifest. He disrupts Marjorie's coaxing by breaking into an attack—completely unjustified: "You know everything" (*IOT*, 39; *NAS*, 203). We have not seen the Marjorie that Nick creates as he criticizes her, but Marjorie is patient under his assault; finally Nick says what he had not had the courage to say—precisely because a part of him did not want to make the break with Marjorie that he had planned: "It isn't fun any more" (*IOT*, 40; *NAS*, 204).

On this night of the big moon and the promised fishing, Marjorie must face the pain of being told that Nick no longer wants her. "Isn't love any fun?" she asks, for she makes the issue perfectly clear; thereby she leaves herself open to the greatest of hurts. "No," Nick replies, using one of the most devastating of words (*IOT*, 40; *NAS*, 204). Marjorie proves her worth by behaving with great dignity. There is no scene, but she knows it is time to leave and does so. Everything in the story has shown to Marjorie's credit.[4] Now that Nick is

4. As I have pointed out, "The End of Something" is the only story published in Hemingway's lifetime where we see Nick alone for an extended scene with a woman. In view of continuing attacks about Hemingway's failure to portray women sympathetically, I would stress Marjorie's dignity. The reader might compare her behavior with Frances Cline's in *The*

older, Hemingway portrays Nick's weaknesses—although
we can understand much about their causation. Many things
have made Nick feel great reservations about marriage. Because he has gotten into complicated territory with Marjorie,
a part of him has been frightened. He is not yet ready for a
big commitment, but after he breaks with Marge he is left
with a sense of great loss.

Clinton S. Burhans is quite wrong when he says that the
point of the story is "less Nick's falling out of love than his
appalled recognition that he can." [5] One may fall in love
quickly, but love seldom dies the quick death Burhans sees.
The something in the story's title is not Nick's feeling for
Marjorie; rather it is their relationship. The story marks the
end of something that means a great deal to Nick, something that he is not even sure he wants to end.

The latter truth becomes clear in the "surprise" ending of
the story. Although his stories are obviously conceived differently from those of an O. Henry, Hemingway frequently
gives us his own brand of the surprise ending—the detail
about the operating tools in "Indian Camp," the news about
Prudie in "Ten Indians," and now the emergence of Bill,

Sun Also Rises. Frances behaves very badly in similar circumstances, as
Robert Cohn does later in the same novel. Several of Hemingway's stories
study a character's reaction to being told by another that their relationship
has ended. See "The Sea Change," "A Canary for One," "Homage to Switzerland." As for Marjorie, I find recent criticism of her completely unjustified.
E. D. Lowry calls her "one in a series of studies in spiritual rigidity." See his
"Chaos and Cosmos in *In Our Time*," *Literature and Psychology*, XXVI (1976),
109. Marjorie is hardly an example of spiritual rigidity. Hemingway knew
a victim when he portrayed one. He had, it needs to be emphasized, accepted the challenge of the female's point of view early in his career; indeed
the lead story of *Three Stories and Ten Poems*, Hemingway's first book, was
from the point of view of a young girl and creates sympathy for her in her
victimization (even though it is mainly self-victimization) because of a romantic love for a young blacksmith. The girl is Liz Coates, and the story is
"Up in Michigan." Had that story been a part of *In Our Time* as Hemingway
had intended, we would have been been more alerted to feelings of sympathy for the woman—feelings awakened in the book by "Indian Camp" and
the vignette "On the Quai at Smyrna"—later added as the opening piece of
the book—and by the later stories of the book "Cat in the Rain" and "Out
of Season."
  5. Burhans, "The Complex Unity of *Within Our Time*," 22.

Nick's friend, from the woods with the question about the departed Marjorie: "Did she go all right?" (*IOT*, 41; *NAS*, 204). The reason Nick did not feel like eating is now evident. Nick, in no earlier story cast in so reprehensible a light, has not been true to himself, to his own feelings. Bill is the questioner here at the end of the story, and his "How do you feel?" is too much for Nick. Whereas the doctor left at the embarrassing moment in "Ten Indians," Nick now must send Bill away.

Bill is the only winner in this story. In contrast to Nick, he feels like eating and walks over to look at the rods. *He* is still interested in fishing. For Nick—and the departed Marjorie—there is only the sense of loss as the story ends. Bill represents the safer world of male camaraderie that Nick has for the time chosen. Bill has been aware of Nick's plan for the night; indeed the story that follows would suggest that he helped plan it. Certainly he had encouraged Nick to make the break.

"The Three Day Blow" is so closely related to "The End of Something" that Burhans feels that the two stories are as connected as the two parts of "Big Two-Hearted River," which slightly overstates the case.[6] "The End of Something" is, of course, a part of the unity of *In Our Time*, but as a story it also contrasts with "The Three Day Blow." It has its own structure, too, its own roundness. It has the Hemingway punch at the end that leaves the reader wondering about Nick's feelings, even as Nick wonders. Although noticeably related to Nick's breakup with Marjorie, "The Three Day Blow" is tonally worlds away. And though the latter story is rich in comic effects, there is no humor in "The End of Something."

"The End of Something" marked the end not only of a love but also of a season, and "The Three Day Blow" effectively picks up the point. In the companion story, it is fall, and the fruit has been picked from the apple orchard. At the opening of "The End of Something" the reader finds Nick

6. *Ibid.*

with Marjorie, but at the opening of "The Three Day Blow" the reader finds Nick alone. Although nature is invigorating, Nick needs human contact at this time of the first of the autumn storms; he walks towards a cottage that has smoke coming out of the chimney.

The cottage turns out not to be a home; there are no Garners there. Rather, this cottage is exclusively masculine. Bill lives there with his father in a freedom that has many appealing aspects, and Nick is a welcomed guest. Even before he gets to the cottage, his friend Bill has opened the door and stands waiting on the porch. Bill's greeting emphasizes their bond: "Well, Wemedge." The name *Wemedge* reminds Sheridan Baker of Wemick, Pip's friend, in Dickens' *Great Expectations.*[7] From his youth, Hemingway liked to play with nicknames, as the world knows from such famous sobriquets as Bumby, Papa, Miss Mary, and the Kraut (the latter for Marlene Dietrich). He also took over into his fiction the values implied in such naming. Dickens' novel makes much happy play on names to suggest relationships—Pip's name (Magwitch's contract specifies that Pip is not to be known by his real name Philip—for reasons practical and symbolic) is a case in point. Pip's closet friend is Herbert Pocket, who calls Pip Handel. Like Dickens, Hemingway uses names to suggest an inner circle, the circle that Nick has chosen over Marjorie.

Since Bill's dad is out hunting, Nick and Bill will be able to talk without any adult to hamper. There will be the frankness of contemporaries. "The Three Day Blow," like the earlier Nick stories (save, in part, "Indian Camp"), makes conversation the essential action. In this story, even more than in the others, nothing happens but the dialogue.

Once they are inside, Bill does the "adult" thing and offers Nick a drink. At the Adamses' drinking was forbidden, and Nick—although he likes the liquor—is comically new to

7. Sheridan Baker, *Ernest Hemingway* (New York: Holt, Rinehart and Winston, 1967), 123. *Wemedge* did not, however, derive from Dickens. See Carlos Baker (ed.), *Ernest Hemingway: Selected Letters, 1917–1961* (New York: Charles Scribner's Sons, 1981), 49.

it. (Drink is a big part of Nick's experience in the war in
"Night Before Landing," the fragment of Hemingway's first
abortive Nick novel. The comedy of the drinking in "The
Three Day Blow" is considerably reduced if we consider the
story, as Young does, as a postwar story.) Nick attempts a
sophisticated remark about the whiskey: "It's got a swell,
smoky taste." Explaining that the taste is caused by peat, Bill
begins a game of one-upsmanship, his game providing the
basis for most of the story's dialogue. If Nick instructed Marjorie in "The End of Something," Bill is instructing Nick here,
certainly trying to—although Nick is ready to spar over the
points. Comically, Bill takes care of Nick in a motherly or
wifely way that would be more noticed if the advice had
come from Marjorie. Consider, for example, what happens
when Nick's shoes begin to steam on the hearth:

> "Better take your shoes off," Bill said.
> "I haven't got any socks on."
> "Take them off and dry them and I'll get you some," Bill said.
> (*IOT*, 47: *NAS*, 206)

As he returns with the socks, Bill (anticipating the comedy
of Neil Simon's *The Odd Couple*) cautions, "It's getting too
late to go around without socks." And when Nick puts his
feet up on the screen in front of the fire, Bill nags, "You'll
dent in the screen," and Nick quickly removes his feet. The
comedy is for the reader rather than the boys, and it has
more point for the reader who has "The End of Something"
in mind.

The conversation turns to baseball. Now that he has taken
up the sophistication of drinking, Nick no longer looks at
baseball with all of his youthful enthusiasm. He would like
to, but the slightly older Bill reminds him of the darker side
of the sporting world. Nick is interested in the underdog St.
Louis Cardinals, who had not ever won a pennant. The New
York Giants had just about won the pennant, which makes
1917 a likely year for the story's action. "'It's a gift,' Bill said.
'As long as McGraw can buy every player in the league
there's nothing to it.'" Nick answers, "He can't buy them all"
(*IOT*, 47–48; *NAS*, 207). Although Nick accepts the more

cynical view of the world that Bill espouses in baseball and in horse racing ("There's always more to it than we know about," Nick says), he still has a strong remnant of his younger dreams: "I'd like to see the world series" (*IOT*, 49; *NAS*, 208).

The baseball discussion provides useful information for placing the story chronologically. Bill says that the World Series is always in New York or Philadelphia now, which would set the story in the hey-day for these teams. New York and Philadelphia played each other in the series in 1905, 1911, and 1913. Philadelphia represented the American League additionally in 1910, 1914, and 1915. New York was there for the National League in 1917. Hemingway allowed no internal evidence to place the story in the post–World War I years. Later Nick says that he and Marjorie had talked about going to Italy. If we use biographical information making Nick the same as Hemingway, that might suggest post-World War I—but not necessarily even then. Since neither "The End of Something" nor "The Three Day Blow" had been published before *In Our Time*, it is likely that Hemingway intended the reference to Italy ironically. Nick will not go to Italy with Marjorie, but alone and as a soldier. The crucial "Nick sat against the wall" vignette is set in Italy.

From the discussion of sports, in which Bill emerges as the one who "knows everything," the youths turn to more intellectual matters—reading. Both are serious readers, but again Bill emerges as the more sophisticated. He is reading George Meredith's *The Ordeal of Richard Feverel*. "It ain't a bad book, Wemedge," says Bill after Nick reports that he could not get into it (*IOT*, 49; *NAS*, 208). Although Meredith's poetic prose might present some difficulties for Nick, Hemingway includes the reference to the Victorian novel as an interesting counterpart thematically to Nick' story. That Hemingway intended those overtones seems clear from later developments in the conversation. Richard Feverel's life has some striking parallels to Nick's. The distrust of the female, particularly because of the mother's conduct, is a major factor in Richard Feverel's life. Richard's father is well-meaning, but uncomprehending of the realities of the world as he attempts to rear his son under a system. He fails, just as Richard fails. Richard makes some tragic mistakes about love and sex and about what it is he really wants in life. In his unfaithfulness to a devoted, lovely, and unsophisticated girl Richard rejects his great chance for happiness, as Nick fears he has in rejecting Marjorie.

Nick is more comfortable with romantic literature than with the style of Meredith. When Nick and Bill turn their attention to Maurice Hewlett's *The Forest Lovers* and Nick questions the practicality of the lovers' going to bed with a naked sword between them, Bill explains that the sword is a symbol. Nick wonders about the validity of an impractical symbol; however, the two prove themselves critics with no irreconcilable differences. Bill agrees to the merits of Nick's candidate for highest honors—Walpole—even as Nick accedes to Bill's choice, G. K. Chesterton. With the alcohol aiding the critical goodwill, they comically prove their magnanimity. Having quoted some lines, Nick says of Chesterton: "I guess he's a better guy than Walpole."

"Oh, he's a better guy, all right," Bill said.
"But Walpole's a better writer."
"I don't know," Nick said. "Chesterton's a classic."
"Walpole's a classic, too," Bill insisted.
"I wish we had them both here," Nick said. "We'd take them both fishing to the 'Voix tomorrow." (*IOT*, 51; *NAS*, 209)

Beyond such agreement, criticism cannot go; hence Bill suggests getting drunk, an adolescent adventure that reveals even Bill's amateur status in such affairs. He has to tell Nick, "My old man won't care," a point on which Nick needs some reassurance. Nick thinks he is already a little drunk, but the wiser Bill (still paralleling the teacher-student aspects of "The End of Something") informs Nick that he is not. They set about remedying the deficiency as Bill provides Nick with some astounding wisdom from his father: it's opening bottles that makes drunkards. Nick is impressed, and the narrator and the reader are amused.

This afternoon of the three-day blow has a relaxed program. There are no pressures of time—such as are present in a later story about recreation "Cross-Country Snow." Preliminary conversation, abetted by the relaxing qualities of the alcohol, moves into more serious matters. Bill's comment about his father and drinking allows Nick to ask, quite naturally and, as the narrator puts it, "respectfully," "How is your dad?" (*IOT*, 52; *NAS*, 210).

Bill's dad, like Dr. Adams, is a hunter, but as an artist he has a different life style. His vocation allows Bill's dad a measure of freedom known only intermittently to most doctors, if at all. Bill's father "gets a little wild sometimes." Although "The Three Day Blow" does not mention specifically Nick's vocational plans, we sense the appeal that the artistic life has for him. He has assessed his father's life and finds it lacking. He wants his own life to be different, to have more of the freedom of Bill's dad. Significantly, Bill's dad is a man without a woman; as far as Nick can tell the painter seems quite content with his life. "He's a swell guy," Nick says of him (*IOT*, 52; *NAS*, 210).

Nick's father is not swell, only "all right." Even as Nick continues his drinking adventure, he tells Bill that the doctor claims never to have taken a drink in his life. Nick says sadly, "He's missed a lot." The line makes perfect sense in light of this story alone, but it gains immensely when we view the story in the light of the other Nick stories as well. Emphasis on the father-son relationship was paramount in the first story of *In Our Time* and is certainly one of the major threads of all the Nick Adams stories.

Bill tries to console Nick over his hurt for his father, as he had tried to smooth over disagreement about books, with acknowledgment that his dad has had "a tough time." The narrator is amused at Nick's easy—and not to be accepted—platitude: "It all evens up" (*IOT*, 53; *NAS*, 211). It is very difficult to think so. And surely Hemingway means for his reader to see that Nick's drinking fellowship with Bill does not make up for the relationship with Marjorie that Nick has sacrificed.

A persistent motif of "The Three Day Blow" is that of

practicality. Nick found Hewlett's having the bedded lovers in his book have a naked sword between them "not very practical" (*IOT*, 50; *NAS*, 209). Bill wants Nick to be practical and put on socks. Now Nick wants to prove that he can "hold his liquor and be practical" (*IOT*, 53; *NAS*, 211). Bill also wants to be "practical"—the two become rivals in even this as Nick comically determines that he will not get drunk before Bill does. Looking at the fire while meditating the "profound truth" that it all evens up, Nick sees that the fire needs another log. Bill maintains his role of giving Nick advice and offers a "practical" suggestion: "Bring one of the big beech chunks" (*IOT*, 53; *NAS*, 211).

On the way back through the kitchen with the log, Nick, showing the effects of the alcohol, knocks a pan of apricots off the kitchen table. He carefully picks up the pan and the scattered apricots off the floor and puts more water in the pan. It is a small mishap, but Nick feels quite proud of himself: he is holding his liquor and being practical, "thoroughly practical" (*IOT*, 53; *NAS*, 211). Bill is also pleased because the beech log, which he has been saving for the bad weather, will burn all night. The drinking can proceed!

Ready to mix and not to worry, Nick finds another open bottle, and still eager to be practical, he goes into the kitchen again for some water. He can be proud that he is able to "fill the pitcher with the dipper dipping cold spring water from the pail." He seems to acknowledge his success by smiling at his face in the mirror which he passes on the way back. "He smiled at the face in the mirror and it grinned back at him. He winked at it and went on. It was not his face but it didn't make any difference" (*IOT*, 54; *NAS*, 212).

Nick is practical enough to think Bill's shots are "awfully big." Bill reassures him: "Not for us, Wemedge" (*IOT*, 54; *NAS*, 212). Whereas opening bottles can make drunkards, Hemingway's comic scene would suggest that making toasts can also. The boys begins drinking to various pleasures: to fishing, to Chesterton and Walpole until finally their drinking ritual peaks.

The moment has come for Bill to broach a subject that

could hardly have been broached earlier, before the preliminary jockeying over baseball, writers, liquor. Using the
special insider's name, Bill says—recasting the practicality
theme most pointedly—"You were wise, Wemedge" (*IOT*,
55; *NAS*, 213). He is talking about the Marge business, and
we are not surprised to find that Nick has some reservations
about *that* practicality. He can only manage: "I guess so." Bill
then takes it upon himself to prove to Nick the practicality of
his action. Marriage would have followed, and Bill comments on marriage from a hardened male perspective, one
that could come from the experience of Richard Feverel's
father or his own father: "Once a man's married he's absolutely bitched" (*IOT*, 56; *NAS*, 213). The line plays on the
earlier Nick stories, not just "The End of Something," even
as it anticipates important moments in many of the stories of
the older Nick.

Whereas the preceding topics of conversation on this
windy afternoon have found Nick trying to match Bill, the
topic of Marjorie brings forth noticeably different results.
Nick may nod, or say "Sure" or "Yes," but mostly he says
nothing. Bill may give ever so many reasons, but Nick is
unsure of their validity. He dislikes the way he behaved to
Marjorie; more important, he dislikes the prospects of a future without Marjorie. "It was all gone. All he knew was
that he had once had Marjorie and that he had lost her"
(*IOT*, 57; *NAS*, 214). Nick can only respond: "Let's have
another drink," for Bill's analysis has taken away the eupho-
ria of the preceding moments. As they start the new drinks,
Bill's statement underscores for the reader that Nick's choice
has been for male adolescence: "If you'd gone on that way
we wouldn't be here now" (*IOT*, 57; *NAS*, 214). The point is
strongly ironic for the reader, but Nick fails to see Bill's possessive streak and the rigidity of his position. Despite the
bohemian life style of Bill's father, Bill is not as liberated as
he thinks. His thinking is painfully narrow: "Now she can
marry somebody of her own sort and settle down and be
happy. You can't mix oil and water" (*IOT*, 57; *NAS*, 213).
Finally, Nick's turn to talk has come, and he lets it out,

picking up the metaphor of the story's title: "All of a sudden everything was over . . . I don't know why it was. I couldn't help it. Just like when the three-day blows come now and rip all the leaves off the trees" (*IOT*, 58; *NAS*, 214). The suddenness that the metaphor emphasizes suggests something unsettling about love, but Nick does not stop with the suddenness of the experience. He accepts blame for the event: "It was all my fault." No three-day blow will take away his pain; nor will the windy efforts of Nick and Bill to justify their treatment of Marjorie blow away Nick's doubts. A naked tree can appear very desolate.

Nevertheless, talking about the experience seems to help Nick temporarily, and the tone of the story returns to the more comic. Thinking about marriage or not, Nick again makes juvenile and naïve observations. They are not only comic, but suggest that Hemingway consciously made Nick younger than he himself was when the counterpointing events in his own life took place.

> "I tell you Wemedge, I was worried while it was going on. You played it right. I understand her mother is sore as hell. She told a lot of people you were engaged."
> "We weren't engaged," Nick said.
> "It was all around that you were."
> "I can't help it," Nick said. "We weren't."
> "Weren't you going to get married?" Bill asked.
> "Yes. But we weren't engaged," Nick said.
> "What's the difference?" Bill asked judicially. (*IOT*, 58–59; *NAS*, 214–15)

The way out of the judicial quandary is to propose more drinking and going swimming, not a very practical suggestion from Nick on this autumn day.

But once Nick's talking machine is going, he finds it difficult to stop it. He is trying to convince himself: "You know what her mother was like!" Showing further the effects of his drink, he repeats himself: "All of a sudden it was over . . . I oughtn't to talk about it." Lady Brett Ashley has a similar problem in *The Sun Also Rises* after she has returned to Jake Barnes at the end of her affair with Romero. "'I won't be one of those bitches,' she said. 'But, oh, Jake, please let's

The Adolescent 67

never talk about it.'"[8] Of course, she has just been bitching to Jake, and she keeps talking about Romero.

The liquor is doing more for the youthful Nick than it could for the more experienced Brett and Jake. Nick is determined to "watch himself," and although Bill does not know it, Nick is already playing with the possibilities that his break with Marge is not as final as the three-day blow is to the leaves: "He felt happy. Nothing was finished. Nothing was ever lost. He would go into town on Saturday. He felt lighter, as he had felt before Bill started to talk about it. There was always a way out" (*IOT*, 60; *NAS*, 215–16). But Nick is also fooling himself, for sometimes a thing is finished—as the title "The End of Something" so poignantly suggests. Some things do get lost.

Momentarily liberated by the afternoon's drink and talk, Nick and Bill, well into their cups, again decide to be practical. "There's no use getting drunk," and they step outside into the wind (*IOT*, 60; *NAS*, 216). Male camaraderie is for more than drinking. Bill's dad is hunting; they will join him. The ending of "The Three Day Blow" is similar to that of "The Doctor and the Doctor's Wife." The boys head through the woods toward the swamp. As they go, Hemingway reminds us of the odd-couple theme that has played so humorously in counterpoint to "The End of Something":

"Let's cut down that way," Nick said.
"Let's cut across the lower meadow and see if we jump anything," Bill said.
"All right," Nick said. (*IOT*, 61; *NAS*, 216)

The ending of the story also reminds us of the end of "Ten Indians" where it was a long time before Nick, hearing the wind on the lake, remembered that his heart was broken. Nick's head is now befuddled and, ambiguously, content: "None of it was important now. The wind blew it out of his head. Still he could always go into town Saturday night. It was a good thing to have in reserve" (*IOT*, 61; *NAS*, 216). The repetition of the town escape clause further convinces

8. Ernest Hemingway, *The Sun Also Rises* (New York: Charles Scribner's Sons, 1926: 1954), 243.

us that in his heart of hearts Nick is not happy with the choice he has made.

Certainly Bill's misogynistic position is not one Nick can easily accept, and Nick's various adolescent wanderings in Michigan cause him to reassess his view of women. The challenge is an important aspect of the controversial "The Light of the World."

Critics have generally considered "The Light of the World" as a Nick Adams story—although Carlos Baker does not mention it in connection with Nick in his *Hemingway: The Writer as Artist*. Most critics have gone along with Philip Young, who named it a Nick story in his influential book and included it in *The Nick Adams Stories*. If Young had been wrong on this point in his book (1952), Hemingway might easily have challenged it if he had felt it worth the while. Locale and character suggest that Hemingway did think of "The Light of the World" as a Nick story, for the unnamed protagonist is very like Nick, the experience is set in Nick's country, and it follows patterns of experience in the Nick chronicle. "The Light of the World" aside, save for "Up in Michigan," all of Hemingway's Michigan short stories are Nick stories.

Some readers may be reluctant to name Nick the protagonist of "The Light of the World" because the story is a first person narrative and the narrator never divulges his name. Third person tended to be the natural voice for Hemingway as he began his career as a short story writer, and all of the Nick stories in *In Our Time* are in third person; in fact, only "My Old Man" of *In Our Time* is in first person. After *In Our Time* Hemingway began to experiment with first person in his short stories, and five (of fourteen) stories in his second major collection, *Men Without Women*, are in first person—including three Nick stories. "The Light of the World" appeared in Hemingway's third major collection, *Winner Take Nothing*. When Hemingway wrote "The Light of the World" he had yet to publish a novel (other than the satiric and brief *The Torrents of Spring*) written in third person. As a novelist he had found first person a more congenial voice, and he achieved his worldwide fame in the two novels from that perspective, *The Sun Also Rises* and *A Farewell to Arms.* He was, in short, a master at creating subtleties in first person when he wrote "The Light of the World." Fully half, seven of the fourteen stories of *Winner Take Nothing,* are first person accounts. Hemingway was a more courageous experimenter than is often recognized. The difference in the effect of the first-person voice in "My Old Man" and "The Light of the World" is immense.

In *Men Without Women* Hemingway used first person in portraying Nick after his wounding in war. How would Nick narrate an experience before that turning point? For Nick, the most important things to write about before the war as well as after it would be those things that had perplexed him. Since Nick has set his goal to be a writer at a young age (a point made explicit in "The Last Good Country"), it is natural to think of his first person accounts as written as it is natural to think of Faulkner's V. K. Ratliff as narrating "Spotted Horses" to a group of listeners. "Big Two-Hearted River," the final story of *In Our Time,* indicated that Nick was already launched on a writing career, and earlier stories of the book prepare us for this step. We have seen Nick's early interest in books ("The Doctor and the Doctor's Wife" and "The Three Day Blow"). Metaphorical thinking is natural to Nick: "I couldn't help it," he had told Bill. "Just like when the three-day blows come now and rip all the leaves off the trees." The metaphor is Nick's as well as Hemingway's. What would be more natural than a narrative from young Nick about his Michigan travels?

Yet "The Light of the World" is much more than the narration of a young man. It is perhaps the most "literary" of the Nick stories, and the title first conveys this aspect of the story's timbre. Readers have been reminded of Jesus' words in John 8:12 ("I am the light of the world") or in Matthew 5:14 ("Ye are the light of the world") and Holman Hunt's famous picture of Jesus holding a lantern and knocking at a cottager's door, but just as likely a source is the gospel hymn "The Light of the World."[9] One source need not rule out another. The multiple possibilities are, in fact, especially appropriate to the story. In many of the Nick stories, as in the body of Hemingway's short stories, the outer action is minimal, often rather quiet, based on the normal. "The Light of the World" deals with the extraordinary. Whereas the Nick stories tend to have precise counterparts in Hemingway's experience, the germ for "The Light of the World" was not personal experience but another literary work. Hemingway advised readers who were interested in his story to read Guy de Maupassant's "La Maison Tellier,"[10] a comic story in which a madame in a small French village takes her five prostitutes on a journey to her brother's house for the occasion of her niece's confirmation—briefly upsetting the contented routine of life in the village. In Hemingway's rendition of five prostitutes in transit (probably for business reasons) the naïveté of the narrator's viewpoint is a useful balance to the complexity of the story's workings.

Naturally, Hemingway felt that he had surpassed de Maupassant, or he would not have invited the comparison. He wanted to have the story in the lead position in *Winner Take Nothing*, but finally had to surrender to Maxwell Perkin's argument that it would invite the wrong kinds of judgments from the reviewers. Hemingway was right in thinking so highly of "The Light of the World," although critics largely ignored it until James J. Martine called attention to some facts about boxing history that Hemingway plays on in the story. After examining the historical context of the story,

9. P. P. Bliss's well-known hymn was copyrighted in 1903 and made its way into numerous Protestant hymnals. The hymn begins, "The whole world was lost in the darkness of sin," a view rather vividly presented in Hemingway's story. The vibrancy and affirmation of the hymn counterpoint the uncertainty portrayed in the story, especially in the refrain: "Come to the Light, 'tis shining for thee; / Sweetly the Light has dawned upon me, / Once I was blind, but now I can see: / The Light of the world is Jesus." I like especially to counterpoint the third line of the refrain to the story.

10. Carlos Baker, *Ernest Hemingway: A Life Story* (New York: Charles Scribner's Sons, 1969), 241.

Martine concluded that "the point of the story . . . is the unreliability of what a woman, any women, says."[11]

Martine's verdict has not gone down easily with succeeding critics, and it is the more unsettling to anyone considering the body of Nick stories. We know that Nick has concluded that his mother is a threat, but that he finds her whole sex untrustworthy is too extreme a conclusion. Marjorie may not have been ideal for Nick in every way, but her example has to count for as much as that of Alice and Peroxide in "The Light of the World." Mrs. Garner from "Ten Indians" does not speak badly for the female sex. And "The Light of the World," after all, is about prostitutes, not wives or all women. The lives of prostitutes, however pleasant they may seem to be in a small French village in de Maupassant's story (and he also indicates that there are drawbacks), is obviously a hard one. Although the need for "pipe dreams" may be universal, as Eugene O'Neill's play *The Iceman Cometh* suggests, the prostitute may have greater need of them than someone like Mrs. Garner.

Honoring the tradition that the narrator is Nick, let us look at Hemingway's story, and view it as fulfillment of Nick's consolation at the end of "The Three Day Blow" that he could always go into town. As "The Light of the World" begins, Nick and a friend, Tom, enter a bar. We are edging farther from "home" and "cottage." With no Marjorie to stake any claims, Nick has begun to explore the surrounding Michigan area. But he is still playing "follow the leader." Tom is the older, wiser head who leads Nick in this exploration, as Bill might on others.

Carlos Baker points out that there is much that is comic in the story.[12] The humor is heightened as the reader views Nick's relationship with Tom in light of his relationship with Bill. Still, the humor teems with dark suggestions, for it is a

11. James J. Martine, "A Little Light on Hemingway's 'The Light of the World,'" in Benson (ed.) *The Short Stories of Ernest Hemingway*, 198. Martine's article first appeared in *Studies in Short Fiction*, VI (Summer, 1970), 465–67.

12. Carlos Baker, *Hemingway: The Writer as Artist*, (4th ed.; Princeton: Princeton University Press, 1972), 140.

fierce world out there that Nick is discovering. As he and Tom enter the saloon, the bartender immediately covers up the two free-lunch bowls. Nick tries to sound like the cowboy who has just entered a saloon in the wild West: "Give me a beer" (*WTN*, 21; *NAS*, 39). The bartender is in no mood to be friendly; he too echoes the western mode turning to Tom with a blunt "What's yours?" The conviviality of "La Maison Tellier" is not to be found here. "What's yours?" is as far as the bartender wants to go with anybody: everyone is a stranger. Tom resents the bartender's attitude. His philosophy is that in a tough world you have to be tough, and he seems intent on showing Nick how it is done as he reaches over and takes off the top of the free-lunch bowl. The bartender is his usual loquacious self: "No." But Tom is not going to back down; he enjoys testing the bartender. He keeps hold of the wood scissors fork and has a smart "You know where" for the bartender, who tells him to put it back.

Nick, in contrast, is noticeably uncomfortable. Who knows where this belligerence might lead? Preferring to be the peacemaker, he puts fifty cents on the counter. "Free-lunch bowl" becomes one of the story's first jokes. Nick is learning that one has to pay one's way in this world. When he orders his second beer, the bartender uncovers both bowls.

So matters might rest. But Tom wants to repay the bartender for the insult of treating him and Nick as kids. He spits out what he has started to eat and says, "Your goddam pig's feet stink" (*WTN*, 22; *NAS*, 40). For the moment the bartender does not say anything; a customer who has drunk his rye does not bat an eyelash, but quickly pays and leaves without speaking to anyone. And he does not look back. Hemingway's model (ironic, of course) for the first scene of the story is the popular western. Before the big fight, the wise retreat—a tradition parodied in Stephen Crane's "The Bride Comes to Yellow Sky" as well as here.

The bartender has not spoken in anger. His words are quite considered, for he has encountered the likes of Tom often: "You stink yourself . . . All you punks stink." Will we get the fight of the western saloon? Tom would like that, and he looks toward his partner: "He says we're punks." Hemingway varies the western formula; Nick is not itching for a fight. He would rather avoid trouble and get to more friendly surroundings—something closer to those he left in "The Three Day Blow." Significantly, at this point, Nick the narrator of the story stops calling his friend "Tom" and reverts to a more friendly and boyish "Tommy." As a character in the story, he advises departure but not cravenly. "I said we were going out . . . It wasn't your idea," he says to the bartender, who has become more belligerent. Tom threatens, "We'll be back" (*WTN*, 22; *NAS*, 40). But Nick does not wish to push the bartender, only to leave the saloon that is anything but a clean, well-lighted place. As the boys leave, "The Light of the World" utilizes the light-dark imagery that is characteristic of many of the Nick stories: "Outside it was good and dark." It has been dark inside too.

Once outdoors, Tom is not the same experienced voice that he was inside. "What the hell kind of place is this?" he asks. Tom's language is always less genteel than Nick's, a point worth noticing not only because we catch the swagger in Tom and his tendency to train Nick in being tough, but because voice—intonations as well as words—has an important effect on the story's tone and final meaning. Perhaps because he would like to hear different kinds of voices, Nick suggests going to the train station. It is dark and cold in town; maybe there will be some light and warmth in another place where human beings gather. Clearly the boys are not going to take a train. They buy no tickets, and they leave before the train comes. They have no timetable.

Inside the train station there is a most unusual gathering: there are five prostitutes, several white men, and four Indians. Nick would have to wait a long time before he could again find five prostitutes gathered in a small Michigan lumber town's railroad station, especially in company with a male homosexual cook. Five is the number of prostitutes who work for Madame Tellier, but there is no Madame Tellier here to resolve any disagreements or to give direction.

Hemingway plays complex games with his readers in this waiting room, for realities shift easily on us. What and where is truth is the question captured in the fiber of the story. Just as the free-lunch bowls turned out not to be free, there is much in the train station that is chimerical, like the dress of the biggest whore: "one of those silk dresses that change colors" (*WTN*, 23; *NAS*, 41). Even Nick seems to change before our eyes. He is only seventeen we learn, and the saloon scene has established him as a very young seventeen. There is something comic about his telling us: "She was the biggest whore I ever saw in my life and the biggest woman" (*WTN*, 23; *NAS*, 41). Nothing suggests that Nick is telling a story a long time after the events. His change from calling his friend Tom to calling him Tommy indicates that the telling is close to the events. Is Nick's comment on whores he has seen a lapse on Hemingway's part? Or is Nick the narrator bragging—unaware that his reader would find his observation comic? We notice too that when Nick and Tom enter the station there are *four* Indians. The fourth one simply disappears, it seems. A bit into the narrative we are told: "Two Indians were sitting down at the end of the bench and one standing up against the wall" (*WTN*, 23; *NAS*, 42). Later on we read: "The ticket window went up and the three Indians went over to it" (*WTN*, 26; *NAS*, 44). One little, two little, three little Indians? Where is the fourth? The puzzle is like Hawthorne's having Old Moodie of *The Blithedale Romance* appear in Chapter X with a patch over his left eye but with a patch over his right eye in Chapter XXI. The discrepancy serves to call attention to the theme of disguise and costume in the story—just as here Hemingway suggests the difficulty of ascertaining reality.[13]

The waiting room of the train station, it turns out, is every bit as hostile as the saloon the boys have just left. "Shut the

13. Barbara Maloy argues in "The Light of Alice's World" that the controlling metaphor of the story comes from Lewis Carroll's *Alice in Wonderland* and *Alice Through the Looking Glass*. See Bates L. Hoffer (ed.), *Hemingway's Experiments in Structure and Style, Linguistics in Literature*, (Spring, 1976), 69–86. I think it likely that Hemingway did have Carroll's work in mind, but using it exclusively as she does, Maloy fails to take us back to Michigan

door, can't you?" (*WTN*, 22; *NAS*, 41) one of the white men says as they enter. Nick looks to see who it is. The speaker is obviously different from the other men gathered, and Nick—an interested observer of the human scene—quickly notes the difference: "He wore stagged trousers and lumbermen's rubbers and a mackinaw shirt like the others, but he had no cap and his face was white and his hands were white and thin." Nick pauses long enough (because he is a keen observer) to cause the petulant voice to repeat the request: "Aren't you going to shut it?" Characteristically wishing to maintain the peace, Nick responds, "Sure," and shuts the door.

Although Nick's compliance is followed with a "Thank you"—words that sound strange in the alien world of the raw "frontier" town—the uncertainty of the meaning of the speaker's politeness is immediately made apparent, for politeness is followed by a snicker and the clear implication that the white man with the white, thin hands is a homosexual. Nick has been looking for a friendly voice in this town, but the one he finds is ambiguous. Nick hardly knows how to respond to the comments made about the homosexual cook. The sense of uncertainty and ambiguity contrasts with the saloon incidents where western formula at least suggested what the next development might be. The saloon was a place where males gathered, and it now seems an uncomplicated arena. In the station, sexuality is immediately a complicating factor, and it is more difficult for Nick or the reader to see where the next move will come or what the one that has just passed means.

The snicker of the unnamed white man becomes laughter at the cook's expense, the first laughter of the story, and a distinctive laughter it is since it comes from the "biggest

---

and the real world. Hemingway's hint of de Maupassant is more productive, finally, than Maloy's. As I have stressed, there are many allusions in the story. (Carlos Baker's comparison of Alice to Chaucer's Alice of Bath is also worth notice: the Chaucerian motif does take us to the real world.) Although it is not amiss to think of Carroll, Nick's experience here is finally more like Hawthorne's Robin in "My Kinsman, Major Molineaux" than like Alice's.

whore" (about three hundred and fifty pounds) that Nick
has ever seen. His observant eye quickly takes in this whore,
two others who are nearly as big (although we are shortly
told that the laughing whore outweighs them by a hundred pounds) and in the same silk dresses that change colors, and two "ordinary looking whores" who are peroxide
blondes—yet another detail to heighten the appearance-
reality puzzle. The biggest whore's laughter is extreme (no
one else is laughing), and the cook's politeness quickly dissipates: "You big disgusting mountain of flesh" (*WTN*, 23;
NAS, 41). But the whore keeps on laughing and shaking
at the comedy she finds in the scene: "Oh, my Christ . . .
Oh, my sweet Christ." Nick observes that she has a "nice
voice"—and voices have been anything but nice up to this
point.

The whore's laughter has diverted the group's attention
from the cook to her, and the lumberjack "who was getting
ready to say something" speaks to Nick very low: "Must be
like getting on top of a hay mow." Nick laughs at the comment (because laughter is expected rather than because the
comment is funny) and repeats it to "Tommy," but Tom, less
careful of anyone's feelings, makes his observation to a
larger audience, apparently. Man of experience that he pretends to be, he must admit the present scene is unusual: "I
swear to Christ I've never been anywhere like this . . . Look
at the three of them" (*WTN*, 24; *NAS*, 42).

When the cook again tries to be friendly, Tom immediately
indicates that his friendliness is not to be trusted. To the
cook's question about the boys' ages, Tom replies with a
crude joke, which only the biggest whore appreciates: "Ho!
Ho! Ho!" Nick is again taken by her "really pretty voice,"
and Nick becomes peacemaker in the station as he had been
in the saloon. When the cook pleads for decency, Nick decides that some friendliness would not be amiss in this hostile atmosphere. To Tom's annoyance he informs the groups
of their green ages, seventeen and nineteen.

Kindness begets kindness, trust begets trust—at least

with most people. In the bar, hostility answered hostility. Here the big whore responds to Nick's gesture and tells him that he can call her Alice. A first name can mean warmth and invite ease and confidence—as "The Three Day Blow" emphasizes. It is significant that in "The Light of the World" Tom and Nick never actually address each other by name— the setting is too public. A name puts a handle on a person, allows others later claim. The theme is used in James Joyce's "An Encounter"—a first person account of an unnamed boy that has several interesting parallels with "The Light of the World." There the narrator instructs his friend with whom he has played truant from school that they should use pseudo- nyms in case the "queer old josser" (a sexually maladjusted man they have met) asks their names. In Hemingway's story wise Tom is skeptical of the whore: "Is that your name?" he asks. The whore knows that truth is elusive sometimes; so she turns to the man by the cook to get verification. "Alice, isn't it?" (*WTN*, 24; *NAS*, 42). Names, crucial for the story's theme, take on increasing importance.

The cook, in obvious competition with Alice, meets her gesture with sarcasm: "That's the sort of name you'd have." Alice quickly declares that it is her real name too. Since Nick the narrator henceforth calls her that in his account, it is clear that he believes her. Even Tom responds to Alice's openness and asks the names of the other girls. Alice is discriminating, for she gives only the names of the other fat whores, who smile. Nick takes the more relaxed atmosphere as encouragement to ask one of the blondes her name, and she answers, but checks the tendency toward friendliness at the same time: "Frances Wilson. What's it to you?" The fifth whore refuses to give her name. In a tone of voice that is easy to imagine, the man who has done most of the talking says: "He just wants us all to be friends . . . Don't you want to be friends?" Peroxide's answers are sharp: "No . . . Not with you" (*WTN*, 24; *NAS*, 43). The idea that anyone would go to these women for "love" is preposterous. Again, we sense the great distance between this world and the community of "La Maison Tellier." Coldness has quickly dissipated warmth; no one cares to ask the boys their names, and only four whores are named in the conversation.

Alice's response to the resurfaced hostility is laughter. "There's nothing funny!" the cook replies—but he is only partly right. "You all laugh but there's nothing funny," he continues, and this time he is obviously wrong. They are not all laughing; only Alice's laughter marks the scene, for only Alice has any perspective on the occasion or provides any healing.

In another attempt to win the boys from Alice, the cook asks about their destination. Tom is too wise (like the narrator of "An Encounter") to tell, but the cook volunteers his destination—hoping to beget trust. He is bound for Cadillac, where his sister lives. His announcement, expectedly, meets with a crude joke. The cook pleads for decency: "Can't you stop that sort of thing?" . . . Can't we speak decently?" (*WTN*, 25; *NAS*, 43). Attempts to speak decently fail repeatedly in this story.

But by declaring his destination, the cook has brought forth a name that produces the climactic discussion of the story. When the shy man mentions that Steve Ketchel and Al Wolgast are from Cadillac, one of the blondes repeats Steve Ketchel's name "in a high voice as though the *name*-[emphasis provided] had pulled a trigger in her." What his name triggers is a highly emotive speech: "His own father shot and killed him. Yes, by Christ, his own father. There aren't any more men like Steve Ketchel" (*WTN*, 25; *NAS*, 43).

As in the other stories of Nick's youth, the skirmishes are verbal. The cook was the initiator of conversation as the boys entered the waiting room; it is appropriate and a part of the subtle battle being waged that he be the one who undercuts, decently to be sure, the impact of the blonde's speech: "Wasn't his name Stanley Ketchel?"

True identity is one of the things hard to come by in "The Light of the World," and the cook's comment went largely unnoticed before Martine did his research into boxing history. There was a Stanley Ketchel and a Steve Ketchel, both boxers. Stanley Ketchel, who was from Grand Rapids, fought Jack Johnson on October 16, 1909, in Coloma, California, and he was shot and killed on October 15, 1910, in Conway, Missouri, but not by his father. A ranch hand shot him in an argument over a girl. Steve Ketchel fought Al Wolgast on July 31, 1915, in Forest Park, Illinois. Hemingway—as the world knows—had a great interest in boxing and would have known of both Ketchels.

Rhetoric can be so effective as to obscure realities, and that seems to be part of Hemingway's point in the story. The peroxide whore tells the cook to "shut up"—the kind of response most questions get in this story—and proceeds to overpower those in the waiting room with one of the longest speeches of the story. She is so effective that the cook (no mean opponent) does not directly press his point; for the moment she is convincing: " 'Steve? Stanley. He was no Stanley. Steve Ketchel was the finest and most beautiful man that ever lived. I never saw a man as clean and white and as beautiful as Steve Ketchel. There never was a man like that. He moved just like a tiger and he was the finest, free-est, spender that ever lived.'" One of the men gives her further opportunity to demonstrate her rhetorical skill by asking if she knew him: "Did I know him? Did I know him? Did I love him? You ask me that? I knew him like you know nobody in the world and I loved him like you love God. He was the greatest, finest, whitest, most beautiful man that ever lived, Steve Ketchel, and his own father shot him down like a dog" (*WTN*, 25; *NAS*, 44).

For the moment the group is nonplussed, although the narrator observes that these speeches had been given in a "high stagey way." Alice again responds in her characteristic manner—seeing the humor of this badly played tragedy. She was beginning to shake again. Nick's allegiance is clear, since—as we now learn—he is sitting by her.

It is again the cook's turn, and he begins to move the group toward skepticism as he cuts Peroxide's authority in an insightful "innocent" remark: "You should have mar-

ried him." When Peroxide replies that she would not want
to hurt his career, the cook is smart enough to detect the
phoniness: "That was a fine way to look at it," and he proceeds to launch a third attack: "Didn't Jack Johnson knock
him out though?" (*WTN*, 26; *NAS*, 44). Cook is nothing if
not persistent.

The cook is leading Peroxide on to trap herself. She declares, romantically, that Johnson took him by a fluke. Her
account gets a punctuation similar to that at the end of *The
Sun Also Rises* when Brett is telling Jake what a good time
they could have had together.

> Ahead was a mounted policeman in khaki directing traffic. He
> raised his baton. The car pressed Brett against me.
> "Yes," I said. "Isn't it pretty to think so?"[14]

In "The Light of the World" the ticket window goes up, and
the three Indians go over to it. Peroxide's bilge is not really
worth listening to. (Hemingway had used Indians similarly
in *The Torrents of Spring*, his 1926 satire of Sherwood Anderson's *Dark Laughter*, as a "red laughter.") To the others she
explains that the knockout came when Steve had turned to
look at her. After someone recalls her earlier remark that she
had not been on the coast, Peroxide must hastily explain
that she had gone out just for the fight.

Peroxide rallies from this implausibility with her rhetoric
after the lumberjack observes that Steve was a great fighter:
"I hope to God he was . . . I hope to God they don't have
fighters like that now. He was like a god, he was. So white
and clean and beautiful and smooth and fast like a tiger or
the lightning" (*WTN*, 26; *NAS*, 45). It is a comic touch that
even Tom is caught by Peroxide's rhetoric, but the Indians
have gone out to the platform. Alice is shaking again, but
Nick does not know how to interpret her special punctuation. Peroxide seizes the moment of her seeming victory for
a final outburst: "He was more than a husband could ever
be . . . We were married in the eyes of God and I belong to
him right now and always will and all of me is his. I don't

14. Ernest Hemingway, *The Sun Also Rises*, 247.

care about my body. They can take my body. My soul belongs to Steve Ketchel. By God, he was a man" (*WTN*, 26; *NAS*, 45).

The words are embarrassing. They have been spoken for public consumption rather than as a reflection of how Peroxide truly feels. It will be up to Alice to confront Peroxide. The cook is replaced as opponent, and the others in the waiting room are silent as the two whores verbally square off. Alice hurls the challenge: "You're a dirty liar . . . You never layed Steve Ketchel in your life and you know it." The fight anticipated in the saloon scene is now forthcoming, although in different form. It, however, will be one that will instruct Nick, whereas the saloon fight would have been merely brawn.

Alice claims that she is the only one in the room who knew Steve Ketchel. "I come from Mancelona and I knew him there and it's true and you know it and God can strike me dead if it isn't true." Alice has countered Peroxide's claim with a rather homely declaration. She claims no California trips, but judges herself solely in terms of her profession: "He said, 'You're a lovely piece, Alice.' That's exactly what he said" (*WTN*, 27; *NAS*, 45).

Although Peroxide calls Alice's statement lies, Nick finds Alice's voice highly persuasive. Readers, at least before Martine, have too: "'It's true,' said Alice in her nice voice. 'And it doesn't make any difference to me whether you believe it or not.'" She is now calm; it is hard not to believe her simple dignity.

But what if the cook is right? What if Alice is remembering incorrectly—Steve rather than Stanley? Must we conclude that Alice's lovely voice is deceptive? Hemingway once described the story as "a love letter to a whore named Alice."[15] If the story is a love letter, then Hemingway obviously approves of Alice's lovely voice. Hemingway went on to explain "the point" in such terms that would indicate his sympathy for, not fear of, women: "nobody . . . knows

---

15. Young, "'Big World Out There,'" 33.

how we were then from how we are now. This is worse on women than on us."

It does not matter if Alice has mixed Steve and Stanley. What is important is that Alice judges herself in terms of her profession. We recall the earlier, "Must be like getting on top of a hay mow." What we learn from Alice is what it *is* like, the kind of claims a whore can and cannot make about her clients. Neither Peroxide's "They can take my body," nor anything she says, indicates a quality-time—even in her harsh profession. Alice (whose name is derived from Adelaide, which means nobility or royalty) judges herself realistically: "I'm clean and you know it and men like me, even though I'm big, and you know it, and I never lie and you know it."[16] Alice has won the fight as Peroxide retreats with "Leave me with my memories . . . With my true, wonderful memories" (*WTN*, 27; *NAS* 46).

Although it is a dark and cold world that Hemingway portrays in "The Light of of the World," Alice casts more than ironical light. Scott Donaldson puts it succinctly: "Nick correctly perceives that the massive whore Alice, despite her profession, is capable of love, the true 'light of the world.'"[17] Nick is learning how to read voices, to distinguish where the true is to be found. The details of a story or a memory may or may not be precise, but there is a heart's truth—as Nick here perceives. Although the narrator makes no reference to "the Marge business," the reader considering Nick's development sees the obvious relevance of Nick's ended romance. Like Alice, Marge had her special nobility, made no

16. Maloy would prefer to have the name come from the Greek *Aletheia*, 29. But it is usually cited as coming from *Adelaide*—noble cheer or princess. The name was a popular one of Romance in the Middle Ages, passed from favor, but was revived in the mid-nineteenth century. Hemingway may also have been remembering a poem of Edmund Clarence Stedman, the influential nineteenth-century American poet and critic. Student of war and war literature that he was, Hemingway may have read Stedman's long poem of the Civil War, "Alice of Monmouth" (1863). The source adds a partly ironic dimension. Consider the lines: "Her slender form is tall and strong: / Her voice is sweetest in the song: / Her brown hair, fit to wear a crown."

17. Scott Donaldson, *By Force of Will: The Life and Art of Ernest Hemingway* (New York: Viking, 1977), 238.

claims beyond what she should: she loved and lost. Nick has learned more about the necessity for "light" in a dark world.

Nick's decision for Alice is so strong that Tom cannot help but notice it as Nick observes Alice's light. He reverses the end of the saloon scene: "Come on. Let's go." Nick and Alice demonstrate the kinship as they exchange goodbyes. The cook is comically persistent, "Which way are you boys going?" Tom restores the reader to the outside world: "The other way from you" (*WTN*, 28; *NAS*, 46).

In order to learn to handle that outside world Nick is going to have to journey on his own. Both Bill of "The Three Day Blow" and Tom of "The Light of the World" are willing, even eager, to tutor Nick, but their limitations are obvious even as they instruct. Thus, Hemingway's placing "The Battler" immediately after "The Three Day Blow" in *In Our Time* carries considerable weight. It also follows "The Light of the World" (although that was written later) in many thematic ways, giving further credence to the validity of the tradition that the "I" of the story is Nick.

"The Battler" begins *in medias res* to give the reader assurance that Nick is going to be able to manage without a Bill or Tom to take care of him. "Nick stood up. He was all right" (*IOT*, 65; *NAS*, 47). At once, Nick is the battler of the title. However, he is not in a literal boxing ring, as the opening sentences might at first suggest. A brakeman has knocked him from a freight car in northern Michigan, not far from Mancelona, where Alice first knew her Steve Ketchel. But Nick is at great psychological distance from Mancelona, for "There was water on both sides of the track, then tamrack swamp."

If someone knocks you down, you should get up before the count—as Nick has. He takes inventory of his person and shows those traits that indicate he is his father's son. We are told that he washed his hands "carefully in the cold water, getting the dirt out from the nails. He squatted down and bathed his knee" (*IOT*, 65; *NAS*, 47). Survival requires precise care, and Nick is already the perfectionist in other things as well as fishing.

With his person checked out, Nick must then evaluate the experience. Although he has learned something about reading character in "The Light of the World," he has just received reenforcement that voices can be deceiving. Recognizing the deceit, Nick thinks of revenge: "That lousy crut of a brakeman. He would get him some day. He would know him again." Nick had been as trustingly naïve as he had been in "The Light of the World." "Come here, kid," the brakeman had said. "I got something for you." But Nick is really angry with himself for having trusted that voice. He tells himself that it was a "lousy kid thing to have done." Nick is determined to put childhood behind him. He has developed a larger sense of the alien world than he had in "The Light of the World": "They would never suck him in that way again" (*IOT*, 65; *NAS*, 47). Consistently applied, such a view might lead to the extreme cynicism of Frederic Henry's reading of the universe at the end of *A Farewell to Arms* as he anguishes at Catherine's deathbed: "Now Catherine would die. That was what you did. You died. You did not know what it was about. You never had time to learn. They threw you in and told you the rules and the first time they caught you off base they killed you. Or they killed you gratuitously like Aymo. Or gave you the syphilis like Rinaldi. But they killed you in the end. You could count on that. Stay around and they would kill you."[18] In "The Battler" Nick is, of course, a good distance from grimness and self-pity. Nevertheless, the sense of a "they" will be reenforced by later events of the story. It seems worth noting here that the context of the story establishes Nick's resolution as a boyish reaction. It is the sort of thing that Nick has learned from Tom. Almost immediately, however, he is thinking better: "Oh, well, it was only a black eye. That was all he had gotten out of it" (*IOT*, 66; *NAS*, 47–48). Already Nick appears ready to invest more of himself in the human arena.

There are more important things than revenge, and

18. Ernest Hemingway, *A Farewell to Arms* (New York: Charles Scribner's Sons, 1929; 1957), 327.

Hemingway's careful description of where Nick is indicates that Nick is more concerned with finding answers than with gaining revenge. Weather and place function metaphorically for Nick as well as for the reader: "It was dark and he was a long way off from anywhere." Nick is a pilgrim, and he seems to sense it. About him is a threatening swamp, "three of four miles of swamp," that looks "ghostly in the rising mist." As Nick walks along, his need for people and fellowship as well as an ultimate goal is implied: "He must get to somewhere" (*IOT*, 66; *NAS*, 48).

Hemingway emphasizes Nick's metaphysical isolation even as he creates the suspense of Nick's plight—alone, with much of the day spent. Nick walks for some miles, until finally he comes to a bridge. As he crosses the bridge, his boots ring "hollow on the iron" and below "the water showed black." The bridge is carrying him to a place half of nightmare—to a place more threatening than that of the saloon or railroad station in "The Light of the World." Up the track Nick sees a fire, which might give him light and warmth, but he knows enough to proceed "carefully." At first the light is very small, finally it is bright. Nick cautiously waits behind a tree and observes a man sitting in front of the fire. Nick apparently debates about the possibility that he might be "taken in" as he was by the brakeman. Finally, however, he decides to take his chances and steps "into the firelight" (*IOT*, 67; *NAS*, 48–49).

What Nick finds in the firelight is as complex as what he and Tom had found in the railroad station. ("The Battler" and "The Light of the World" are similarly structured. In each story, Nick—seeking for light and fellowship after harsh treatment from a stranger—comes into "grotesque" company to find in that company new insight about the nature of love. As each story ends, Nick is walking away from the grotesques—with a companion in "The Light of the World" but alone in "The Battler," ready to test his new knowledge.) If the brakeman, in retrospect, is as easy to decipher as the bartender in "The Light of the World," Nick will be longer puzzled by the man sitting by the fire whom he has already been watching for some moments. The man sits there like some Ethan Brand "looking into the fire." He is not a person who belongs to the everyday world. The man is so intent on what he sees in the fire that he does not notice Nick, who has stopped quite close to him, and Nick must break the man's trance with a "Hello!" (*IOT*, 67; *NAS*, 49).

Nick is not the only battler of the story, although the fact that he is one is his badge of entry into the circle. The first thing the fire-watcher notices about Nick is his black eye: "Where did you get the shiner?" Nick gives the honest answers that we would expect of him; he is as guileless as he was in "The Light of the World." The man's reaction presents a perspective on the world's hostility that Nick has hardly formulated for himself: "It must have made him feel good to bust you." Nick quickly reverts to his revenge posture, but it is only posture. When the man declares, "You're a tough one, aren't you?" Nick sounds very like the youth of "The Light of the World." "No," is his simple answer. He clearly is not a tough one, but he would like to practice what Tom preaches. "You got to be tough" (*IOT*, 68; *NAS*, 49), he affirms.

The reader discovers later—a revelation that is a shock for Nick—that the man who sets such priority on toughness is the boxer Ad Francis. In "The Light of the World" both Tom and Nick are reverential toward boxing heroes: they admire the courage of the professional battler. Tom is grateful that he had seen the movies of Ketchel's fight against Johnson. At that moment, however, Nick is aware only that he is looking at a very strange person. In *Winesburg, Ohio* Anderson's George Willard learns much from his experience with people Anderson designates "grotesques"—people who look or act strangely by the norms of society but who may nevertheless have special insight into life. Certainly, now that he is close enough to observe Francis in detail, Nick sees something strange. Although Nick sees gradually, we must assume that he takes in a great deal—since Hemingway's handling of point of view in the story has emphasized the process of internal analysis from the beginning: "The man looked at Nick and smiled. In the firelight Nick saw that the face was misshapen. His nose was sunken, his eyes were slits, he had queer shaped lips. Nick did not perceive all this at once. He only saw the man's face was queerly formed and mutilated. It was like putty in color. Dead looking in the firelight" (*IOT*, 68; *NAS*, 49). If Nick in "The Light of the World" could categorize three-hundred-fifty-pound Alice as the "largest whore" he has ever seen, he hardly knows what to say or think as he takes in the special death of the face in the firelight. Ad Francis is proud of his badges, and takes of his cap to show Nick that he has only one ear. Hardly immunized against such a sight, Nick is a little sick. "I could take it" (*IOT*, 69; *NAS*, 50), Ad says. But the missing ear is good for more than adding to visual grotesquerie: what Nick learns later strongly suggests that Hemingway wanted to remind his readers of Vincent Van Gogh's missing ear and Van Gogh's unhappy love affair.

Nick has never met anyone like Ad—he obviously regrets having come to this campfire. His remarks are terse, and he would like to make a retreat. Ad, however, wants to talk: "They all bust their hands on me . . . they couldn't hurt me." He invites Nick to sit, to eat, to call him Ad—the kinds of invitations that came so reluctantly if at all in "The Light of the World"; and Ad has an announcement that could not totally surprise Nick: "I'm not quite right." When he confesses to Nick that he is crazy, Nick feels like laughing, but the line initiates a strong motif for *In Our Time* and for Nick's own career. Nick's lot will have much in common with that of this strange looking fire-watcher. Anticipating much of Nick's future agony, Ad asks: "Listen, you ever been crazy?" (*IOT*, 69; *NAS*, 50).

It is at the point when the topic of sanity is raised that Ad reveals to Nick who he is. "Honest to God?" Nick replies, and Ad can see Nick's shock. "Don't you believe it?" What is new in the Nick stories with "The Battler" is the idea that a human character could change so dramatically, so noticeably. The Ad Francis that Nick knew about was a fighter, a win-

ner, someone heroic. What Nick now sees both frightens
and sickens him. No more was Ethan Brand always the de-
mented and frightening character that little Joe Bartram
finds in Hawthorne's short story.

The eeriness becomes even greater as Ad, a man of
strange pride, tells Nick how he was able to "beat them." He
explains that his heart is slow, beating forty a minute, and
invites Nick to take hold of his wrist and take his pulse.
Nick does so, but we hardly think Tom or Bill would have.
The touch leads to no epiphany or communal fellowship, as
it might have in an Anderson story. Nick wishes merely not
to cross this strange person, and he arrives at the prescribed
forty per minute, whether that was the count or not, whether he counted or not.

A man like Ad, who has so single, so narrow a truth for
life, would hardly be capable of taking care of himself, and
Nick's anxiety is relieved by the arrival of Ad's caretaker,
Bugs, a black man whom Ad greets warmly: "Hello, Bugs!"
Ad seems happy as he makes the introductions: "This is my
pal Bugs . . . He's crazy, too" (*IOT*, 71; *NAS*, 51).

But Bugs is not crazy. He immediately asks where Nick is
from and what his name is (as no one bothered to do in
"The Light of the World"). Nick does not name the Michigan
lake of his parents' cottage as his home, although he might
reasonably have done so. He responds more impressively
with Chicago—a tough city, city of the big shoulders as Carl
Sandburg definitively described it. There is no designation
of any Chicago suburb, where we find Nick in a later story—
"The Killers."

Ad Francis, of course, is not impressed with Nick's designation of Chicago, for he can see that Nick is not tough. But
Nick has told him something he has found impressive: "He
says he's never been crazy, Bugs." We are reminded of Bugs's
race as he quietly responds: "He's got a lot coming to him."
As a Negro, Bugs has also had to be a battler. But there
is something reassuring about Bugs's method of battling.
As he tells Ad, he hears "most of what goes on." No fire-
watcher, Bugs has been busy, and he goes about his busi-

ness and unwraps a package by the fire. Nick finds the
normalcy reassuring. Having earlier refused an invitation
from Ad to stay to eat, he responds differently to the invitation now that Bugs is there although the invitation is again
from Ad: "Are you hungry, Nick?" Nick admits that he is
"Hungry as hell" (*IOT*, 72; *NAS*, 52).

The difference between Bugs and Ad is seen in the cool
efficiency of Bugs. Bugs has been away to get food; now he
is cooking it. Later he will take care that Ad's aggressive
stance does not go too far. Their voices (Bugs's voice is soft
and gentle) further distinguish them—as well as their use
of language. Ad did not ask Nick's name, but he too quickly
seizes upon it once he learns it: "Are you hungry, Nick?"
Bugs knows the value of distance and proprieties. He
speaks of Nick as "the gentleman" and addresses him as
"Mister Adams." He uses language to help control his companion: "Just close that sandwich, will you, please, and give
it to Mister Francis" (*IOT*, 73; *NAS*, 53). Bugs is wonderfully
skilled in reading the words and silences of his companion.

Ad Francis not only has changed from what he used to be,
but he changes abruptly before us in the story. Nick misses
the precise moment of the change. "Let me take your knife,
Nick," Ad says. Nick, who is cutting bread at Bugs's request,
would likely have responded with the same trusting "Sure"
with which he answered Bugs. That would have been in
keeping with his general affability, especially after Bugs's
arrival. Certainly he remains enthusiastic about the meal
under preparation even after Bugs has told him not to give
Ad the knife. "Do you like to dip your bread in the ham
fat?" Bugs asks. Nick seems to have sensed little danger:
"You bet." Shortly he is eating with gusto; we learn that the
"hot fried ham and eggs tasted wonderful." But we have
read Nick's danger in the one-sentence paragraph after Bugs
told him not to surrender the knife: "The prizefighter sat
back" (*IOT*, 72; *NAS*, 52).

Ad says nothing from then on, breaking the aura of fellowship, until Nick is made nervous. If words sometimes
unsettle, so can silence. Finally Ad's hostility breaks out in a

torrent of words, uninterrupted by the polite Bugs and with only the briefest and most noninflamatory responses from Nick. It is not Nick, obviously, but many things from the past that Nick's youth and innocence kindle in Ad's mind that lead to his outburst: "You come in here and act snotty about my face and smoke my cigars and drink my liquor and then talk snotty. Where the hell do you think you get off?" What can one say to such craziness"? Nick says nothing, but Ad's hostility is not to be checked by Nick's passivity: "I'll tell you, you yellow-livered Chicago bastard. You're going to get your can knocked off. Do you get that?" Nick's prudent response is to "step back"—which even Tom might have done at this moment, although he would not have taken the verbal abuse so quietly.[19] The odds are about like those Dr. Adams faced with Dick Boulton. As Ad presses Nick to the fight, the strongest Nick can manage is "Cut it out" (*IOT*, 74–75; *NAS*, 53–54).

Fortunately for Nick, the sadistic quality present in most of the observers in "The Light of the World" is not part of Bugs's character. He does not wish to see Ad "feel good" by busting his hands on Nick. As Ad goes into his fighting stance, Bugs skillfully taps Ad on the base of the skull with a cloth-wrapped blackjack. He then carries Ad to the fire and lays him down "gently." After he proceeds to care for Ad with characteristic efficiency and gentleness, he apologizes to Nick: "I'm sorry, Mister Adams," and explains that he did not know how well Nick could take care of himself. Besides, he did not wish to hurt or mark Ad up any more than he is. He has had to intervene before: "I have to do it to change him when he gets that way" (*IOT*, 75–76; *NAS*, 54–55).

In "The Light of the World" Nick was an observer of a battle. In "The Battler" he avoids being a participant in one, but he is able to ask questions this time, and he discovers in Bugs a voice that he can trust. Alice's voice was "lovely" and

19. Mary Kay Willis is quite correct in stressing that Ad is like a child in seeing violence as a positive solution. See her "Structural Analysis of 'The Battler,'" *Hemingway's Experiments in Structure and Style*, 63.

reassuring. Bugs's voice continues to be soft, "low, smooth, polite." Hemingway stresses the uniqueness of each. Nick here is able to share the solace and communion of a cup of coffee with Bugs and to find there is light and warmth by the campfire in the swamp after all.

Whereas early in the story Ad asks Nick questions, Bugs soon takes over and asks the questions and gives gentle commands. Late in the story Nick can ask questions. His "What made him crazy?" is the one that interests him and us, both for this story and for the Nick stories to come.

Bugs relates a complex history in which physical battles of the boxing ring are minor. Ad has been hurt in love. His female manager (Hemingway is punning as well as relating unusual fact—surely there were few female boxing managers) looked like his sister. And after Ad married her, other people made a lot of "unpleasantness" about it. Certainly, others created the atmosphere in which "they commenced to have disagreements, and one day she just went off and never came back." The end of something, we are reminded, can be traumatic. As Bugs explains, "He was busting people all the time after she went away and they put him in jail" (*IOT*, 77; *NAS*, 56). That is where Bugs met him. Bugs had apparently been in many battles himself (he was in jail for cutting a man), and he finds Ad a pleasant companion: "I like to be with him and I like seeing the country and I don't have to commit no larceny to do it" (*IOT*, 78; *NAS*, 56). With Ad, Bugs can live like a gentleman.

The reason Bugs does not need to commit larceny reveals just how complicated love can be. Ad had made a lot of money, but "they" took it away from him. However, Ad's former wife sends them money, and Bugs admits that she's a "mighty fine woman" (*IOT*, 78; *NAS*, 56). Sometimes people love and care for people at great remove, as Ad's former wife tries to do. Separations may come, but three-day blows do not take care of the hurt that results.

Ad's and Bugs's life together is one of retreat from the hostilities of the world out there. It is not what either would have chosen, but it is about the best either could hope for from now on. Both are men without women; they manage to live away from people much of the time. "I have to sort of keep him away from people" (*IOT*, 78; *NAS*, 56), Bugs explains. If the experience of "The Light of the World" causes reflection on Nick's relationship to Marjorie, so does Nick's encounter around this northern campfire. In "The Three Day Blow," Bill defended the wisdom of Nick's breakup with Marjorie by stressing the obligations that would follow marriage, particularly the burden of Marjorie's family. However, "The Battler" emphasizes that any human relationship involves obligations. Ad's wife meets her obligation—and Bugs meets his. The alliance between the two men is one of the most durable relationships to be found in *In Our Time*.

Some readers have found the relationship ominous, seeing in the swamp the threat of homosexuality.[20] Of course, some have found the specter of homosexuality earlier than this in the Nick stories, seeing Nick's turning from Marjorie to Bill a more important raising of the issue.[21] Male comradeship was important to Hemingway, but homosexuality he found abhorrent (some say he protested too much). But to be a man without a woman was not for Hemingway to be a man who looked for male sexual companionship. There are adolescent dimensions in Nick's turning to Bill, for women do complicate things. Nevertheless, Nick in those stories does not turn to homosexuality but to a nonsexual camaraderie. Similarly in "The Battler," Ad and Bugs have not sought each other out for sexual reasons. Life has beaten them enough that they must take it on simpler terms. Bugs's voice is not threatening, nor is it deceiving. Bugs is like Alice in his honesty—letting Nick know exactly why he was in

20. The suggestion that the Ad-Bugs relationship is homosexual first came from Philip Young. It has been accepted by a number of others. See, for example, Robert W. Lewis, Jr., *Hemingway on Love* (Austin and London: University of Texas Press, 1965), 13. More recently E. D. Lowry's "Chaos and Cosmos in *In Our Time*," 112, says that "Ad may be a homosexual." Carlos Baker, meanwhile, has made known Hemingway's objection to any homosexual theme in the story. See *Ernest Hemingway: A Life Story* (New York: Charles Scribner's Sons, 1969), 509.

21. See Joseph Whitt, "Hemingway's 'The End of Something,'" *Explicator*, IX (June, 1951), Item 58.

jail. He shows the marks of the true professional that
Hemingway always admired. His cooking "tasted wonderful." He is a man who cares about quality. He believes in the
ritual of food and explains to Nick that dipping bread in the
ham fat is "better at the finish of the meal." The vibrations
from Bugs are quite positive. He would like to ask Nick to
stay the night, but that would be too much for Ad when he
awakened. Food was withheld at the beginning of "The
Light of the World." It is proffered and accepted at the end
of "The Battler." Bugs wishes Nick "Good-bye and good
luck!" (*IOT*, 79; *NAS*, 57), as Nick departs.

The light in "The Light of the World" was not immediately
evident, although it was there. In "The Battler" Nick finds
further evidence that even if the world is hostile and fierce
there are caring hands and caring voices. That Nick senses
these is evident in the final sentence: "Looking back from
the mounting grade before the track curved into the hills he
could see the firelight in the clearing" (*IOT*, 79; *NAS*, 57).

As we leave Nick on his journey to "somewhere" at the
end of "The Battler," he has been exposed to harshness,
cruelty, and the complexity of the outer world. Realization of
the horror of evil is still ahead of him. His first encounter
with it in its bare form occurs in what must be the most
famous of all the Nick Adams stories—"The Killers." This
story was not only the basis of a popular film—the first
portrayal of Nick in that medium—but became a classic text-
book piece for classroom analysis. In several ways, however,
"The Killers" is an atypical Nick story, even if it is frequently
taken as a norm for the Hemingway method. Hemingway
was ever conscious of the contrapuntal within a story and
between stories. Significantly, he was working on "Ten Indians" at the same time that he was writing "The Killers." [22]
The one emphasizes the familial, the natural, the normal;
the other, isolation and the unabashedly criminal. The pace
of the one story is leisured and calm; the pace of the other is
quick, and time is clearly of the essence. The technique of

22. Baker, *A Life Story*, 169.

"The Killers" owes much to the dramatic arts—its chief metaphors are comparisons to the movies and vaudeville. Description is minimal (but certainly important); dialogue makes up almost all of the story.

Taking "The Killers" by itself, the reader might almost miss the fact that Nick is the central character—as he surely would not in any reading of "Ten Indians." In the body of the Nick stories, we become accustomed to studying Nick as an observer. As Nick gets older, we are even more occupied with studying him in the role of observer and listener. Both "The Light of the World" and "The Battler" build on this pattern. In "The Battler" Bugs tells us a great deal about those who survive when he declares: "I hear most of what goes on" (*IOT*, 72; *NAS*, 52). We have seen that both stories emphasize the quality of voices. Similarly, both stress sight. The action of both occurs in half-lights and shadows. Nick, who gets a black eye at the opening of "The Battler," watches Ad Francis for some time before he ventures into the firelight. And the last line of the story insists on the sight motif: "Looking back from the mounting grade before the track curved into the hills he could see the firelight in the clearing." In "The Light of the World" there are dresses of changing colors and disappearing Indians. Interpretation of voices is also crucial to the story's meaning. Hemingway uses the Indians to heighten the motifs of sight and sound; the Indians say nothing, but they are listening and watching. By their actions they comment on the society that has dispossessed them.

In "The Killers" Nick is for a time almost hidden as a character. The story is ultraspare, even for Hemingway. The majority of the action of stories of Nick's youth takes place outdoors. Most of the action of "The Killers" takes place indoors, and the outdoors plays only on the periphery of our vision. Hemingway begins as if he were writing a moviescript—or a play.[23] The rewriting necessary to

23. The play as technique was on Hemingway's mind as he worked on "The Killers." (See Baker, *A Life Story*, 169.) Concurrently he was writing the short play "Today Is Friday." It bears some interesting resemblances to "The

change the opening paragraph (and the whole story) to playscript form would be minimal: "The door of Henry's lunch-room opened and two men came in. They sat down at the counter" (*MWW*, 78; *NAS*, 58). Thereafter, almost all of the clues to the story's meaning will come from the dialogue. Most of what is not dialogue could easily be printed as stage directions. The story has three similes in non-dialogue matter, but modern plays frequently provide novelistic comment (sometimes many comments) in their stage directions to help directors and readers.

That Hemingway's conscious model in this story is the play becomes even clearer when we watch how he handles identification of speakers. The reader of the Nick Adams stories is accustomed to heeding not only a name, but also to how it is given. "What is your name?" is an important motif in the Nick stories that take him beyond the confines of family and close friends. George, who is running the lunchroom, is identified as he opens the dialogue, but the two men whom he addresses are not. The two men immediately create something of the atmosphere of vaudeville and the movies by their costume (an item given minimal attention in the earlier stories save for "The Light of the World"). Hemingway identifies them by name only after the name each goes by (and only a first name) is used by one of them in dialogue. For several speeches the lines are spoken by "Max" and "the other." After Max finally uses Al's name, the narrator begins using it.[24]

Counterpointing the objectivity of the dramatic method,

Killers," but is also instructive for consideration of Hemingway's interest in the objective method of drama, what the drama could teach the writer of fiction. Hemingway apparently thought of "Today Is Friday" as a short story, for it later counted as one in *The Fifth Column and the First Forty-nine Stories*. Hemingway had continued his interest in the dramatic format by writing his single full-length play, which he reprinted with the stories.

24. George Bernard Shaw's *Pygmalion* provides a good example of how dramatists use this device. As the play opens, lines are spoken by The Daughter, The Mother, The Flower Girl, The Gentleman, and the Notetaker. Once the character is named in conversation, the identifications become Mrs. Hill, Clara, Eliza, Pickering, and Higgins. Freddy is named from the beginning since the daughter uses his name in the opening speech.

Hemingway indicates that Nick is to be the central character of the story by making him the only character in the opening scene to be given a whole name—exceptional even in the Nick stories. As Al and Max, dressed "like twins" and looking "like a vaudeville team," enter Henry's lunchroom, Nick immediately senses the unusual—not only from the looks of these men but from what they say and how they say it. The two men study the menu and in a highly artificial dialogue discuss what they will eat. Hemingway says, "From the other end of the counter Nick Adams watched them" (*MWW*, 78; *NAS*, 58). We are invited to watch with Nick—as we watched unusual characters with him in "The Light of the World" and "The Battler." Of the characters in "The Killers" only Nick and Ole Andreson are identified by a surname.

The duo that looks like a vaudeville team proves to be anything but that. Max insists to Al that they have to amuse themselves in their business; their business, however, is not entertainment. In "The Light of the World" and "The Battler" some unlikely looking characters had their own special light. It is very different with Al and Max, who are as unlike Ad and Bugs as possible. They do not care for each other or anyone else. They are—as the blunt title warns—killers. They will kill for pay, concerning themselves with the prospects of a good dinner as they wait to do a wicked deed.

Although the action of "The Killers" takes place inside, we are nevertheless conscious of the world outside. What we see from the window of Henry's recalls the atmosphere of both "The Light of the World" and "The Battler." As the killers enter the lunchroom, we are told that "Outside it was getting dark." Modern plays often use lighting in subtle ways to reveal something about the world beyond the set. As the killers speak, the arc light comes on outside the window. Since it is still only early evening, just five o'clock, we know that we are in the late fall season. Winter and death are imminent. In the stories of Nick as a young boy ("Indian Camp," "The Doctor and the Doctor's Wife," "Ten Indians") the season is summer. In the adolescent stories we move from the transitional "The End of Something" (which takes place in late summer) to the autumnal "The Three Day Blow." "The Battler," while less specific as to season, also evokes the autumnal. The mists are threatening; Nick feels urgency in getting somewhere; the fire and food and hot coffee are especially welcome. "The Light of the World" decidedly takes us into a November mood; there as Nick and Tom move from the saloon towards the station it is dark and cold and the puddles of water in the road are freezing at the edges. Four times in "The Killers" Hemingway reminds us of the darkness in the world out there, a world badly in need of a little light.

"The Killers" is the last of the finished stories to portray Nick as adolescent and the only one not set in Michigan. However, Hemingway had first set the story in Petoskey, the lovely Michigan resort town where Hemingway went to write after World War I.[25] By moving the locale from Petoskey to a Chicago suburb, Hemingway was adding verisimilitude to his story. Petoskey is far removed from the centers of boxing, and an unlikely place for a boxer who got in wrong to be waiting to be murdered. Readers associate such events with big cities—especially Chicago.

But, more important, the change of the locale from Petoskey, Michigan, to Summit, Illinois, was a happy switch for a rounder portrait of Nick. "The Light of the World" and "The Battler" show Nick as interested in boxing and boxing figures. But as in "The Three Day Blow" he can only wish to get to a world series, he has not until "The Killers" had much more than newspaper acquaintance with what goes on in the sporting world. In "The Battler" Nick had told Bugs that he is from Chicago, but we find him instead a boy of the suburbs. He is still without a defined course for his own life. We do not find Nick in the one "Chicago" story of the Nick canon in a gymnasium or protecting himself from homosexual advances. He is far different from the pose that Hemingway created of himself in oral fictions for the likes of

25. Baker, *A Life Story*, 169.

Gertrude Stein and Sylvia Beach. We find Nick very much as we have always found him—as an observer and talking with a friend, slightly older, who will give him advice. Nick is not at Henry's to eat, but to talk with his friend; Nick himself is not employed. George—as the story bears out—is geared toward an accepted pattern of life. He is going to be more like Charley Simmons of "Soldier's Home," a man with a job and probably destined to be married. Nick is at loose ends in Summit, an ironic name for the hum-drum town. His restlessness is present as the story opens, but is a muted theme. By the story's end, the theme becomes insistent and carries frightening overtones.

The atmosphere of "The Killers" is charged with the potential of fast, violent action. But story time is finally given over exclusively to the "action" of waiting. It is colored by the frame of Nick's waiting for a direction for his life, the desire to control his life more than he ever has before. Then Al and Max enter the lunchroom, and Nick is caught in events that he cannot at all control. Only in "The Battler" was Nick himself under serious threat from the outside world, but here the threat is even greater: almost from the beginning of the story it is clear that Nick may lose his life in a gruesome execution. He comes very close to it. After the killers determine that Ole Andreson is not coming, Al does not like leaving Nick, George, and the cook, Sam, knowing so much. "It's sloppy," Al tells Max. But Max is feeling magnanimous. Al tells George, "You got lots of luck" (*MWW*, 88–89; *NAS*, 65).

The first scene of waiting lasts a full two hours, and during much of it Nick does not know what is happening. Moreover, he does not know why it is happening. The reader is privileged to get information earlier than Nick does since Max informs George of their assignment to kill Ole Andreson and of their plan to kill the prizefighter as soon as he arrives at the lunchroom. During most of the two hours Nick is tied and gagged, along with Sam, off stage as it were. Nick is victim—merely in the wrong place at the wrong time.

But whereas Nick does not hear Max's explanation, he has seen and heard quite enough before he is tied up to know that this is no game, no mere entertainment, that he is not watching the movies. Al and Max start by bullying their way, and neither George nor Nick knows what to do.

"You're a pretty bright boy, aren't you?"
"Sure," said George.
"Well, you're not," said the other little man. "Is he, Al?"
"He's dumb," said Al. (*MWW*, 80; *NAS*, 59–60)

From then on George is "bright boy" to Al and Max. They never bother to ask his name; *boy* carries an insult that George knows he must tolerate. Hemingway gives further indication that Nick is the central character of the story by having Al ask Nick his name. Nick also feels that it would be practical for him to answer these insulting voices, but he tries to be tough about it. "Adams" is his reply. In "The Light of the World" there was some choice about answering questions, but there is none in this lunchroom encounter. Of course, Nick's identity does not finally matter to Al or Max— any more than Ole Andreson's matters to them. Al will shortly again ask Nick's name—at the moment he and Max prepare to arrange their expected climax to the evening's waiting. Although they are indeed killers, Al and Max are also conscious showmen.

Just as Nick gets certain information in "The Killers" after the reader does, the reader also has a delay in getting certain information. The reader, although not with Nick for every moment of the story, experiences things much as he does. As far as the killers are concerned, Nick is merely excess baggage. Certainly they feel no need to "explain" things to him. Their plan—and Nick's hope for survival—depends on George's wisely playing the role assigned to him.

Hemingway's handling of names as if he were writing a play prepares the reader for the technique of continually delaying information. Ultimately, we will not get information that Nick does not get—no last names for Al and Max, for example—and there is information that we never get.

Why is Ole Andreson to be killed? We can only guess. The technique of delaying information (and sometimes not giving it at all) adds to the horror that the story conveys.

We have noted that Al and Max bully the boys by the sheer aura of their presence and through language. But as the killers begin to prepare for action after they have eaten, they do not hesitate to reveal that they have more than verbal weapons. Hemingway heightens the horror of the threat facing Nick and George by not mentioning the gun at all when it is first displayed.

> "Hey, bright boy," Max said to Nick. "You go around on the other side of the counter with your boy friend."
> "What's the idea?" Nick asked.
> "There isn't any idea."
> "You better go around, bright boy," Al said. Nick went around the counter. (*MWW*, 82; *NAS*, 60)

The narrator does not mention the sawed-off shotgun that is behind this command until several pages later.

Whereas in "The Battler" there were many questions and answers that fit them, in "The Killers" we get few explanations: we view impersonal evil. When the narrator says that Al is "like a photographer arranging for a group picture" (*MWW*, 84; *NAS*, 62), he underscores the impersonal professionalism. Al and Max have no individuality—call me Al or call me Max, it makes little difference. Both believe that force rules. They have perverted the natural, and their language teems with sexual insult. Max tells Nick to go around the counter "with his boy friend." Told to bring Sam out from the kitchen, George asks Al what they are going to do to him. "Nothing. Use you head, bright boy. What would we do to a nigger?" (*MWW*, 83; *NAS*, 61). Al and Max seem to specialize in sexual innuendo. They also enjoy insulting each other. From the kitchen later Al warns Max against talking too much to George:

> "Well, I got to keep bright boy amused. Don't I, bright boy?"
> "You talk too damn much," Al said. "The niggers and my bright boy are amused by themselves. I got them tied up like a couple of country girls in the convent."

"I suppose you were in a convent."

"You never know."

"You were in a kosher convent. That's where you were."
(*MWW*, 86; *NAS*, 63)

Such efforts to fill the time of waiting do not amuse. The jokes are cruel, and not only at the expense of the trapped but of the killers themselves. The world seems reft of human values.

The waiting finally ends, however, when it becomes clear that Ole Andreson is not coming in for dinner. George has played the role assigned him by the killers well; so he survives, as do Nick and Sam. The killers depart.

After George unties and ungags Nick and Sam, Nick exposes his youth even as he seeks to cover it with a tough response: "'Say,' he said. 'What the hell?'" (*MWW*, 89; *NAS*, 65). Offstage for the waiting that occupied the first two-thirds of the story, Nick will be more profoundly affected by the evil of the killers after he talks with the intended victim, as he realizes that the waiting at Henry's has a counterpart in another waiting—that of Ole Andreson. Sam the cook, who has met the brutality of the world before, advises Nick not to do anything about warning Andreson. But for Nick there is no hesitation about following George's advice. Even though he must have known that a visit to Andreson was not without risk, Nick makes the hard walk in the ominous dark. Having recognized the evil of the world ("He had never had a towel in his mouth before"), Nick feels compelled to act, to counteract that evil.

At Mrs. Hirsch's rooming house Nick finds Ole Andreson fully dressed, lying on his bed, and waiting—Nick learns— for the courage to leave, to make up his mind to take what he knows is coming. For it happens that Nick can tell Andreson nothing that he does not already know. The shocking news that Nick learns from Andreson is that he sees flight as futile, but Nick gets no details. He learns only that the fighter "got in wrong" and that Andreson is "through with all of that running around" (*MWW*, 93; *NAS*, 67). Andreson does not even look at Nick, but he thanks him for coming.

The fighter continues to lie on his bed looking at the wall; he has come to a place of no exit.

In their influential analysis of "The Killers," Cleanth Brooks and Robert Penn Warren argue that Hemingway brings the horror of Andreson's waiting to a high pitch by including a homely exchange between Nick and the woman who had shown him up to Andreson's room. The effect of the exchange, they say, is much like that of the incident of the knocking at the gate after Macbeth has murdered Duncan. It returns the reader to the normal.[26] The point is well taken, but the exchange also serves to emphasize, I think, that the normal is not to be relied upon, that assumptions can be wrong. We have not completely left the atmosphere of "The Light of the World." Mrs. Bell, not Mrs. Hirsch, is running Mrs. Hirsch's boardinghouse. We do not find any Henry in Henry's lunchroom; George is in charge. Furthermore, we learn that Henry's had been made over from a saloon. That transformation aids plot by accounting for the mirror that Max utilizes as he manages the show at Henry's, but it also serves to mirror a world view. The clock of the lunchroom is twenty minutes fast—clearly not very helpful unless you are one of the inner circle who frequent Henry's. The printed menu is not of much value either unless the patron understands the clock since the menu does not become valid until six o'clock. With the arrival of Al and Max, the stage invades life—but is disturbingly different. The vaudeville team metamorphoses into paid killers who carry a gun that is not at first recognized, but it is made prominent when Al leaves: "The cut-off barrels of the shotgun made a slight bulge under the waist of his too tight-fitting coat" (*MWW*, 89; *NAS*, 65).

It is no wonder that Nick when he returns to Henry's is baffled and overwhelmed by the experience with Ole Andre-

---

26. Cleanth Brooks and Robert Penn Warren, "The Killers," in Benson (ed.), *The Short Stories of Ernest Hemingway: Critical Essays*, 190. This influential essay first appeared in *American Prefaces* VII (Spring, 1942), 195–209, then with revisions, in Brooks and Warren (eds.), *Understanding Fiction* (New York: Appleton-Century-Crofts, 1943), 316–24.

son. The movies, in their way, had given at least a kind of predictability to what went on at Henry's. In the movies, however, there would have been a shooting or some dramatic culmination. "The Killers" moves toward thought, the implied action being death for Andreson and retreat (at least momentarily) for Nick. It is not Hemingway's business to tell us that Andreson was killed, as a more traditional storyteller would have. Whereas Nick doubtless found a certain dignity in the doomed Andreson, it is not dignity that has most impressed Nick. After we are told that Nick had never had a towel in his mouth before, we see a swaggering Nick, but he is not swaggering at the end of the story. Hemingway reminds us of the earlier swagger by having George reach for a towel to wipe the counter, emphasizing the telling silence after Nick declares, "It's an awful thing" (*MWW*, 95; *NAS*, 69). Here Nick gives the genuine, not the rehearsed response. He gets close to the question that he had asked his father at the end of "Indian Camp": "Is dying hard, Daddy?" Nick finds it "too damned awful" to think of Andreson waiting in his room knowing he is going to be killed. George ends the story with his famous line: "you'd better not think about it" (*MWW*, 96; *NAS*, 69). But the fact of evil cannot be dismissed by leaving town. We know that no three-day blow will ever wipe this memory from Nick's mind. We know further that Nick is too imaginative a person ever to respond to such events as a George or a Sam would. He appears quite unable to make a separate peace.

At the end of "The Killers," then, Nick is markedly changed from the young man he was at the beginning of the story. At the start of the story he was anticipating bidding farewell to all of the scenes of his youth—to the Michigan summers and the Illinois winters. But any sense of high adventure is decidedly checked because of the events of a few hours. Nick has previously learned something about the precariousness of all life, but he had never comprehended the potential for total evil in human nature, the potential for impersonal destruction—sometimes released in war—a kind of destruction that Nick will learn about as he leaves the

familiar terrain of his boyhood and youth. "The Killers" is
also prelude to Nick's experience in the devastation of World
War I.

Nevertheless, it should be recognized that the Nick who
discovers in human nature utmost darkness also shares
something of that dark in himself. In the stories of his
boyhood, Nick was essentially the innocent observer. In
"Ten Indians" he is the victim of Prudie's unfaithfulness, but
in the stories about his adolescence he becomes more ac-
tively a participant in the human drama; his numerous wanderings reveal that there is a strong desire to understand, to
explore the human condition. Nick betrays both himself and
Marjorie, reversing the situation of "Ten Indians." He causes
pain for someone he has loved. And that experience makes
him a more perceptive observer and listener to the strange
events he experiences and hears about in "The Light of the
World" and in "The Battler." It is useful to recall the light of
those stories in the face of the grimness at the end of "The
Killers." For Nick has found meanings; he is, furthermore, a
battler. Even though the world is a darker place than Nick
had before guessed, he is not in Andreson's frame of mind—
merely waiting for the end. In time, Nick may come to cast
his own special light. Surely he will seek to do so in his relationship with others and in his writing.

Chapter Three
The Soldier

The most traumatic of Nick's experiences are those he had as a soldier, especially the trial of battle and his wounding in battle. Yet those are the experiences Hemingway was most hesitant to treat directly. Hemingway could, of course, write vividly of men in action. The one novel that shows his hero as a man in action in war, however, is *For Whom the Bell Tolls*, which did not appear until 1940 and was not about Nick's war. *A Farewell to Arms* (1929), which was about Nick's war, portrayed more of retreat than of battle. Hemingway tended to be more concerned with revealing consequences than with dramatizing military combat; certainly that was his interest in the Nick stories.

The piece of fiction that takes Nick closest to battle is also the shortest piece—Chapter VI of *In Our Time* (chapter 7 of *in our time*).[1] The fame of this interchapter rests more on its relationship to *A Farewell to Arms* than to its place in *In Our Time*, for the wounding is similar to Frederic Henry's. (Hemingway described Frederic's wounding with considerable detail and vividness, as he had not Nick's *In Our Time*.) Furthermore, there is a comrade named Rinaldi present; and Nick mentions "a separate peace." Students of the novel naturally find this interchapter interesting—along with "A Very Short Story"—as the embryonic material for the novel.

1. Like other readers, I rely on the context of *In Our Time* in making the Nick of the interchapter Nick Adams. D. H. Lawrence, on the other hand, when reviewing *In Our Time* assumed that the Nick of Chapter VI is an Italian soldier. But since Nick speaks mainly in English, mixing in some Italian, he is not convincingly Italian.

But the chapter is also crucial for *In Our Time* and for students of the Nick chronicle.

In Our Time has established Nick's character by Chapter VI. The story immediately preceding the interchapter is "The Battler," and the metaphor easily carries over into the arena of war. The various interchapters of *In Our Time* had counterpointed Nick's life as a boy with the harsh picture of war—a reality that Nick would ultimately have to measure his life against. Chapter VI stands out because it is the only interchapter about Nick. The protagonists of some of the other interchapters, for example the first, are potentially Nick, but Hemingway sensed the advantage in preserving for the reader the aura of Nick's primal innocence. It would not do, then, to name the soldier of Chapter VII Nick. There is a thematic link between the praying soldier and Nick, but the praying soldier is not wounded, and since the chapter follows the one in which Nick is wounded, it is evident that Hemingway means to mirror the experience of many soldiers. The soldier in Chapter VII is not Harold Krebs, either, even though the story that follows Chapter VII is the one about Krebs, "Soldier's Home." Krebs had been at a different front. Nick is like Krebs in some ways—but Hemingway saves Nick (certainly through the stories of *Men Without Women*) for less reprehensible circumstances than those of Krebs, who, at the end of the story, capitulates to his mother and denies thereby the validity of his own experience. With Nick we usually maintain a larger sense of Adamic wonderment. The experience of other soldiers, then, may suggest Nick's, but beyond that Hemingway does not wish to go. The possessive pronoun of his title, *In Our Time*, gains considerably because of the restricted use of Nick in the interchapters.[2] Nick becomes one of many—and the title

---

2. Because a story is based on Hemingway's experience (some Nick stories are not—*e.g.*, "Indian Camp") it does not automatically qualify as a Nick story. E. D. Lowry calls Nick the protagonist of "A Very Short Story" in "Chaos and Cosmos in *In Our Time*," *Literature and Psychology*, 26 (1976), 109. Even though the story follows the Nick interchapter, the unnamed "He" should not be considered Nick. There is none of Nick's sensitivity in the protagonist. In *In Our Time* the episode does not follow the "Nick sat

reminds the reader that it is also his own world that has been defined.

That Nick would go to war is implied in the structure of *In Our Time*: the events of his Michigan youth are interspaced with war vignettes. Soldiering is also in keeping with the progress of the prewar adventures. That progress becomes increasingly more rapid, more staccato. There is a heightened sense of restlessness in the stories of Nick's adolescence, and the stories after Nick's breakup with Marge suggest a new urgency. Baffled by the existence of evil in "The Killers," Nick feels compelled to study the larger arena of killing in the world. There may not be anywhere he can go to avoid the realities Al and Max represent. Since mankind appears so incomprehensible, study of man in the most stressful of circumstances—war—might help Nick better understand the human predicament. Paradoxically, there could be advantage in deliberately seeking the distressful.

Several years after *In Our Time*, Hemingway, in talking of his own experience as a writer and student of the human scene, intellectualized what for Nick had been instinctive. Hemingway observes in *Death in the Afternoon*: "The only place where you could see life and death, i.e., violent death now that the wars were over, was in the bull ring and I wanted very much to go to Spain where I could study it. I was trying to learn to write, commencing with the simplest things, and one of the simplest things of all and the most fundamental is violent death." [3] Nick had gone to war because he wanted to see life and death. The equating of the bullring with the conflict of war had been built into the structure of *In Our Time* as bull-fighting interchapters replace interchapters of war after "Soldier's Home." Chapter VIII connects the violence of war with the kind of violence

---

aginst the wall" piece. It should be observed that Hemingway also chose to leave the *he* of Chapter 11 unnamed when he became "The Revolutionist" of *In Our Time*. Hemingway uses the unnamed *he's*, *we's*, and *I's* to stress the impersonality and scope of modern warfare.

3. Ernest Hemingway's *Death in the Afternoon* (New York: Charles Scribner's Sons, 1932), 2.

we find in "The Killers"; and the final vignette, "L'Envoi," reminds us of war and revolution. Nick was a student of war, revolution, violence.

Jake Barnes (also a former soldier) was a Hemingway hero who found the study of man in the bullring of immense value in his personal struggle to order his life. Jake was a writer, and Nick will become a writer, as Hemingway has intimated and finally makes unequivocal. Hemingway prepares us for considering Nick in terms of this profession from the beginning. The stories repeatedly cast Nick as a keen observer. Quietly, but firmly, Hemingway makes us feel that Nick's eventual occupation is inevitable. Nick is unique among Hemingway heroes in embodying in his experience the idea that Hemingway spoke of later about the special value of war for the writer. In *Green Hills of Africa*, speaking as himself, Hemingway asserts his belief in the great advantage to a writer of having experienced war: "It was one of the major subjects and certainly one of the hardest to write truly of and those writers who had not seen it were always very jealous and tried to make it seem unimportant, or abnormal, or a disease as a subject, while, really, it was just something quite irreplaceable that they had missed."[4] Because he has the writer's instinct, Nick has sought this "quite irreplaceable" experience.[5]

We have become accustomed to meeting Nick just before or after an event. Ole Andreson has not been killed when "The Killers" ends; no one has. In "The Battler" we begin

4. Ernest Hemingway, *Green Hills of Africa* (New York: Charles Scribner's Sons, 1935), 70.

5. Harold Krebs of "Soldier's Home" is a useful contrast to Nick on this score. Nick goes to war because he feels the compulsion to study man, even though he would probably not have articulated this need at the time he went to war. Krebs, on the other hand, was caught up in a movement. That son of Middle America tended to go along with the crowd. As a portrayal of war, "Soldier's Home" is much more affirmative than the Nick war stories. In war Krebs gained a great deal. He found out things about himself and the world that he needed to know. There is no sense that the war itself was shattering for Krebs. Krebs was shattered after he got home and was not true to what he learned as a soldier. Nick's experience in war is altogether otherwise.

with Nick's picking himself up from the ground. Thus it is
not surprising that in what most critics take as the crucial
event of Nick's life, Hemingway has again selected the moment just after action. There is not even a story to mark the
event, just one of the brief interchapters of *In Our Time*.
When we find Nick at war, his battle days have just ended.
He has been hit in the spine—this time there is no picking
himself up. Others have propped him up against the wall of
the church—the prayer for peace implied in Hemingway's
title, *In Our Time*, takes on a keen irony. There is little grace
for Nick in this posture as his legs "stuck out awkwardly"
(*IOT*, 103; *NAS*, 143). He, as if recognizing that all has been
utterly changed, sits up and observes carefully the physical
details of this special place: "Nick looked straight ahead bril-
liantly." He notes that the "pink wall of the house opposite
had fallen out from the roof, and an iron bedstead hung
twisted toward the street." He shows that he recognizes
particular meaning in the event for himself, other than the
fact that he has been wounded. He tries to make the same
meaning apply to the wounded Rinaldi, who can hardly
breathe: "Senta, Rinaldi, senta. You and me, we've made a
separate peace." It is an odd comment, for Nick can hardly
speak for Rinaldi. "We're not patriots," he had said. But it is
Rinaldi's country, not his. No wonder Rinaldi makes a disap-
pointing audience. In fact, as we will see, Nick does not
know what to do with his separate peace. For the moment
he can smile "sweatily," and he feels relief that he will not
have to get close to the fighting again, but there is no real
benediction here. Nick will be a long time coming to terms
with the event. By avoiding portrayal of the big event in
Chapter VI, Hemingway gives only the very tip of his immense iceberg—leaving it to other stories in *In Our Time* to
reveal just how much is below the surface.

A later Nick story—a story not to appear until Hemingway's third major volume of short stories, *Winner Take
Nothing* (1933)—gives some of the detail about Nick's soldiering in flashback. Clearly, the handling of Nick's war experience did not come readily to Hemingway. But by the time of

"A Way You Will Never Be" Hemingway had written about a similarly crucial wounding in memorable detail—although the experience was Frederic Henry's and not Nick's.

Probably Hemingway had intended to describe the experience as one of Nick's when, after the publication of *In Our Time*, he started to write a novel about Nick and the war experiences largely implied in *In Our Time*. He managed in that novelistic attempt only some of the key moments before Nick's career in battle (as a soldier not an ambulance driver) began. The fragment of this abortive Nick novel was tentatively called "Along with Youth," a title Hemingway borrowed from his poem "Along With Youth" that had been published in his first book, *Three Stories and Ten Poems*. It appears as "Night Before Landing" in *The Nick Adams Stories*. Hemingway had intended to recount Nick's European war activity from landing to a time in Paris, then Milan, Nick's wounding in battle, and return to Milan for a love affair.[6] He did not write very much of this novel and stopped the narrative before Nick got to the European coast. A major reason for his setting it aside was, undoubtedly, the magnitude of his own wounding that Nick's mirrored. He needed time before he could use this material.

But Hemingway may also have delayed because he was hesitant to lose too much of Nick's primal innocence—as the novel appeared destined to do. As character in a series of short stories, Nick repeatedly had vast suggestive value. The major character in a novel is more fully rounded—and it seems strange to read "Night Before Landing," a piece that has only a touch of the suggestive force of the Nick stories. The fragment does give some of Nick's character, for he had a definite enough reality in Hemingway's mind. In writing a Nick novel, however, Hemingway faced the task—if the novel were to come to satisfactory fruition—of bringing in the past and the sense of character that he had already created in the stories of *In Our Time*. There is so strong a

6. Carlos Baker, *Ernest Hemingway: A Life Story* (New York: Charles Scribner's Sons, 1969), 147.

sense to the being of Nick in *In Our Time* that the novel
character presented a vastly different kind of challenge. It
would have been easier, certainly, to start with a new character. As Hemingway worked on his Nick novel, it may have
become apparent that the short story was the right vehicle
for Nick. Hemingway, confident of his achievement in the
short story genre, was eager to write his first novel, but why
should he restrict himself through the use of a character
who already had a fictional life? Not surprisingly, he abandoned the Nick novel.

Nevertheless, the fragment is long enough to reveal several major threads. As "Night Before Landing" begins, Nick
is aboard ship, headed for France. He, along with other
young men, is restless. Since it is now dark, the waiting is
even more difficult, and rumor is that they land tomorrow. It
is certain that Nick is to be the focal character. Nick's eye—
as in most of the Nick stories—will provide the reader his
angle of vision: "Nick sat in the empty chair and looked out
at the men passing against the light from the sea" (*NAS*,
137). But the details take on meaning only because we know
Nick from the earlier stories. The canvas of a Nick story
never seemed so crowded. Nick is one of equals here, and
there is not enough detail to give the reader the sense of
startled innocence that is major in so many of the stories.
Nick sounds rather like a high school boy as he says, "It will
be fun to see all the planes and that stuff" (*NAS*, 141). The
line is partly bluff, of course. Other lines reveal that Nick
has learned something of the world. When his friend Leon
tells him that "they say" their ship will never be sunk since
it carries German mails, Nick replies, "Maybe . . . I don't
believe it" (*NAS*, 138).

There is prefigurement of a strong love interest for the
novel. There is one woman, named Gaby, on board. Because
of a family connection, she is traveling on this ship for a
reunion with her family in Paris. Hemingway's story "A Way
You'll Never Be" reveals that this Gaby was a famous movie
star and dancer. The soldiers on ship also talk a great deal

about girls. Nick claims to be engaged and to have been to whore houses, but he is idealistic about the girl to whom he claims to be engaged.

Hemingway intended, of course, that his novel be realistic. He would show aspects of war that were upsetting to the likes of Mrs. Krebs in "Soldier's Home." She knew that soldiers frequently were sexually active. It had been so in the Civil War, she knew, but fiction before the armistice of 1918 had underplayed this aspect of soldiering. In addition to dealing with such details, the Nick novel (it would seem from "Night Before Landing") would revolve around the issue of cowardice at the front, the war as a measurement of manhood. Nick fears that he will not be any good as a soldier. When he naïvely says, "I wonder if I'll be scared" (*NAS*, 141), Hemingway recalls to his readers Nick's attitude toward dying at the end of "Indian Camp." Nick tells a fellow soldier: "Other people can get killed but not me. I feel that absolutely" (*NAS*, 142), and his words are close to what Nick feels in the last lines of that early story.

Self-doubt seems to be the norm on the ship. Another soldier, Carper, has admitted to being scared. Carper is dealing with his fear by drinking, and Galinski says that Carper has been drunk for two weeks as the fragment ends. Nick and Leon are also drinking heavily, hidden in a lifeboat. The use of alcohol as a means to blunt fear was the revelation of the first interchapter of *In Our Time*. It begins: "Everybody was drunk" (*IOT*, 13). The Nick novel would surely shock the folks back in Oak Park, Illinois, the upper middle-class suburb where Hemingway had lived (save for those Michigan summers) until he graduated from high school.

Hemingway might lose more than he would gain from a Nick war novel. He had never used Nick to expose anything. That kind of novel about World War I had already been written when Hemingway started "Along with Youth." Probably no novel could give us a more powerful sense of what war had done to Nick than "Big Two-Hearted River" and the memorable short stories of Nick's war experience that were to come. "Big Two-Hearted River" already existed as the last story of *In Our Time*. That story—as Hemingway later wrote in *A Moveable Feast*—was about the war but never mentioned it. *Men Without Women* (1927) contained two Nick war stories, although in one of these first-person narratives Nick's name is never used. Their placement in *Men Without Women* is informative. "In Another Country," the second story of *Men Without Women*, never uses Nick's name. It follows "The Undefeated," relating the book to *In Our Time* as the reader is reminded of the connection between the arena of war and the arena of bullfighting that had played throughout the earlier book. The last story of *Men Without Women*, "Now I Lay Me," takes place before "In Another Country." There Nick's name is used twice, but not immediately. Hemingway intends our understanding of Nick to involve an exploring. The reader who does not see that the stories are about the same soldier has not paid attention. In a sense Nick's war plight frames the book. In the middle of the book is "A Simple Enquiry," the only story in the book that takes place during the war. It is not a Nick story, but it reminds us of the complex war arena. There are two other Nick stories in the book, however, both stories of the prewar Nick—"The Killers" and "Ten Indians," in that order. By jumbling chronology, Hemingway forces the reader to supply crucial contexts; his giving us the prewar Nick and the wounded Nick strengthens the ironic perspective of the book. In the case of "In Another Country" and "Now I Lay Me," Hemingway can surely expect his reader to know Nick when he appears. The "I" method partly veils the experience, but decidedly serves to intensify it. In "Big Two-Hearted River" Hemingway does not mention the war: in "In Another Country" he does not mention Nick. In "Now I Lay Me" he does so only belatedly. In one of the last Nick stories that he wrote, Hemingway is most specific about Nick's actual experience at the front, and then he not only names him, but he expands his name to Nicholas Adams. This late story—"A Way You'll Never Be"—appears in the volume *Winner Take Nothing*.

In the stories that Hemingway wrote about Nick after *In*

Our Time, he tended to choose titles that make strong allusions. The title "Now I Lay Me" suggests experience more elemental than that evoked by the more sophisticated allusion of "In Another Country." "Now I Lay Me" emphasizes that the narrator has reached back to earliest responses. The prayer that the title echoes is a child's prayer. Again, the question that Nick asked his father about dying comes ringing to the fore. Indeed, once we get to the Nick war stories, his past becomes increasingly important as an element of the stories. He becomes a character with a past—hardly a significant aspect of the early boyhood stories or the teen-age exploration stories. The hand of the past now makes new claims. The narrator lies down, not to sleep, as in the child's prayer, but to pray and to think about others. It is because of the nature of some precise memories that we would know unquestionably that we were reading a Nick story, even if Nick were not named.

Whereas "Now I Lay Me" builds on Nick's memories of his youth, the reader should always bear in mind that the action of the story is also a memory. The narrative point of view is, finally, affirmation. Nick had been working out his problems, but was in a very bad way during that summer of 1918 that he is telling about. Writing is a process for finding order, and "Now I Lay Me" as a first person story suggests more that Nick has written what we are reading than that he is speaking it. The narrative recounts the methods that the wounded Nick used in 1918, when he could not write, to deal with his fears and doubts, especially with his fear of death.

Hemingway's title carries a heavy irony because during the summer Nick remembers he did not even want to go to sleep at night. War had upset the very rhythm of life. He wanted desperately not to go to sleep at night—precisely because he feared that he would die. Never before, probably, has the experience of sleep as a type of death been more believably rendered in prose fiction. Nick says, "I had been living for a long time with the knowledge that if I ever shut my eyes in the dark and let myself go, my soul would go out of my body. I had been that way for a long time, ever since I had been blown up at night and felt it go out of me and go off and then come back" (*MWW*, 218; *NAS*, 144). So "by a very great effort" he prevented himself from going to sleep at night. As he lay on his cot, his eyes were wide open. He would sleep only by day or on the nights when he could have a light.

In interchapter six of *In Our Time* Nick has been wounded "in the spine" and in bright daylight, but in "Cross-Country Snow"—also in *In Our Time*—Nick's war wound is a leg injury. Probably Hemingway intended the reader to think of Nick as having been wounded more than once, and in "Now I Lay Me," John, Nick's hospital roommate, says, "You been wounded a couple of times" (*MWW*, 230; *NAS*, 152). But in "Now I Lay Me" Hemingway altered the wounding of the interchapter (the wounding that put Nick out of the war) dramatically, in part, probably, to make Nick's wounding different from Frederic Henry's—but also for the artistic pur-poses of "Now I Lay Me"—a night piece recounting night conversations and night thoughts. To have Nick report that he had been "blown up at night" heightens the night-terror emphasis of many of the Nick stories; night shadows pro-vided a threatening backdrop in several stories of Nick's adolescence—"The Light of the World," "The Battler," and "The Killers"—and provided the basis for the first story of Nick's boyhood, "Indian Camp." Night would be a time of heightened fear for soldiers since what cannot be seen is usually more threatening than what can be seen, and death—ultimately—is the final great night.

Although the particular nights that Nick tells of in "Now I Lay Me" occurred some time—probably weeks—after his wounding, time seems to have stopped as he lies there "re-cuperating." There is only present and past time—not future time, save for that implied in the point of view. Nick's hospi-tal is not far from the front, some seven kilometres, and he can hear the noise of the fighting. He has no curiosity about the war—merely the sense that it has been going on for a long time and will continue going on—but without him.

The noises of war are not the noises that make the biggest impact on Nick and therefore the reader. Listening has been tuned to a very fine art for Nick as he lies "in hospital." The opening sentences speak volumes for decribing Nick's night-time state: "That night we lay on the floor in the room and I listened to the silk-worms eating. The silk-worms fed in racks of mulberry leaves and all night you could hear them eating and a dropping sound in the leaves" (*MWW*, 218; *NAS*, 144). As the reader later learns, when Nick can hear these slight rustlings, he is in a very depressed condition.

Nick is trying to follow George's advice of not thinking about what is bothering him. Trained as he was in the north woods, Nick has learned the value of order. Lest chaos come, he has discovered that he needs a careful ordering of his night thoughts. He has been in his makeshift hospital long enough to have developed several rituals. At the best times, he goes trout fishing with the Michigan of his youth on his mind. Michigan is, to borrow the metaphor that Hemingway later made famous in his memoirs of the 1920s, a moveable feast. In his mind he fishes carefully the whole length of the streams he fished in his youth. He is deliberate about all of the details of that fishing, always stopping at noon to eat his lunch, always eating it slowly, and watching the stream as he eats. He never takes more than ten worms when he starts, and he must improvise after that bait is gone. The improvisations are so detailed that we find the imaginary fishing totally real. But even Nick's fishing in his Michigan streams (the best of his nighttimes) does not take us completely away from the horror of battle, killing, and death. Nick, in seeking bait, once came upon a salamander under a log. The salamander was small, neat, agile, and was "a lovely color." With his tiny feet, the salamander tried to hold on to the hook. After that, Nick never used a sala-mander although he found them often. Nick tells us, "Nor did I use crickets because of the way they acted about the hook" (*MWW*, 220; *NAS*, 145).

With so revealing a detail, we are not surprised that some nights the fishing does not work for Nick. He lies "cold-awake." On those nights he says his prayers over and over, trying to pray for all the people he has ever known. He conveys no sense that he feels that God hears his prayers, but the ritual provides some comfort—at least a way of dealing with the night. In the "Three Shots" fragment Nick's religious heritage is Protestant. There it is the singing of a Protestant hymn, "Some day the silver cord will break," that gave him his first intimations of mortality. "Now I Lay Me" is also a Protestant prayer. By the time that he is in Europe, Nick has turned from the religion of his upbringing towards the older tradition of Catholicism, whose ritual brings him greater consolation. As he prays for "all the people" he has ever known, he uses the "Hail Mary" and "Our Father" format for each. He does not improvise his prayers.

Nick's praying is another kind of fishing. It is also carefully controlled. Although Nick uses standard prayers, he has to exercise his mind, for he not only tries to pray for all of the people he has ever known, he tries to do so in a proper order. He keeps pushing his mind to find his earliest memories. He prays in a chronological order. By thus fishing the streams of his mind, Nick serves as his own good psychiatrist, uncovering just the sorts of things he needs to uncover. He fishes and refishes these streams of time, but he always stops when he reaches the war. That black swamp he will save for a later time.

In the course of this fishing, Nick uncovers his earliest memory, and as the first it is obviously significant. He remembers the attic of the house where he was born. In it he recalls his mother and father's wedding cake in a tin box hanging from a rafter. There are also jars of snakes and other specimens that his father had collected as a boy and preserved in alcohol. It is this house that Nick needs to come to terms with—from basement to attic. And by eschewing the present, he may paradoxically come to understand it.

The early Nick stories return to echo in our minds, as Nick remembers. Some of these echoes are to "Big Two-Hearted River," since that story had been published previously—although we are now exploring an earlier period in Nick's life. "The Doctor and the Doctor's Wife" unquestionably comes back into play. In that story, even though Nick's mother was abed she was able to undercut the doctor's position in his house and to undercut his self-esteem. Nick remembers moving from the house he was born in "to a new house designed and built by my mother" (*MWW*, 222; *NAS*, 146). It is clear from what Nick remembers that his mother can act with energy and decisiveness—and that her actions can be thoughtlessly (to give them the best interpretation) destructive. Nick's early memory centers upon an image of fire and destruction. His mother, heedless of the feelings of others, specialized in "cleaning things out." Nick's memory of such a cleaning is essential for understanding the final half of the story when Nick is not remembering the past but is talking about the future with his hospital roommate.

Nick's recollection—letting us know how life was to go in the big new house designed by his mother—is of the time just before the move to the new house, when his father was away on a hunting trip. The doctor returns to find a fire that is feeding on the mementos of his past. The story has only one line from the mother: "I've been cleaning out the basement, dear" (*MWW*, 223; *NAS*, 147). The line is the more painful because the mother stands there smiling. We recognize the chilling (to us) *dear* of "The Doctor and the Doctor's Wife." We also find the doctor's reaction to his wife's managing ways familiar. He says nothing to her, but instead looks at the fire to see what might be salvaged. He tells Nick to get a rake and then begins raking "very carefully in the ashes," and that response may have been practical advice to Nick as he lies abed "raking carefully in the ashes." We have already seen the care and precision of the doctor in "Indian Camp." He again elicits Nick's aid, telling him to take his gun and game bags into the house and to bring him some newspapers. Nick is not at all reluctant to comply. His boy's heart is responding with instinctive sympathy. Again, the doctor's advice to Nick on that day carries useful suggestions for the Nick in his bed. Nick had tried to carry his father's shotgun and the two game bags in one trip and found the going difficult. He father instructs: "Take them one at a time . . . Don't try and carry too much at once" (*MWW*, 244; *NAS*, 148). Nick proceeds without murmur to put down the game bags, carry in the gun, and return with newspaper—and then watch his father arrange and wrap the mementos of his past. Nick's mother has long since gone into the house. There is a tremendous sense of loss as the doctor summarizes the results of his efforts: "The best arrow-heads went all to pieces," and then walks alone into the house. How acutely sensitive Nick was to the event and how deep his empathy for his father is unmistakable: "I stayed outside with the two game-bags. After a while I took them in" (*MWW*, 224; *NAS*, 148).

The nights of imaginary fishing in Michigan streams are clearly easier for Nick than the nights of praying and raking up such memories. But there are even worse nights—nights when the praying will not work, when Nick cannot even remember the prayers. The night of "Now I Lay Me" is such a night. It is "the night" of the opening sentence, the kind of night when Nick listens to the silkworms eating the mulberry leaves. Such nights start with Nick's strivings for order through remembering animals, birds, fishes, cities, food—but finally those nights give way to just listening; and there were always, Nick reports, things to hear. Emphasizing that Nick's past is now the issue, the story's present does not begin dramatically until very late—a departure from the pattern of the earlier Nick stories. We have a spare, uncluttered scene. Insomnia in war is not unique with Nick, even if his case is severe. His roommate is also awake this night. He too has been trying to lie quietly. John reenforces a pattern of several of the Nick stories. He is several years older than Nick, but since he lived ten years in Chicago, they share a frame of reference. Of Italian descent, John had been visiting in Italy in 1914 and by this bad luck has been conscripted for the duration of the war. His age and experience count for less in the story than they might have, since John is Nick's orderly. John gives Nick advice, however. But since Nick has been in the war, his relationship with tutors and would-be tutors has changed drastically.

In no earlier Nick story has preparation for the present moment of a story been so prolonged. The delay has served the function here of rendering time as a force, almost a character. Once the dialogue begins, however, it proceeds, almost unbroken, until finally John falls asleep.

The talk, although it takes some new twists this night, is also a part of a pattern. Nick and John have had other conversations on these nights, and there is a sense of repetition, ritual. It does not matter much to Nick what they discuss. Talking about things they have discussed before may even ease the pain. As Nick talks, we recognize a tone of voice never present in the earlier stories. Modulations are different. These are night voices. He repeatedly admonishes John to talk quietly. Nick is weary, subdued, seemingly worldly wise—but at very great cost. Talk about Chicago, Nick tells John. Talk about how you got married. But these are things they have already talked about, and John is not as depressed as Nick.

For want of an agenda, Nick suggests that they smoke. So they talk briefly about smoking, a subject they cannot take very far. They both agree that it is not good for them. The smoking also reveals to us something about the state of Nick's nerves; we have never seen him smoking in the pre-war stories. Nick has developed as a person who exults in the senses. Smoking dulls the senses of smell and taste and the big woods. Nick's gusto has been for good food, fishing, hunting, sport. Talk of smoking even allows Nick to feel that he has made some recovery, for he tells John that he has just about stopped smoking. The present smoke is a social affair—a way to fill in the awkwardness of having nothing to say.[7]

7. The smoking motif and the emphasis on the sense of smell provides another strong link between Hemingway and Nick. In *Green Hills of Africa* Hemingway says: "Then as the stream made a bend and we came out of the high grass to the bank I smelled game very distinctly. I do not smoke, and

When the smoking is finished, the silkworms become a presence. John hears them, too, and he would prefer to return to the talking. Whereas Nick's plan for conversation has been to have John talk about his life, John reverses the program and changes the focus to Nick's life. Talking about one's life, the real thing, is usually the most difficult kind of talk. It is something Hemingway's heroes are reluctant to do. There were extended preliminaries in "The Three Day Blow" before Nick could talk about what was on his mind. In "Now I Lay Me" the darkness probably helps, and John is not aggressive, but he has noticed Nick's insomnia. Because there have been certain preliminaries of conversation and the smoking, it now seems natural for him to ask Nick about his condition. Nick briefly reports to John, but by no means with the specificity of the account that Nick the narrator (removed from the story) has provided for the reader.

The reader is also in a privileged position for understanding the answer to another of John's questions. He wants to know why Nick was in the war. Nick responds: "I don't know, John. I wanted to, then" (*MWW*, 228; *NAS*, 150). It will take Nick some time before he can satisfactorily answer that question—and it will not be within the time of the story. It will probably take the writing of stories like "The Battler," "The Light of the World," and "The Killers" before he can explain to himself why he is where he is.

John, of course, does not find Nick's response very informative. Having failed to elicit information about Nick's past, he reasonably enough turns the conversation to Nick's future and asks what Nick is going to do in the States "when it's over." In one of the story's affirmative notes, Nick replies quickly: "I'll get a job on a paper" (*MWW*, 229; *NAS*, 151). He does not know where, but he knows that he is going to

---

hunting at home I have several times smelled elk in the rutting season before I have seen them and I can smell clearly where an old bull has lain in the forest. The bull elk has a strong musky smell. It is a strong but pleasant odor and I know it well, but this smell I did not know," p. 97. Hemingway had smoked, however, in younger years.

write. For the moment the immediate goal appears to be only journalism, but Nick's need to write is much greater—as "Big Two-Hearted River" makes clear. By the time of "Now I Lay Me" Nick has already had some newspaper experience, it seems, although he downplays it. John mentions a Chicago columnist, Arthur Brisbane. Nick tells John that he knows his work, has seen the man, but has not met him. But by the use of first-person point of view, Hemingway suggests that Nick's bent is for more than journalism.

Nick, picking up from John's reference to his wife, is able to divert the conversation from himself—briefly. He asks how John's children are. John can report their well-being, and he tells Nick that his wife and three girls have been of great practical value to him in the war. Were it not for them and his ability to speak English, John would not now be Nick's orderly. John keeps coming back to Nick. He cannot get over Nick's being unable to sleep. He does not believe Nick's declaration that he does not worry—and advises him to stop worrying. From John's point of view, Nick has much going for him—he is young, good looking, and has war decorations. He is certain that Nick would have no trouble getting a nice, rich Italian girl to marry him. "Over here, the way they're brought up they'll make you a good wife" (*MWW*, 231; *NAS*, 152). John feels very confident about the advantages of being married: "A man ought to be married. You'll never regret it. Every man ought to be married." Bill's advice in "The Three Day Blow" reverberates across the ocean: "Once a man's married he's absolutely bitched." There is, of course, no mention of Bill. Nor does Nick remind the reader of the wedding cake in the attic or his mother's thorough cleanings. Nick politely tells John that he will think on his advice but now suggests that they get some sleep.

The sleep comes to John, for whom marriage has worked so well. He is soon snoring. With his marked concentration Nick listens to John snore "for a long time" and then blocks the snoring from his mind to listen to the silkworms eating. He realizes that he has a new thing to think about—all the girls he has ever known and the kind of wives they would make. But the girl-thinking gets complicated, and Nick reverts to trout-fishing and prayers.

Nick also prays for John—whose good luck holds. John's class is removed from active service, and he misses the October offensive. He visits Nick later in the hospital in Milan and is disappointed that Nick has not married. At the end of the story it is clear that John's advice has counted for little. From the narrative present, a great distance from the episode he has just described and from Milan, Nick reports: "I know that he would feel very badly if he knew that so far I had never married. He was going back to America and he was very certain about marriage and knew that it would fix up everything" (*MWW*, 232; *NAS*, 153). With that punch line, Hemingway found the exactly right line to end the collection *Men Without Women*. It is not, however, a final note about Nick; rather it harks back to the earlier Nick stories and anticipates those to come.

In *Winner Take Nothing* Hemingway sent Nick close to the front again before sending him to Milan and the hospital experience mentioned at the end of "Now I Lay Me." Philip Young, quite reasonably, places "A Way You'll Never Be" after "Now I Lay Me." In *Men Without Women* Hemingway was studying Nick in relation to the larger theme of the collection and was counterpointing "Now I Lay Me" with "In Another Country." It is, then, somewhat jarring to read "A Way You'll Never Be" immediately after "Now I Lay Me"—although this would have to be the chronological ordering of the stories. Hemingway does not echo the earlier Nick stories quite as deliberately in "A Way You'll Never Be" as he had in "Now I Lay Me." There are, however, some points that would be puzzling to the reader unfamiliar with the earlier Nick work. Nick's past in "A Way You'll Never Be" is mainly the immediate past, the past of the war and Europe. The story dwells precisely on the things that in *Men Without Women* Nick consciously choked off from his thinking. The story is closer to the themes and attitudes of the abortive Nick novel than to the earlier stories. Sheridan

Baker finds the first use of *Nicholas* for Nick a signal of Hemingway's new attitude toward Nick. He even suggests that Hemingway may have begun to tire of his hero.[8]

However, a variation in Nick's Christian name is not the most radical indication that Hemingway was going to view Nick differently in this story. Hemingway alters dramatically certain aspects of Nick's experience at the front. The reader of *In Our Time* viewed Nick initially as suffering from a spine injury, but then a leg injury. In "In Another Country" Hemingway seemed to have settled definitively on a knee injury, much as he had given Frederic Henry. But in "A Way You'll Never Be" Nick's wounding has been literally and figuratively of the head. As the story begins the reader sees Nick riding his bicycle—a shocking beginning since Nick has already been wounded. In "In Another Country" we find him undergoing therapy for his knee, but in "A Way You'll Never Be" his legs give him no apparent trouble as he rides or walks. To be sure, when he gets up from a nap, he swings his legs down carefully for "they stiffened any time they were out straight for long" (*WTN*, 54; *NAS*, 162). Such a phenomenon could be the result of the head injury, but it is likely that Hemingway intends that his reader think also of a leg injury since Nick admits to having been wounded "in various places" (*WTN*, 56; *NAS*, 163). Otherwise, Hemingway makes no reference to Nick's legs in the story. If Nick is to need further hospital treatment, it will be for a head wound. The reader is informed of this fact when Nick tells the commanding officer, who has asked about his condition, that he cannot sleep without a light of some sort. The officer replies, "I said it should have been trepanned. I'm no doctor but I know that" (*WTN*, 52; *NAS*, 159). In trepanation, or trephination, the surgeon perforates the skull with a surgical instrument, a trephine, in order to relieve pressure on the brain. Nick explains that the doctors "thought it was better to have it absorb." As the story unfolds, Nick must deal with the pressure on his brain—explaining on the literal level the

8. Sheridan Baker, *Ernest Hemingway: An Introduction and Interpretation* (Holt, Rinehart and Winston, 1967), 34.

commander's concern that Nick not go out into the heat and that he lie down.

By Hemingway's own testimony, the account of Nick in "A Way You'll Never Be" was intended as something of an object lesson to a young girl who was "going crazy." He would show her a young man who was crazier than she would ever be.[9] Although Hemingway's explanation does not fully account for the story, it is the kind of statement Hemingway did not usually make. Hemingway's stories were written because he had to write them for himself—and Nick's stunned acquaintance with a harsh world had repeatedly served him as a worthy vehicle. He wanted to portray the sensitive boy of the Midwest who went to war and became a writer. Perhaps Hemingway felt an obligation to bring Nick in closer contact with the war—something he had once intended to render. Unquestionably, the Nick of "A Way You'll Never Be" has seen a good deal of combat. By the time of *Winner Take Nothing*, Hemingway also may have wished to counteract biographical readings of Nick. In "A Way You'll Never Be" Hemingway portrays Nick's mental condition in terms of the horror of war. He casts Nick's feelings about his own wounding and the fear of death in a light not seen in "Now I Lay Me." Nick in the later story is the observer of war, and what he views is too staggering for sanity to continue unchecked.

However, no Nick story, particularly one about war in Italy, that Hemingway would put into print could exist merely to cheer up some girl or to correct critics. The impetus of the story, Hemingway also said, came on a very hot day in Havana that put him in mind of the summer of 1918, a summer of crisis for him before it became so for Nick Adams. The intervening years had not dimmed Hemingway's memory of the hell of combat.

When we read "A Way You'll Never Be" immediately after "Now I Lay Me," we get an added forceful indication of how far Nick had to go before he could ever write such an ac-

9. Carlos Baker, *A Life Story*, 228.

count as "Now I Lay Me." For "A Way You'll Never Be"
Hemingway did not use a first person narrative; he wished
to take the reader directly into Nick's mind with the guns of
the enemy not far away; revelation will come not only
through dialogue but through extended use of stream-of-
consciousness technique. Hemingway has, of course,
evoked the quality of Nick's mind in other stories, but
through essentially objective description of what Nick saw
and what was said. Here he shows us the alarming state of
Nick's mental processes.

The story begins in the objective Hemingway style, describing a moment shortly after an attack and shortly before
other attacks come. The key words of the opening paragraph are "Nicholas Adams saw" (*WTN*, 47; *NAS*, 154). Nick
had not been a part of the recent attack; after many nights of
listening to silkworms, he is returning to the front—ostensi-
bly to bring comfort to the Italians because he is wearing an
American uniform. He can do the fighting Italians no practical good, but it has been suggested that he may soon aid the
war effort by taking postcards, cigarettes, and chocolates to
the soldiers. Nick has no commitment to serving as an er-
rand boy or even to aiding the allied cause; rather he wants
to prove to himself that he can return to the front and keep
hold of his sanity.

As Nick arrives near the front shortly after an attack, he
appears to be a careful observer, for what "Nicholas Adams
saw" is described in great detail. The reader of *Winner Take
Nothing* will be mindful of the scene of death that Nick has
observed as he reads a later story of the volume, "A Natural
History of the Dead," a story that tells with similar precision
what it is like to encounter dead bodies after battle. The
stories share some of the same details, although "A Natural
History of the Dead" is a heavily satiric piece, told by a
narrator who is full of bitterness toward effete humanists
who do not really know what war is like. "A Natural History" surveys several war areas whereas "A Way You'll
Never Be" gives only the one. But the two link closely when
the satiric piece becomes dramatic in portraying a hospital

scene near the front. War and putting away the dead and caring for the wounded make men act irrationally. Battle in the final part of "A Natural History" has not brought men into ideal brotherhood—as earlier war fiction tended to assume. The doctor in charge of the many wounded and the artillery officer who brings the wounded in begin to attack each other verbally. The artillery officer accuses the doctor of being crazy, but he is himself soon totally out of control: "F—— yourself," he said. "F—— yourself. F—— your mother. F——your sister" (*WTN*, 105). The doctor throws a saucerful of iodine into the lieutenant's face. In the final line of the story the doctor is telling the stretcherbearers to hold the lieutenant tightly: "He is in much pain. Hold him very tight" (*WTN*, 106). On balance, the doctor has acted very ably in the most difficult of circumstances; he is most the professional in his final line, for he can indeed understand the circumstances that have caused the lieutenant to act as he has.

"A Way You'll Never Be" also instructs humanists on how it is after battle. Nick passes through the deserted town with its many dead and the debris that typically surrounds the dead. Even after Nick's journey through the scene of the attack and after he finds other living soldiers, the atmosphere is almost surreal. The few men who guard the outposts are asleep. Nick seems to be in some kingdom of the dead.

Adding to the surreal atmosphere, Nick's coming arouses at first only one person. In "A Natural History" the narrator repeatedly felt that the grimness of the war he had viewed required a Goya to depict it. A Goya could also do much with the opening of "A Way You'll Never Be," with its city of the dead through which Nick rides, absurdly, on his bicycle. Goya could also catch a memorable moment when Nick meets the first living soul on this journey, the young second lieutenant "with a stubble of beard and red-rimmed, very bloodshot eyes" (*WTN*, 49; *NAS*, 156) who is pointing a pistol at him.

The moment is dramatic when the second lieutenant stops

Nick, and the officer's action further stresses the absurdity of Nick's journey. Nick could easily lose his life on this trip. In war the danger, the threat, does not come only from the other side, as the ending of "A Natural History" also stresses. Furthermore, the episode with the young soldier helps to prepare us for Nick's flashback. Nick has not been present at the attack whose aftermath he has just witnessed, but the young soldier has. The Nick stories have featured the confrontation of the young with ugly realities. There is no doubt that the attack was not a glorious adventure for the young soldier: "the face of this officer looked like the face of a man during a bombardment. There was the same tightness and the voice did not sound natural. His pistol made Nick nervous" (*WTN*, 50; *NAS*, 157). Had Nick been the soldier present at the bombardment, he might have acted much as this soldier does. It is to Nick's credit that he handles the second lieutenant so well and can persuade him to take him to Captain Paravicini to verify that he is not a spy. On the other hand, the incident undermines what Nick hopes to achieve on this venture, for his nerves are put to a hard test.

Captain Paravicini is something of a father figure for Nick, and he greets Nick with a familiar "Nicolo." Paravicini belongs to that select group of characters in Hemingway's fiction who seem totally professional—they are aware of the limitations and injustices of life, but they act with honor and dignity in the face of those limitations and injustices. Paravicini is a sensitive man, formerly an architect, well mannered, considerate, tactful. He is in the tradition of such characters as Count Mippipopolous (*The Sun Also Rises*) and Count Greffi (*A Farewell to Arms*). His age and the sense that he conveys of knowing how to live are reassuring to Nick— and in obvious contrast to both Nick and the young second lieutenant. Aware of the effect on Nick of what he has just seen, Paravicini tries to direct Nick's mind by talking about the battle with reference to a map—by looking at the war in military rather than personal terms. And he talks about Nick's unexpected arrival with as much tact as anyone could, although Nick is too alert not to realize that Paravicini sees exactly what the situation is.

Ever the gentleman, Paravicini offers Nick some Grappa, which he politely refuses. In offering the Grappa, the Italian has unknowingly touched a nerve. The first interchapter of *In Our Time* shocked in its emphasis of the prevalency of liquor as a means to blunt fear, and the motif is present in the fragment of the early Nick novel. Now, although he is in stress, Nick politely refuses. The captain reassures Nick that the Grappa has no ether in it. The mention of ether "suddenly and completely" (*WTN*, 51; *NAS*, 159) makes Nick taste it—and remember the past he dared not remember a short time ago. He begins talking about himself in a surprisingly confessional bluntness. Nowhere have we found Nick so full of self-condemnation. "I was stinking in every attack," Nick says and appeals shortly thereafter to Paravicini: "Let's not talk about how I am . . . It's a subject I know too much about to want to think about anymore" (*WTN*, 52; *NAS*, 159). He then confesses that he cannot sleep without a light of some sort. Typically, in this dialogue Hemingway suggests rather than states the facial expressions and voice tones of his characters. Paravicini has been quite matter of fact about his view of the treatment of Nick's wound. Nick's abrupt response is telling: "What's the matter? I don't seem crazy to you, do I?" Paravicini knows that Nick needs to rest; so he suggests that Nick lie down. He urges Nick to be practical: "You oughtn't to go out in the heat now—it's silly" (*WTN*, 52; *NAS*, 160).

Because he knows how he is, Nick lies down—but not to the careful rituals of "Now I Lay Me." The memories before which Nick always stopped in that story are now starkly revealed. Nick's fishing program, though it helped, has not been entirely successful. The reader is plunged for the first time into Nick's mind for a long passage of direct thought flow—the first such in the Nick canon. Nick, in mentally tasting etherlike Grappa, opened the memory gates for re-creation of his time at the front. Present participles and remembered dialogues create immediacy—but not in the

order that was present in the early memory the controlled
narrator recounted in "Now I Lay Me." The issue, however,
is clear—Nick's sense of fear, even cowardice. The Nick stories began on such a note although Hemingway rejected the
too obvious emphasis of the "Three Shots" prelude when
Uncle George observed of Nick: "I know he's an awful coward." The issue of cowardice is also present in "The Doctor
and the Doctor's Wife"—although not as the simple matter
critics have sometimes assumed. One can be fearful and
even retreat, but can he do so in terms that do not negate
his self-esteem? Clearly, Nick in his initiation into war could
not. He remembers, with great shame, the one time he went
into battle without the aid of alcohol. "Making it cold, no
time to get it, he couldn't find his own after the cave-in, one
whole end had caved in; it was that started them; making it
cold up the slope the only time he hadn't done it stinking"
(*WTN*, 53; *NAS*, 160). It is difficult to imagine precisely the
scene Nick remembers, but it is clear that he is disgusted
with himself. Because we are in Nick's disturbed mind, there
are not always stated antecedents for pronouns, but the passage reveals Nick's reliance on alcohol for his courage. His
first attack of craziness came after the cave-in that prevented
his finding his Grappa: "it was that started them." It is also
clear that there was a gruesome repetition of dealing with
the wounded and the dying: "And after they came back
the teleferica house burned, it seemed, and some of the
wounded got down four days later and some did not get
down, but we went up and we went back and we came
down—we always came down" (*WTN*, 53; *NAS*, 160–61).

Nick's mind switches momentarily from the horror of the
front to his days in Paris before going to Italy. The passage
portraying this flashback is somewhat perplexing to present-
day readers. It seems deliberately obscure, ready-made for
some new humanist to explain with footnotes: "And there
was Gaby Delys, oddly enough, with feathers on; you called
me baby doll a year ago tadada you said that I was rather
nice to know tadada with feathers on, with feathers off, the
great Gaby, and my name's Harry Pilcer, too, we used to

step out of the far side of the taxis when it got steep going up the hill and he could see that hill every night when he dreamed with Sacré Coeur, blown white, like a soap bubble" (*WTN*, 53; *NAS*, 161). The Gaby is in all probability the Gaby on board ship in "Night Before Landing." The name Gaby Delys is not even obviously feminine to most present-day readers. But in 1918 Gaby Deslys (Gabrielle of the Lilies) was a famous movie actress and dancer (Hemingway misspelled her name). She was reported to have been engaged to Harry Pilcer, a famous dancer—a report (one of many that circulated about the flamboyant celebrity) familiar to Nick. When she died in 1920 of throat cancer, the circumstances were sensational like her life: She wanted no operation that would disfigure her throat. Born in 1884, she was too old to have been a serious love for Nick. His attraction to her was youthful infatuation for a celebrity. What he remembers is an image; Nick has probably never even met Gaby. She is singing the first two lines of the chorus from "A Broken Doll," music by James W. Tate, words by Clifford Harris: "You called me Baby Doll a year ago. / You told me I was very nice to know." The song about a broken romance was from the British show *Samples*, copyrighted in 1916. When Hemingway wrote "A Way You'll Never Be," the references were already dated, but they are appropriate to Nick's thinking at the time of World War I.

The passage building on the song owes something to other sources, too. Hemingway's method evokes an atmosphere reminiscent of parts of T. S. Eliot's *The Waste Land*, though Nick could not be remembering it, for the poem did not appear until after the war. The method of disorientation and abruptness so important in *The Waste Land* is like what goes on in this flashback centered on Gaby, who is like the hyacinth girl, and Gaby in Nick's mind is also part of some "Burial of the Dead." The "tadada" seems to play on the pub scene in Part II of *The Waste Land*, "A Game of Chess." "Tadada" may also catch dadaism of the war years—although it also carries into postwar Paris, as does the play on F. Scott Fitzgerald's titles, as Gaby becomes "the great Gaby," and "we used to step out on the far side of the taxis." The taxi's going up hill turns Nick's thought back to the hill of battle, and his nightmare vision is again suggestive of the Eliotic nightmare as Nick "dreamed with Sacré Coeur, blown white, like a soap bubble." The song "A Broken Doll" corresponds to Nick's disastrous love affair in Europe (planned for the abortive novel "Along with Youth"); the "we" is not Nick and Gaby, but Nick and his girl (someone like the Luz of "A Very Short Story"). Nick's experience with a girl was another disaster: "Sometimes his girl was there and sometimes she was with some one else and he could not understand that." The passage puts an edge on Nick's discussion with John in "Now I Lay Me" about possible marriage.

The girl provides a transition to the most evocative symbol of the flashback, the image of the yellow house in a terrain that is strangely quiet—the essence of nightmare, recalling the town through which Nick has just come, a town of the dead: "Those were the nights the river ran so much wider and stiller than it should and outside of Fossalta there was a low house painted yellow with willows all around it and a low stable and there was a canal, and he had been there a thousand times and never seen it, but there it was every night as plain as the hill, only it frightened him. That house meant more than anything and every night he had it" (*WTN*, 53; *NAS*, 161). Nick's dreams always take him to the same place, not far from where he now is. And every night he awakens when he reaches the house. The frightening yellow house marks, apparently, the spot where Nick was when he was wounded. As such, it becomes the dream prefiguration of his death.

When Nick awakens now—upon reaching the yellow house in his dream—he is embarrassed, for others have witnessed the awakening. He tries to show his control through talking, and his talking is very unlike that he has done in the past. His speeches have usually been few and lean. The contrast with "Now I Lay Me" is especially useful. "A Way You'll Never Be" gives even more specific reasons for Nick's reticence. He is possessed with a great deal of self-loathing as he informs the adjutant that other Americans will be coming: "Oh, Absolutely. Americans twice as large as myself, healthy with clean hearts, sleep at night, never been wounded, never been blown up, never had their heads caved in, never been scared, don't drink, faithful to the girls they left behind them, many of them never had crabs, wonderful chaps. You'll see'" (*WTN*, 55; *NAS*, 162). And the usually reticent Nick continues talking, showing how badly frayed his nerves are; his talk finally erupts into a torrent of words as he begins to lecture on grasshoppers, insects—he says—that "at one time played a very important part in my life" (*WTN*, 56; *NAS*, 164). The speech is easily the longest spoken by Nick in any Nick story, and it is about as long as the flashback to the dream he has just had. It ends in a similarly chaotic manner. It is also the part of the story that most pointedly connects with other Nick stories, emphasizing in the use of the grasshopper the plight of the victim of war—an important symbol in "Big Two-Hearted River" and in "Now I Lay Me."

On Hemingway's testimony, a part of the impetus for "A Way You'll Never Be" was the heat of a Havana day. The detail of the heat at Fossalta is a part of the realism of the story. Nick, hot and sweaty now because of his nightmare as well as the heat of the day, has removed his helmet and announces that he is going to the river to wet it. In view of the military situation and Nick's dream, the suggestion carries dark implications. In Nick's dream the river was Styx-like with its boat waiting to carry him to the house that he "needed." Without the dream sequence, Nick's intention would be nothing more than realism. It is, of course, a good bit more.

Fortunately, Paravicini—the good guide and the example of grace under pressure—arrives. He knows that Nick is in no condition to go anywhere alone. Nick does as his mentor tells him, returns inside to sit. He also takes us back to the opening scene of the story when he tells Paravicini that he has seen helmets "full of brains too many times." The captain, addressing Nick with a fatherly *Nicolo*, advises him to return to his hospital and not to come back until he has the supplies. He becomes, then, thoroughly stern and practical and professional: "There's nothing here for you to do. If you moved around, even with something worth giving away, the men will group and that invites shelling. I won't have it" (*WTN*, 58; *NAS*, 166).

Nick cannot argue against this practicality, but he feels another siege coming on and must finally let it out: "The trouble is you have a damned small battalion to command. As soon as it gets to strength again they'll give you back your company. Why don't they bury the dead? I've seen them now. I don't care about seeing them again. They can bury them any time as far as I'm concerned and it would be much better for you'" (*WTN*, 58; *NAS*, 166). Although considerably shorter than the lecture on grasshoppers, the paragraph shows the same tendency towards disjunctiveness. It is a paragraph only because it is faithful to the state of Nick's mind and the fashion of his delivery—which is irrational. Nick is seeing the war in personal terms—as if the carnage were somehow to punish him. The paragraph also shows rationality: Nick is something of a student of this particular war. Nowhere else do we find Nick concerned with the politics of war. His statement about how the system treats capable men like Paravicini is more like the thought of Colonel Cantwell in *Across the River and Into the Trees* than of the Nick we have usually seen. The late Nick story, then, adds an interesting dimension. More to be expected is Nick's profound revulsion before the dead—the natural history that has been kept out of the books on war. Nick ends by trying to be practical about it ("It would be much better for you"), but the impact of the speech stems from Nick's revulsion against war with its overwhelming disregard of life.

Paravicini, of course, has more pressing things to be concerned with. The dead will have to wait a little while. The battallion is confronted with fortifications against new attack. And Paravicini cannot worry about the politicians. More immediately, he counsels Nick to lie down again for a while.

Nick is soon dreaming again of "long, yellow house with a low stable and the river much wider than it was and stiller" (*WTN*, 59; *NAS*, 167). This time Nick senses that he should leave, but not towards the river. The time with Paravicini has helped. As measured against the outburst on the grasshoppers, the second outburst had been more rational and more honest. As he has many times before—following the basic rhythm of the Nick stories—Nick turns from disaster towards the future. Paravicini agrees to let Nick go alone, "as a mark of confidence." Retreat is here advancement. The final line of the story reenforces an old Nick theme as Nick again starts out on a journey where retreat is progress, telling himself: "I don't want to lose the way to Fornaci" (*WTN*, 59; *NAS*, 167).

Like "A Way You'll Never Be," "In Another Country," the story that recounts the next stage in Nick's recuperation, has as one of its aims the portrayal of experience vastly different from that of the reader. "A Way You'll Never Be" is one of Hemingway's more cryptic titles—hence his explanation of its genesis as an illustration for the young girl who was going crazy. For the ordinary reader, the implication is that he would never know Nick's state save to the extent that he would see the examples of death in war that Nick has. War is the ultimate experience. Similarly Nick as the narrator of "In Another Country" stresses the great gulf that exists between those who have been at the front and those who have not. His statement is explicit: "we felt held together by there being something that had happened that they, the people who disliked us, did not understand" (*MWW*, 62; *NAS*, 170). The wounded are all "in another country," even the soldiers who are from Milan. In the communist quarters there is verbal abuse for all of them; the citizens in that quarter know the abstractions of politics, not the realities of war.

"In Another Country" is one of Hemingway's most evocative short story titles. It and the narrative voice create a special poetry of the still sad music of humanity. The memorable opening sentence immediately makes the title do more than comment on geographical boundaries: "In the fall the war was always there, but we did not go to it any more" (*WTN*, 58; *NAS*, 168). Nick describes the routine of the wounded as they make their regular journeys to the hospital, where the official propaganda is that they are going to be made as good as new. Style and tone make apparent how the experience of war has been decisive for these young men. Having told us of their routine, Nick repeats: "We only knew that there was always the war, but that we were not going to it any more" (*MWW*, 61; *NAS*, 170).

At the point of repetition the narrator sets up still another remove. "But this was a long time ago," he says. Time plays a role in this story similar to the role it plays in "Now I Lay Me"—the story with which it is most closely aligned. The sentence is also a transition to our seeing the story as a Nick story, for the narrator is prepared to talk about himself with great honesty, and the things he tells us about himself correspond so exactly to the details of "Now I Lay Me" that there need be no hesitation in seeing this as a Nick story.[10] Not to see it as a Nick story would be to miss a great deal.

The transitional sentence to more immediate consideration of Nick also places the literary allusion of the title. It comes from Christopher Marlowe's play *The Jew of Malta*. Hemingway got the lines from Marlowe by way of T. S. Eliot, who had used them as an epigraph for his poem "Portrait of a Lady": "but that was in another country / And besides, the wench is dead."

The allusion is, of course, less obvious than the allusion in the title "Now I Lay Me." But it is useful on that score for placing the story at a further remove from the time when Nick is still close to the front. He is now in Milan and mak-

---

10. Earl Rovit takes a purist line in discussing this story in his *Ernest Hemingway* (New York: Twayne, 1963), 60, 61–65. He leaves the first-person narrator unnamed, using him simply as an example of the tyro. The inventory of the Hemingway manuscripts provides compelling evidence for the identification. A near-final draft of "Now I Lay Me" carries the title "In Another Country—Two: A Story." See Philip Young and Charles W. Mann (eds.), *The Hemingway Manuscripts: An Inventory* (University Park and London: Pennsylvania State University Press, 1969), 44.

ing some progress in his difficult task of sorting matters out. The narrative Nick is writing in the present reflects that progress by his ability to treat his problems more comprehensively. He talks about himself with an honesty that pulls the reader to deep sympathy—although that is not what Nick is seeking. He is sharing with the reader the realities of war's aftermath—and seeking for himself answers to some long-standing questions.

In contrast to the heat of the summer of "A Way You'll Never Be," the mood of "In Another Country" is colored by the cold of the fall in Milan. Nick and his comrades walk though the town and feel the wind coming down from the mountains. Because we experience with Nick the daily walks to the hospital, we feel the strength of his character. The walks are important—they are, in part, rituals. There is an orderliness about the walks—although there is some variation in the routes (there are three bridges that contain the choices), for the ending is always the same: the hospital. Nick recognizes that the building is stately and impressive. He can appreciate man's edifices as well as he can appreciate nature: "The hospital was very old and very beautiful, and you entered through a gate and walked across a courtyard and out a gate on the other side" (*MWW*, 58–59; *NAS*, 168). The boy Nick in "Indian Camp" felt that he would live forever. The pictorial rendering in "In Another Country" creates the hospital and death as normal to the human condition. Nick knows that now. He tells us that there were "usually funerals starting from the courtyard." Many roads lead to one end.

Still, the journey of life that the journey to the hospital suggests is worthwhile; or at least this conviction is a strong one in Nick, and it persists. In the first paragraph Nick reports that it was "pleasant along the streets looking in the windows" (*MWW*, 58; *NAS*, 168). There are pleasures to be found. Along one of the routes to the hospital there was a woman who sold roasted chestnuts: "It was warm, standing in front of her charcoal fire, and the chestnuts were warm afterward in your pocket." Clearly, Nick is not just a young man who fears death. His very perceptions and delight in his senses help to explain the degree of his fears.

That Nick does not relate any names in the story mirrors his keen sense of isolation. For even as he insists on the fact that men who have been to war are set aside from people who have not, Nick also feels isolated from his comrades with whom he walks through the streets of Milan. Even in their company he is "in another country." He reports, "I was a friend, but I was never really one of them" (*MWW*, 63; *NAS*, 171). Nick's wounding was, he realizes, an accident. He is left wondering about his own bravery—could he have done the things that three of his comrades did to get their medals? He has his doubts: "The three with the medals were like hunting-hawks; and I was not a hawk, although I might seem a hawk to those who had never hunted; they, the three, knew better and so we drifted apart" (*MWW*, 63–64; *NAS*, 171). A fourth comrade, a young boy who "wore a silk handkerchief across his face because he had no nose then and his was to be rebuilt," is a comfort to Nick, for the boy had been wounded immediately upon his arrival at the front and so had not been tested in battle. But walking home through the streets thinking about the deeds of the three, Nick is honest with himself. "I knew that I would never have done such things, and I was very much afraid to die, and often lay at night by myself, afraid to die and wondering how I would be when I got back to the front again" (*MWW*, 63; *NAS*, 171). Always a reliable observer of others and of events, Nick Adams has become a keen observer of himself.

There is no easy optimism for Nick. The boyish eagerness of "The Light of the World" has been gone out for a long time. A controlled skepticism has taken over, but it is expressed in terms that show the value of routine in dealing with harsh realities. Nick reports that he and his comrades "were all very polite and interested in what was the matter, and sat in the machines that were to make so much difference" (*MWW*, 59; *NAS*, 168). Even while using the machines Nick was skeptical of what difference the machines would or could make. Hemingway contrasts Nick with an ebullient, very talkative doctor, who promises that he "will play football again like a champion" (*MWW*, 59; *NAS*, 169). Nick is not here the talker of "A Way You'll Never Be," but more like the terse speaker of "Now I Lay Me." He answers the doctor politely but briefly.

Although point of view in "A Way You'll Never Be" sets it apart, the three stories of Nick at war bear significant structural similarities. In each Nick is quizzed by an older man who also gives Nick advice. Each story proceeds from description to a variation on the catechetical method. Paravicini's professional skill is markedly in evidence. In "Now I Lay Me" Nick outranks John, and although John is older than Nick and kindly, he is decidedly an ordinary sort of person. But he also queries Nick and gives him definite advice. In the context of *Men Without Women* Hemingway obviously planned that the reader upon hearing John's advice would recall very different advice from a different sort of tutor. The ending of *Men Without Women* was to take us back to the beginning.

The tutor of "In Another Country" is a major, unnamed in the story—as all of the characters in the story are unnamed. The device of having all the characters unnamed heightens the "in hospital" sense of the story—the sense of a hospital's, any hospital's, being in another country. The gulf between the wounded and the whole is immense.

The major has the temperament of the ironist, and overhearing the doctor's pep talk to Nick, he asks: "And will I too play football, captain-doctor?" (*MWW*, 60; *NAS*, 169). The major's withered hand is "like a baby's," and he does not have any confidence it will ever be otherwise. Still, he goes through the prescribed treatments, and he believes that a sense of humor is not amiss.

That defense cannot be easy, for before the war the major had been the greatest fencer in Italy. He is obviously, then, a man of great self-discipline—and he would have great appeal for Nick, who consistently has been approving of the skilled—in boxing, baseball, fishing, and writing. Nick real-

izes what it must mean for a man like the major to have to
cope with the kind of "industrial accident" that he has had.

Like Paravicini, the major has sensed Nick's quality, too.
Instructing Nick in Italian becomes one of the major's ways
of coping with his own frustration and tedium. Nick, as we
discovered in his warm relationship with Paravicini, has
some facility for the language. In advising Nick to marry an
Italian girl, John told him that he speaks the language "fine,"
but the major has higher standards than John. He thinks
Nick should "take up the use of grammar." Language becomes a discipline: Nick learns, the major instructs, and it is
good for both of them.

Hemingway's own disciplined use of language, of course,
is what gives this story the power that it has. We can be
reminded of it when Nick describes the new hospital discipline of language lessons. He takes the story from vivid
details of daytime patterns to the dramatic presentation of a
particular daytime, as in "Now I Lay Me" the pattern of various nights gave way to dramatic presentation of a particular
night. The transition in "In Another Country" comes in a
surprising, but effective passage of indirect discourse. It is
not a usual tool of Hemingway's short fiction, as it is in
Joyce's *Dubliners*. In "In Another Country" it marks the major's cracking point: "There was a time when none of us
believed in the machines, and one day the major said it was
all nonsense. The machines were new then and it was we
who were to prove them. It was an idiotic idea, he said, 'a
theory, like another.' I had not learned my grammar, and he
was a fool to have bothered with me" (*MWW*, 65; *NAS*, 172).
The major's outburst is similar to Nick's at the end of "A Way
You'll Never Be" when he admonishes Paravicini to bury the
dead.

The indirect discourse, because of its uniqueness in the
story, is useful for suggesting Nick's stunned reaction to the
major's outburst. Nick has always found the major admirable in his control of his emotions and actions and in his
careful speech. And, of course, Nick has appreciated the
major's thoughtful concern for him; the major never mistook

Nick for a hawk. Puzzled, Nick does not protest his mentor's abuse. He remains the dutiful student.

The story switches from indirect to direct discourse when the major asks a question that is important for the whole body of the Nick stories—and the same question that John asks in "Now I Lay Me." The major snaps, "What will you do when the war is over if it is over? . . . Speak grammatically!" (*MWW*, 65; *NAS*, 172). In addition to its play on "Now I Lay Me" the question is also a moving echo of the opening sentence and the pervading atmosphere of eternal sameness and stopped time. Can Nick, or anyone, think of the future?

Nick tells the major, as he had told John, that he will return to the States. Perhaps because he has thought of John's advice, Nick also tells the major that he hopes to marry. The major's reply is the exact opposite from John's firm belief. He retorts: "A man must not marry" (*MWW*, 65; *NAS*, 172). The right answer for "Now I Lay Me" is the wrong answer in "In Another Country"; Nick naturally seeks for an explanation.

The major's explanation is vastly different from Bill's cynical verdict in "The Three Day Blow." Marriage, for the major, has been the relationship that has brought him the greatest satisfaction. But it has also made him vulnerable to the greatest of pain. He expresses his agony memorably when he warns against a man's marrying: "If he is to lose everything, he should not place himself in a position to lose that. He should find things he cannot lose" (*MWW*, 65–66; *NAS*, 173). And somewhere in the back of Nick's mind there must have been echoes of a night in an Indian camp when he had intimations of the risks of love. Nevertheless, winners may take nothing, as the title of Hemingway's third major book of stories asserts, but that is a hard lesson for Nick—and the major—to grasp. In what terms can Nick, or any man, be a winner? The Nick stories have built up to this question, so crucial to Hemingway's work. The major has sought for true value and for the permanent. Do they ever come together? The major's experience suggests that they do not, and Nick's own experiences have impressed on him the impermanence of things human.

The major is so shattered by the loss of his wife that he almost shouts at Nick and then feeling how far out of control he is, he leaves the room. He returns later wearing his cape and his cap, looking very military, again in control of himself. Military discipline is a stay for him. The major has survived the war and even a wound that effectively puts an end to his fencing career. It is as if the gods were probing to find the place where this admirable man might crumble—one more testing for Job. They have found that point of vulnerability, causing the woeful "A man must not marry."

Having regained his composure, the major realizes that he owes Nick an apology, and he apologizes with all the usual grace and dignity that Nick has found to be characteristic of him. He explains to Nick, "My wife has just died" (*MWW*, 66; *NAS*, 173). Nick feels "sick" for the major, who stands there "biting his lower lip." The tears do not seem unmanly as the major cries: "I am utterly unable to resign myself." Nick has learned, apparently for the first time, how hard someone's dying can be for those who remain. He now understands the world as he never has before. As he views the major, he takes with him from that afternoon a powerful image: "And then crying, his head up looking at nothing, carrying himself straight and soldierly, with tears on both his cheeks and biting his lips, he walked past the machines and out the door" (*MWW*, 67; *NAS*, 173).

Many Nick stories end with a departure, usually a walk, but a journey or a new turning. But as a first-person narrative told by Nick sometime later, "In Another Country" needs the more contemplative rather than the dramatic ending. It parallels its companion "Now I Lay Me" in using the generalized, comtemplative ending, rather than any dramatic end for the particular day or night. Furthermore, both stories gain by returning to the atmosphere of the hospital and the sense of stalled time, the sense that the war was always there.

In the final paragraph of "In Another Country" we learn several new things. The major had not married his young wife until he had been "invalided out of the war" (*MWW*, 67; *NAS*, 174). The war has been an immense cheat for the major—taking nearly everything from him. His wife's death has been a biological accident, like Catherine's in *A Farewell to Arms*. Hemingway's metaphor of the world as a hospital and a place of dying extends beyond the war and the wounded. The bereaved are also people "in another country." The machines can do nothing for the major, who nevertheless returns to them after three days, wearing the appropriate black band on the sleeve of his uniform—the military man again taking support in ritual. The final sentence of the story conveys no movement at all. The image is frozen. The major sits looking out the window. He sees, apparently, nothing.

There is more for us to see, however—particularly as we view the Nick stories as an artist's progress, for Nick is not where he is at the end of "Now I Lay Me." It is significant that in "In Another Country" Nick, who has talked a great deal about his feelings and self-doubts, ends the story with such profound empathy. We have seen Nick as a keen observer and a keen listener. He could feel for Ole Andreson, but he thought of him only as he affected Nick himself. "I can't stand to think about him," he had told George. Now Nick is thinking about the major and the major's loss. The story bodes well for Nick's future—especially for his aspirations to be a writer—one who will be capable of evoking empathy for his characters.

Whereas Hemingway had maintained that the "quite irreplaceable" experience of war is difficult to write about truly, most readers have found the stories treating Nick as a soldier "truly" rendered, powerful in their conveyance of the horror of war and the effects of war on men. Nick's war experience was no escape from the issues that had earlier bothered him—his relationship with his family and his uncertainty about the possibility or desirability of deeply loving another person. If anything, Nick's war experience brought those problems more revealingly to his consciousness and into a context that is finally adult. And although the experience of war brought Nick to the very threshold of death and at times across the boundary of sanity, it also taught Nick greater compassion and sympathy. Especially in "In Another Country" Nick demonstrates marked empathy for another. That two of the Nick war stories are in the first person suggests that Nick as writer has indeed gained from his experience at war.

Chapter Four
Soldier Home: "Big Two-Hearted River"

When Hemingway came to arrange the stories of *In Our Time*, there was probably no question about which would come last. Four stories to appear in the book would be new; three of them were about Nick, insuring that readers would find him the most important character of the book. Although the final story would not be one of the new ones, it would be about Nick—the Nick story that showed best what the group as a whole meant. That story is, of course, "Big Two-Hearted River." It is unquestionably the most brilliant of the collection. It is also the story that had cost Hemingway the most labor, but it provided unmistakable proof that its young author had mastered his craft.

"Big Two-Hearted River" in the final placement also has the advantage of balancing Nick's trauma in the opening "Indian Camp" with the resolution to his trauma in war. It should not be forgotten that Hemingway had published "Indian Camp" under the Joycean title "Work in Progress." Throughout his career Hemingway gave high praise to Joyce, whom he considered a true master. *Dubliners* was partly a model as he arranged *In Our Time*. He knew from it, as well as from *Winesburg, Ohio*, that a book of stories could be more than a collection; so he vigorously protested well-meaning efforts of his publisher to alter the unity, as he saw it, of *In Our Time*. His book, because of its incorporation of *in our time* into the structure, would be unlike either Anderson's book or Joyce's, but it would owe as much to *Dubliners* structurally as it owed to *Winesburg*. *Dubliners* begins with three stories, arranged chronologically, about a boy. The boy disappears thereafter, but the reader may well remember the boy's peculiar disposition when he reaches the final story of the book, "The Dead." The intervening stories are arranged into groups illustrating various aspects of Dublin life, many of them heavily satirical. *In Our Time*, similarly, moves from the early Nick stories to a grouping about three young men who come to crucial experience in war and revolution. It is followed by a grouping of stories about young married couples (all set in Europe). The two groupings have a good bit of satire in them. "My Old Man" stands somewhat alone. It is set in Europe, too, but it recalls much of the youth and innocence of the boyhood stories at the beginning of the book—and plays also on the theme of the shattering of innocence. More than any other story Hemingway wrote, it shows the influence of Sherwood Anderson. But "My Old Man" (one of the stories of *Three Stories and Ten Poems*) would not have served as satisfactory coda. We need to come back to Nick. Joyce had originally ended *Dubliners* with "Grace," but he was not satisfied with the total effect of the book. There were aspects of Dublin life he had not shown, and the book seemed too disparaging about Dublin, in some sense not true to what Joyce knew about Dublin and life. He countered with "The Dead," the longest story by far in the collection and a masterpiece. Hemingway would also end his book with a major story—something uniquely his. It would not remind readers of anyone but Hemingway.

Hemingway stressed the importance of "Big Two-Hearted River" to *In Our Time* by dividing it into two parts and listing each part in the table of contents. He further insisted on the division by having an interchapter between the two parts. Together the parts are the longest Nick story we have. It is unique in being almost totally descriptive and in having only one human character present—Nick. While he was working on the story, Hemingway explained to Gertrude Stein that he was "trying to do the country like Cézanne."[1] He was trying to do in fiction what had not been done before, and he knew he was succeeding. In "Big Two-Hearted River" his hero was also dealing, more meaningfully than he had ever done before, with the issues of life and death—as was Joyce's Gabriel Conroy in "The Dead." Finally, Hemingway was giving us the most affirmative note of *In Our Time* in that concluding Nick story, as his title "Big Two-Hearted River" emphasizes—the more so since it was doubly given.

Late in his career, reviewing his Paris years for what came to be *A Moveable Feast*, Hemingway described the effect he was trying to achieve in "Big Two-Hearted River":

> What did I know best that I had not written about and lost? What did I know about truly and care for the most? There was no choice at all. There was only the choice of streets to take you back fastest to where you worked. . . .
> I sat in a corner with the afternoon light coming in over my shoulder and wrote in the notebook. The waiter brought me a *café crème* and I drank half of it when it cooled and left it on the table while I wrote. When I stopped writing I did not want to leave the river where I could see the trout in the pool, its surface pushing and swelling smooth against the resistance of the log-driven piles of the bridge. The story was about coming back from the war but there was no mention of the war in it.
> But in the morning the river would be there and I must make it and the country and all that would happen.[2]

At least one of the things "Big Two-Hearted River" is about is the trauma of war, although the story never mentions the war. The reader of *In Our Time* has a large frame of reference against which he should evaluate "Big Two-Hearted River"—the war experience for Nick and others being major in that background. Probably no other Nick story illustrates how greatly Hemingway was concerned with Nick's career as a whole, as an on-going thing, as "work in progress."

1. Charles Fenton, *The Apprenticeship of Ernest Hemingway* (New York: Viking Press, 1958), 157.
2. Ernest Hemingway, *A Moveable Feast* (New York: Charles Scribner's Sons, 1964), 76.

"Big Two-Hearted River" cannot stand alone in the way "The Dead" can stand alone. *In Our Time*, from the first interchapter on, and after 1930 from "On the Quai at Smyrna" on, had insisted that war and revolution are the central fact of our time. As we have seen, one interchapter specifically places Nick as a part of the great conflict of his time.

In *Death in the Afternoon* Hemingway eloquently explained a central component to his theory of writing, a theory that had been basic to his method from the start: "If a writer of prose knows enough about what he is writing about he may omit things that he knows and the reader, if the writer is writing truly enough, will have a feeling of those things as strongly as though the writer had stated them. The dignity of movement of an ice-berg is due to only one-eighth of it being above water."[3] The theory is helpful for describing no story more than "Big Two-Hearted River"; however, when we apply the theory to the story we may be reminded that the reader, like the writer, sometimes has to know some things not mentioned in a particular story. Understandably, "Big Two-Hearted River" has been anthologized frequently, for anthologizers like to include the best of a writer if they can get it. But if the reader does not already know Nick, he will miss much of the story's impact—even though he would probably enjoy reading it. He could get a great deal from the story by itself—and still not think of World War I. "Big Two-Hearted River" gains immeasurably from the context that Hemingway meant us to have.

The opening of Part I recalls "The Battler"—where Nick also had been traveling alone by train. There Nick's destination was vague, but here it is precise, and his purpose is precise. He intends to go fishing alone on the Big Two-Hearted River. Previously Nick had been hoboing; this time he has paid his fare, and he does not need to pick himself up from the ground. Indeed, the action here is quite the

3. Ernest Hemingway, *Death in the Afternoon* (New York: Charles Scribner's Sons, 1932), 192.

reverse. The baggageman pitches his baggage to him from the baggage car. But almost immediately Nick sits down— and from shock. The opening anticipates the course he will take in Part II when he is actually fishing. The narrator does not tell us that Nick is shocked, but we know that he is. We experience the shock with him. Sheridan Baker puts it effecively: "It is almost as if the Nick of this story, not Ernest Hemingway, had written 'The Big Two-Hearted River.'"[4] And if we have read "A Way You'll Never Be" the shock also takes us backward in time, for it is like the shock at the start of that story where we see what Nick Adams saw at Fossalta. The first sentence of the story leaves Nick alone surrounded by destruction: "The train went up the track out of sight, around one of the hills of burnt timber" (*IOT*, 177; *NAS*, 177). Sitting on the bundle, Nick, almost like some Waste Land fisher king, surveys the wreckage around him. Seney, Michigan, has been burned to the ground. Only the foundation of the Mansion House hotel shows above the ground. "Even the surface had been burned off the ground." This destruction perforce reminds Nick of the earlier destruction he has seen. His journey has begun ominously, for he has not found what he expected, but what he sought to forget. He is immediately tested.

The river of the title, never mentioned in the story, counteracts the image of the destruction of the opening paragraph. The river is there and the railroad bridge. The fire has not, after all, destroyed everything man-made. Nick reaffirms the conviction that started him on this journey; he has to build his life on what is there, not on what is not. The quest is to find what is there, what he can be certain of. In this frame, the simplest sentence can take on the profoundest meaning. "The river was there" (*IOT*, 177; *NAS*, 177). More, it is alive, moving. It swirls against the log spiles of the bridge. Having returned to the States from Europe

4. Sheridan Baker, "Hemingway's Two-Hearted River," in Jackson J. Benson (ed.), *The Short Stories of Ernest Hemingway: Critical Essays* (Durham: Duke University Press, 1975), 157.

(which his training had presented as possessing the greatest traditions of civilization), Nick turns to nature to see if he can find there a sustaining force.

For a long time Nick is a man at the bridge. He looks down at the trout he means to fish, and they become more than objects of sport—they are, in the terms of Santiago of *The Old Man and the Sea*, brothers. Nick would like to be like them. They are beautiful as they keep themselves "steady in the current with wavering fins." Although not called so, the river running through Seney immediately becomes a big two-hearted river.

As Henry David Thoreau put it in *Walden*, "Time is but the stream I go a-fishing in." Rivers inevitably—and certainly here—make us think of time. Man lives his day in time, and some men even survive for many days—like the big trout at the bottom of the pool. Hemingway establishes that the theme of time will be an important one in the story: "It was a long time since Nick had looked into a stream and seen trout" (*IOT*, 178; *NAS*, 178). Time moves on, but man is the only creature who can stand on a bridge and get a perspective on his unique place in the stream of time. Thus, while "Big Two-Hearted River" takes place on a particular day in fully realized country, a part of the experience of the story, paradoxically, is moving out of time. Like Nick, we cannot be rushed, or we will miss what we should find. Nick did not at first see the big trout. The kind of experience Nick has in "Big Two-Hearted River" is similar to that Robert Frost presents in "Directive." Both works are concerned with quest. Nick's experience is like that which Frost describes as the necessary starting point in the quest for wholeness:

> Back out of all this now too much for us,
> Back in a time made simple by the loss
> Of detail, burned, dissolved, and broken off
> Like graveyard marble sculpture in the weather. . . .

Nick's search becomes more significant as we sense what he leaves behind. Even though he journeys to an unnamed destination, he could hardly seem to be acting more precisely by directive. There is no grail image for what he seeks, but his quest is nonetheless religious. The other Nick stories—continually suggestive in their titles and imagery and motifs of the problem of good and evil and the possibility of faith—should help to prepare us for consideration of "Big Two-Hearted River" in terms of religious quest. Even the very act of fishing has established symbolic value for Western civilization, especially the challenge of Jesus to become fishers. The fish is an established icon for Jesus.

The reader of "Big Two-Hearted River" may at first be puzzled about where Nick is. Seney will be found in only the most specialized of gazetteers. Once notorious in its region, the town is now most famous because of Hemingway's story. Because the first paragraph mentions Seney's thirteen saloons, the reader of *In Our Time*, having just finished several expatriate stories, would take the American usage *saloon* as indication that Nick was back in his beloved north woods, and this belief would soon be confirmed. The reader can also gradually place Seney, somewhat but only gradually. We discover that Nick is in Lake Superior country—hence it must surely be Michigan's upper peninsula. Only when Nick prepares his meal near the end of the day do we discover the route he has traveled to arrive at Seney. He came by way of St. Ignace. It is worth pausing over this geographical lesson.

"Big Two-Hearted River" is the only Nick Adams story—indeed the only story by Hemingway—set in the upper peninsula. Nick knows the Big Two-Hearted River, but it is not in his country. The Adams-Hemingway country is the area around Little Traverse Bay—Walloon Lake, Lake Charlevoix, Horton Bay (called Hortons Bay in the stories), Petoskey. Nick has not gone to Seney from Chicago, but from his northern country—an area filled with the ghosts of many summers. He needs a further remove. In Nick's time, to get from the Little Traverse Bay area to Seney was no easy task—you had to want to get there. "Big Two-Hearted River" begins with a great deal of travel already behind Nick, and certainly travel more primitive than that to which modern readers are accustomed. Nick had to travel to Mack-

inaw City and then await a ferry to cross the four miles of
the Straits of Mackinac to St. Ignace. (Even after World War
II and the construction of a great bridge the trip could not be
recommended for those in a hurry.) The upper peninsula
remained remote and sparsely settled country. It was too far
for Michigan's downstaters to go for weekend respite. Nick
is the only human we actually see in "Big Two-Hearted River"; the baggageman has already tossed down his baggage,
and the train is going out of sight as the story begins. Such
isolation is just what Nick has been seeking. He has traveled
far, and he will travel farther—this time by foot.

The kind of experience that Nick is having might appropriately be called primitivistic, and many literary historians
have noted the importance of the doctrine of primitivism in
American literature. *Huckleberry Finn*, the work Hemingway
found basic in American literature, is the classic representa-
tion. In nature, away from civilization, Huck finds what is
truly his own view, what *he* feels rather than what society
has told him he ought to feel. Nature is good; civilization is
corrupt. In twentieth-century literature this faith is not
unique to Hemingway. Faulkner at least saw the appeal of
such a view, and Nick's experience in the upper peninsula
can be compared profitably with Isaac McCaslin's in *Go
Down, Moses*, especially in "The Bear" and "Delta Autumn"
stories of that novel. There, the hunters feel a yearly need to
tap elemental roots, to reaffirm somehow their connection to
the forest and its life. The task becomes more difficult as the
years pass and the wilderness vanishes. In "The Bear," Ike,
as a young boy, must divest himself of the implements of
modern civilization before he can see Old Ben, the bear who
symbolizes the wilderness. And he must meet Ben alone. In
"Big Two-Hearted River" Nick does not need to use his map
after he leaves Seney. And he needs no compass. He can tell
where he is from the position of the river.

Nick here is older than the Ike of "The Bear," and "Big
Two-Hearted River" is not an initiation story. Nick's needs
are not the same as Ike's. Nick is seeking himself by losing

himself—as Frost's poem and the biblical admonition have
it. It may be helpful to see Nick's experience in terms of that
of René Descartes, the first of the modern philosophers.
Descartes' method was philosophical and abstract. Nick's
approach is to suspect the abstract, to deal with the con-
crete. (Because the reader experiences Nick's progress so
vividly, he will hesitate using a label like primitivism which
seems to lessen the experience.) Nevertheless, Nick and
Descartes are not far apart.

In seeking to prove God's existence, Descartes started by
doubting everything that could be doubted. He decided that
he could not even trust his senses, for they gave him conflicting information about a single piece of data. Finally, Descartes was left with only himself. He could not doubt his
own existence. "I think," he declared, "therefore, I am."
Having reduced everything to an undeniable assertion, Descartes felt that he could then move forward. At least to his
own satisfaction, he was subsequently able to verify God's
existence.

Nick is not interested in syllogisms. Thinking is what he
wishes to avoid. But he is modern man in the sense that
faith in the Old World and in himself has been taken from
him. Hence he has tried to reduce life as much as he can, to
get away from people, memories, his personal needs: "He
felt he had left everything behind, the need to think, the
need to write, other needs. It was all back of him" (*IOT*, 179;
NAS, 179). Nick will rely on his senses, on what he feels. He
will start where Descartes started, with what he could absolutely trust. Then—like Descartes—he can move forward, to
find—perhaps—what he cannot lose, maybe even God.

Despite the setback at Seney, all the evidence mounts to
indicate to us that Nick's program of reduction before advancement is working. As the trout moves, Nick feels
"all the old feeling" (*IOT*, 178; *NAS*, 178). There are things
he has not lost, despite the trial by fire. Nick bears a
heavy burden, even "too heavy" a burden the staccato
rhythms insist, as he begins the walk "up-hill" (*IOT*, 179;

NAS, 179), leaving the burned country. Paradoxically, the burden becomes easy, even a joy. Twice we are told that Nick feels happy.

There is a complex poetry here, and the repetitions are an important part of it. They function to make us share in shouldering Nick's burden in his climbing and in the joys of his success. Repetition also connects this day with the day recounted in "A Way You'll Never Be." Nick is at least one year from his time at the front, probably more—it has been "a long time since Nick has looked into a stream and seen trout" (*IOT*, 178; *NAS*, 178). We know that Nick refers to more than calendar time, for other Nick stories have stressed that psychological time is different from calendar time. Hemingway emphasizes the heat of the day during the action of "A Way You'll Never Be." Nick is reminded of that heat, but he will not let himself deliberately think on it. Seney is associated with Fossalta: we are told that Nick is "leaving the burned town behind in the heat" (*IOT*, 179; *NAS*, 179). Hemingway the symbolist is obviously at work. In terms of naturalistic probability, Nick would not inevitably find the kind of hot day in the upper peninsula that he does find. As likely as not, a bright summer's day will be invigoratingly chilly. On any day of the summer, a swim in Lake Superior will be very brief.

Hemingway is doing more than creating country in the story; he is showing us man in country. As Nick commences his climb, the description is at once precise and suggestive: "He hiked along the road, sweating in the sun, climbing to cross the range of hills that separated the railway from the pine plains" (*IOT*, 180; *NAS*, 179). He is a man against the sky, although more immediately rendered than any character in Robinson's philosophical poem. He is Bunyan's Christian, although the allegorical is replaced with a naturalism and we see Nick clearly as a creature of our time. The descriptions of Nick's climb can also remind us of another famous climb up a hill—even as we sense echoes of promises of easy burdens. Hemingway's handling of scene in "Big

Two-Hearted River" is unmistakably assured, and the scenes are never mere photographic realism. From the top of the hill Nick's view reveals the joy of accepted challenge. From the height, Nick can put Seney (and Fossalta) in perspective. He is like Descartes, now ready to move forward: "Seney was burned, the country was burned over and changed, but it did not matter. It could not all be burned. He knew that" (*IOT*, 180; *NAS*, 179). Nick has completed an important piece of thinking.

Having made such judgment, Nick is ready for advancement, and he proceeds, like the road, "always climbing." The pictorial aspect of the story shifts. We have been aware of Nick as a character in the scenes. The country is made to be majestic and to call for the hand of a painter. Now we look with Nick, who already has a part of his reward: "Ahead of him, as far as he could see, was the pine plain. The burned country stopped off at the left with the range of hills. On ahead islands of dark pine trees rose out of the plain. Far off to the left was the line of the river. Nick followed it with his eye and caught glints of the water in the sun" (*IOT*, 180; *NAS*, 179). Nick can see nothing but the pine plain until far in the distance arise the "far blue hills" of the Lake Superior height of land. Because of the heat-light, the vista reminds us even more of a painting—perhaps of a Cézanne. If Nick looks too steadily, the blue hills are gone, but if he only half-looks, they are there, "the far off hills of the height of land." Furthermore, Hemingway's description echoes a famous poem of A. E. Housman's *A Shropshire Lad*, "Into My Heart an Air That Kills," and Nick's postwar frame of mind resembles the disillusionment of Housman's narrator.

> Into my heart an air that kills
>   From yon far country blows:
> What are those blue remembered hills,
>   What spires, what farms are those?
>
> That is the land of lost content,
>   I see it shining plain,

The happy highways where I went
And cannot come again.

It may be, however, that Nick will find more contentment
than did the Shropshire lad. Hemingway makes the importance of Nick's view of this wilderness country unmistakable. Nick sits down, as he had earlier upon arriving at
Seney. The destruction he witnessed there is perforce recalled to our minds. Nick will take in this scene, too. In his
epigraphs to *The Sun Also Rises* Hemingway would later play
off Gertrude Stein's famous "lost generation" indictment
against the affirmation of the statement from Ecclesiastes,
"but the earth abideth forever." Here, for similar effect, we
contrast the two scenes Nick views.

The second scene looks forward as well as backward. Nick
now sits leaning against a charred stump, and his legs are
stretched out in front of him. Both details recall the description of war in interchapter VI where Nick sat against the
wall. Here he notices a grasshopper and then many other
grasshoppers—to discover that they have been made black
by the burned-out country side. (Sheridan Baker reports that
in realistic terms this is an improbability: the detail is not
likely to disturb the reader since it is so symbolically right.[5])
Nick, wondering how long they would stay that way, may
make us think not only of his state but that of other soldiers.
The grasshoppers also bring to mind Nick's lecture on them
in "A Way You'll Never Be." Since his attention is here on a
particular grasshopper, we are also reminded of Nick's experience with a particular salamander in "Now I Lay Me"
when he engaged in his ritualistic night fishings. The salamander seemed too human as he "tried to hold on to the
hook" with his tiny feet. "Now I Lay Me" also echoes because Nick smokes a cigarette as he sits. His smoking reinforces our idea of the tautness of his nerves.

Smoking also anticipates other events of the story. Nick
will smoke whenever he wishes to slow down his responses. The vista Nick surveys is given a special punctuation by

5. *Ibid.*

his stopping to smoke. Hemingway's "war" story that does not mention war creates country; it creates country as antidote to the horrors of destruction.

Nick shows compassion to the grasshopper he has so carefully examined—as in "Now I Lay Me" he had decided not to use the crickets for bait because of the way they were about the hook. Nick is hypersensitive to the simplest forms of life after his encounter with mass destruction. That hypersensitivity is emphasized when Nick speaks to the grasshopper, for there is almost no use of speech in this longest of the Nick stories. When used, speech must then receive more than ordinary attention. "Go on, hopper . . . Fly away somewhere" (*IOT*, 181; *NAS*, 180). Nick tosses the hopper into the air and watches him sail away. He has seen himself in that hopper. As soon as Nick sees the hoppper land, he arises and again commences to travel. Provocatively, Hemingway repeats the opening sentence of "The Battler": "Nick stood up."

There is something at work other than Nick's earlier war memories. We know there has been no speech in the story before the episode with the grasshopper, and Hemingway calls that lack of speech to our attention, stating that Nick was "speaking out loud for the first time." He is, in part, telling us to pay heed to later speaking, but he is not giving us new information. More important, he is emphasizing the verbal atmosphere of the whole story. "Big Two-Hearted River" is Hemingway's account of Genesis. That "for the first time" is haunting. The biblical and religious overtones of the story are insistent.

Nick will need no map as he goes into the country he has just viewed. Like Adam, he will keep his direction by the sun. He starts walking again, and soon the road and the fire line are behind him. Nick makes judgments on his experience that have a pristine quality: "Underfoot the ground was good walking" (*IOT*, 182; *NAS*, 180). The word *good* comes in for frequent play in Part I. *Good* in Genesis is God's verdict on the world He has created. Nick's senses will likewise continuously assert that life is good: "Then it was sweet

fern, growing ankle high, to walk through, and clumps of
jack pines; a long undulating country with frequnt rises and
descents, sandy underfoot and the country alive again"
(*IOT*, 182; *NAS*, 181).

Few stories attempt to call all of the reader's senses into
play as fully and as continuously as does "Big Two-Hearted
River." Usually a story seems to be underway when the dialogue starts, when what characters say engages us intellec-
tually. Even Hemingway stories sometimes work that way.
Not here. We feel the heat of the day, the weight of Nick's
pack, and we come with Nick to look with primordial wonder at the world. We rediscover our senses. The fern smells
sweet, and Nick makes that good count. He breaks off some
sprigs and puts them under his straps so that he can relish
the smell as he walks. Only the sense of sound is underplayed: there is little attention to forest or river sound in
"Big Two-Hearted River." Consequently, as we have seen,
the breaking of the silence by the human voice has a powerful effect, partly Adamic but also useful for reminding us of
Nick's past. Ultimately, the muted sounds of "Big Two-
Hearted River" are a powerful means of reminding us of the
clamor of war, of the sounds that Nick means to forget or
minimize on this trip. The silences of "Big Two-Hearted
River" contrast with the sounds of the Nick war stories discussed in the previous chapter, stories that often build on
the sounds of war and depend on dialogue to carry large
sections of the narrative.

As Nick makes his journey through the forest, it is evident that he wants to get tired, since he wants to go "as far
upstream as he could go in one day's walking" (*IOT*, 183;
NAS, 181). But there is much to discover as he goes, and
there are places that have special meaning and accent the
healing silences Nick has sought. The fishing is not everything; the getting to the place of the fishing is as worthy of
our attention as is the fishing action of Part II.

In describing one place with special meaning for Nick,
Hemingway evokes one of the most memorable scenes of
The Red Badge of Courage, the scene in which Henry Fleming

after his flight from battle finds temporary solace in nature. Under the boughs of great pines Henry is reminded of a chapel, but the religious feeling the setting has aroused is dissipated when he finds a corpse ugly in its state of decay; Henry, appalled, is soon in flight. In Hemingway's story, Nick deliberately seeks an island of pine, and he, too, finds a chapel-like place. There is, however, nothing to appall him in it, nothing to make him flee. After Nick has passed through his chapel he pauses as if to mark the quality of the experience. He lies on his back and looks into the pine trees: "The earth felt good against his back" (*IOT*, 183–84; *NAS*, 182). The creature is at one with the creation. Sleep comes blessedly to Nick—Nick for whom sleep in war was something he often wished to avoid.

When he awakens, stiff and cramped, the sun is nearly down, but he feels no panic. He takes up his heavy pack again, comes to a meadow, and then the river. Nick was "glad" to get to the river. It has been his point of reference—he knew he could always get to it. He has journeyed by faith.

The joy at anticipation of the fishing reasserts itself. Again, the story pauses. Before going down to the river, Nick stops on the spot of high ground near the end of the meadow where he will make camp. He looks down at the river in the light of early evening. The insects from the swamp across the stream have come to the river. The river is silent, but is fast and smooth and full of significant life. The trout jump high out of the water for the insects. The meaning of the trout at the opening of the story is again to the fore—for Nick and the reader. The pictorial view—and again the long view—serves to vindicate the faith behind Nick's journey: "As far down the long stretch as he could see, the trout were rising, making circles all down the surface of the water, as though it were starting to rain" (*IOT*, 185; *NAS*, 182).

Thus assured, Nick is ready to set up camp. We are told exactly how he does so and why he does it as he does. Hemingway's prose in its steady detail mirrors the values that

Nick is seeking in his life—order, neatness, purpose. Nick makes camp before he cooks, exemplifying the kind of discipline that he believes should mark the good life. Much later, in *A Moveable Feast*, Hemingway will say that hunger is good discipline. So it is here. Work never seemed more purposeful or more rewarding than when Nick sets up camp. The process takes on the aura of ritual. Although he does not think of it in these terms, Nick is thoroughly Pauline. In I Corinthians 14:40 Saint Paul admonishes: "Let all things be done decently and in order." Such values have been passed on to Nick by his father. Work carries its own reward, as we feel when we go inside the tent with Nick:

> Inside the tent the light came through the brown canvas. It smelled pleasantly of canvas. Already there was something mysterious and homelike. Nick was happy as he crawled inside the tent. He had not been unhappy all day. This was different though. Now things were done. It had been a hard trip. He was very tired. That was done. He had made his camp. He was settled. Nothing could touch him. It was a good place to camp. He was there, in the good place. He was in his home where he had made it. Now he was hungry. (*IOT*, 186; *NAS*, 183–84)

The crawl inside the tent builds on the essential rhythm of Part I, with its stop-go quality. There has been movement, then pausing to survey, for varying lengths of time, what is there. After such pauses Nick can make a sound judgment, as he does here—pronouncing the place good. Nick has arrived someplace; twice Hemingway uses the word *home*. Home is paradoxically the traditional goal of every pilgrim who ever shouldered a heavy load. And Hemingway is at pains to suggest these religious connotations: "Already there was something mysterious and homelike." *Mysterious* with *homelike* is powerfully evocative. In its way, the tent prefigures Hemingway's later "A Clean, Well-Lighted Place," although this one is more reassuring. How blessed it is to have arrived where Nick is: "Nothing could touch him." And the whole tent scene is couched in the symbolic shadows of evening: "It was quite dark outside. It was lighter in the tent." The Nick stories have repeatedly used light-dark imagery. Hence, the lines are even more forceful.

Again, the story moves from contemplation to action. Now Nick will eat. "He did not believe he had ever been hungrier" (*IOT*, 187; *NAS*, 184). In the context, that is an immensely positive statement. Eating has been an important literary motif in most of the Nick stories. In "The Light of the World" the story beings with the denial of food, except for pay. In "The Killers" Al and Max mock "the big dinner" and eat with their gloves on. Marge and Nick have a joyless night meal together in "The End of Something." The vibrations are more positive in "Ten Indians" when Nick's father serves him dinner—but ambiguity shrouds that less than satisfactory ending to an otherwise happy Fourth of July. Nick and Bill do not eat together in "The Three Day Blow"— they only drink, and this suggests that Nick's opting for male camaraderie is only temporary. There is the breaking of bread together in "The Battler," and tasty it is. Nick takes from that campfire a sandwich—reenforcing the positive qualities of the light he had found in the clearing of Bugs and Ad.

The eating in "Big Two-Hearted River" is even more memorable—in both Parts I and II. Eating is another good for Nick. The reader, too, is likely to become hungry and relish the cooking and the eating, for the cooking is as important as the eating. The fare is quite simple, but it is something to be remembered for a long time afterwards.

When Nick takes from his pack a can of pork and beans and a can of spaghetti, he speaks for the second time in the story: "I've got a right to eat this kind of stuff, if I'm willing to carry it" (*IOT*, 187; *NAS*, 184). He finds his voice strange in the darkening woods and so does not speak again. The strangeness comes because the verbal expression somehow violates the sense of mystery and blessedness that the erection of the tent in the good place has produced. At the same time Nick's words, comic on one level, reenforce the primitivism that the cans seem to violate.

With Nick, we experience the food through sight, smell, and, finally, taste. Nick stirs the beans and spaghetti together over the fire: "They began to bubble, making little bubbles that rose with difficulty to the surface. There was a good smell" (*IOT*, 187–88; *NAS*, 184). Hemingway makes the most of the taste experience. After Nick spreads the beans and spaghetti on his plate, he sets it aside so that the food can cool: he knows the food is too hot. Fire becomes potentially an enemy—almost hobgoblin. Nick looks from the fire to the tent (the symbol of order and home): "he was not going to spoil it all by burning his tongue." There are rumblings from the past: "For years he had never enjoyed fried bananas because he had never been able to wait for them to cool" (*IOT*, 188; *NAS*, 185).

Hemingway does not falsify the world as it is, even as he insists that there is a place for Nick to build from. Another ominous image appears—taking us back to "The Battler" as well as anticipating the rest of the story: "Across the river in the swamp, in the almost dark, he saw a mist rising" (*IOT*, 188; *NAS*, 185). Turning from the swamp and mist, Nick looks at the tent once more, and he cannot doubt that he has found what will fortify. He speaks for the third and final time—not to be denied. (There is no speaking in Part II.) "Chrise," he says, "Geezus Chrise," and Hemingway adds the adverb *happily*. Nick's words are not in isolation—he has taken his first mouthful; hence the expression is appropriate to the action of tasting the hot food and to the faith that he feels as regards the future. He again judges what has happened as a "good."

Coffee time follows the meal. It is a more leisured time traditionally. After the diners have satisfied initial hunger, the pace of most meals slackens. Nick also seeks to end his meal on the relaxed key of coffee and dessert. The activity sets the tone for the ending of Part I—extremely different from the earlier portions when Nick was expending so much energy. Nick must go down to the river to get water before he can make the coffee. The challenge of the river and its complex associations are reasserted. Nick finds the other

bank in "white mist." As he kneels on the near bank the
grass is "wet and cold." When he puts his bucket in the
water, we are reminded of the strength of the current, for
the bucket bellies and pulls hard. The water is ice cold. The
contrasts with the heat of the day and the long walking are
stark. "Up away from the stream" Nick finds it "not so cold"
(*IOT*, 189; *NAS*, 185).

As Nick begins making the coffee, the point bores deeper
that he has not been camping for a long time. The story had
begun on such a note. Now Nick tries to recall the proce-
dure for coffee making. Other people, by design not included in the excursion, enter Nick's consciousness. In a
very deliberate and qualified way, "Big Two-Hearted River"
becomes a remembrance of things past. The making of coffee had once been an issue between Nick and his friend
Hopkins. Nick and Hopkins had once argued about everything. Argumentation would not, however, be desirable on
this outing: as we have observed, Nick is seeking something
more elemental. And in Nick's thinking, now, Hopkins is no
threat; hence Nick makes the coffee in Hopkins' way. While
he waits for the water to boil, he has his dessert—apricots.
He again trusts what his own experience (and memory) reveals: the canned apricots are better than fresh apricots.

When Nick takes the coffee from the grill, he judges it a
triumph for Hopkins. Nick's stream of memory touches on
Hopkins, and his melancholy side becomes evident as he
recalls the good times he, Hopkins, and Bill had had in
earlier years on other Michigan fishing trips. Hopkins is one
of the things he has lost. After Hopkins inherited money,
they never saw him again. But since Nick decidedly feels
that was a long time ago, the memory is not now stinging.
We again get suggestions of the lost camaraderie and of
Nick's sense of humor in the remembered use of nicknames.
Hopkins was "The Hop Head" and his girl "The Blonde
Venus"—the latter reference the only one to women in the
story. Nick will choke off his thinking before it gets to the
complications of women and love. (In "Now I Lay Me" Nick
reports that thinking of girls turned out unsatisfactorily, so

he "gave up thinking about them almost altogether.") Nick's mind seems to work with Hemingway's to insist on the religious qualities of the day's happenings. Nick thinks of the coffee as "straight Hopkins": it was coffee made "according to Hopkins." These are playful references to the four gospels—and Nick can take his own jokes, for the coffee (too soon judged a triumph) proves to be bitter. He laughs— viewing the ending with ironic amusement, seeing it as part of a story and himself as writer: "It made a good ending to the story" (*IOT*, 191; *NAS*, 187). The bitter coffee has not ruined the evening.

Nick has handled the memories of other Michigan fishing days very well. But his mind is clearly starting to work, and it is time to choke it off; Nick lights another cigarette. He will not rush his memories. It is time for sleep. From the tent, Nick watches the glow of the fire. It bodes well for the night's sleeping that the swamp is "perfectly quiet." Only a mosquito in the tent threatens to disturb Nick's rest, but with a match he gets rid of the mosquito. It makes "a satisfactory hiss in the flame" (*IOT*, 191–92; *NAS*, 187). There will be no humming in his head this night—no listening to mosquitoes or to silkworms. Nick lies down to blessed sleep. "And the evening and the morning were the first day" (Genesis 1:5).

By dividing his story into two parts, and so labeling it, Hemingway emphasizes the two-heartedness of the river, and he also reenforces the rhythm of Genesis. The story will give us one day exactly. Nick is like Adam at creation, for sleep has—the structure indicates—brought no disturbing dreams. A part of the two-heartedness of the river comes from the abundant sense of renewal that Hemingway's story conveys. The imagery at the opening of Part II suggest birth: "Nick crawled out under the mosquito netting stretched across the mouth of the tent, to look at the morning. The grass was wet on his hands as he came out." He is like Adam gazing out on creation, and we have another broad perspective, since we look with Nick: "The sun was just up over the hill. There was the meadow, the river and the swamp. There were birch trees in the green of the swamp on the other side of the river" (*IOT*, 195; *NAS*, 187). The swamp has been rendered considerably less ominous than it seemed as the shadows lengthened in Part I. The greenness associates the swamp with the forces of life. And the greenness comes from the leaves of the white birch. No cause for alarm here—especially when Nick observes a mink cross the river on the three logs that cross the river into the swamp.

Nick's awakening conveys to us the exhilaration of the aubade—joy in the morning. Even though Hemingway tells us he could never read Thoreau, it is difficult for those who have done so not to think of him when they read "Big Two-Hearted River." In *Walden* Thoreau declares that there are parts of us that are alive in the morning that slumber the rest of the day. In any event, Nick is full of expectancy as he considers the possibilities of the day: "He was excited. He was excited by the early morning and the river" (*IOT*, 195; *NAS*, 188).

Nick has to check his enthusiasms: he has to remind himself to be practical (practicality being an aspect of his character that received comic treatment in "The Three Day Blow"). He knows that he needs a good breakfast before he goes about the day's business—fishing. Nick will be thoroughly practical about that, too. He makes his fire and puts on the coffeepot. While he waits for the water to boil, he goes searching for the grasshoppers he needs for bait before the sun dries the grass. Time (but not clock time) has been of the essence from the beginning of the story and will continue to be so. Without the dew Nick knows it would take him all day to get a bottleful of good grasshoppers—and he would have to be "messy" in doing that, having "to crush many of them, slamming at them with his hat" (*IOT*, 196; *NAS*, 188). Such destruction Nick would avoid; he intends to be a good fisherman. He soon has his hoppers, and the reader may get here—as elsewhere in the story—practical suggestions for fishing. Nick puts a pine stick in the bottle as a cork: "It plugged the mouth of the bottle enough, so the hoppers could not get out and left plenty of air passage"

(*IOT*, 196; *NAS*, 188).[6] But more than getting practical suggestions, the reader should be aware that with these hoppers Nick will be testing his fragile nerves and his reluctance to use bait like salamander or crickets "because of the way they acted about the hook" ("Now I Lay Me," *MWW*, 220; *NAS*, 145).

Having gathered the hoppers with dispatch, Nick turns his attention to preparation of his breakfast. On a hasty judgment, "Big Two-Hearted River" is sometimes described as a story in which nothing happens. Actually, a great deal happens, as attention to such details as bait reveals. "Big Two-Hearted River" might more precisely be termed a story of significant action. Therein lies its true distinction. We have seen deliberateness in the gathering of the hoppers—and now we see it in Nick's preparation of his breakfast.

6. Nick's search for hoppers may meaningfully be set against an event that Frederic Henry tells us about late in *A Farewell to Arms* as Catherine is dying. Henry says: "Once in camp I put a log on top of the fire and it was full of ants. As it commenced to burn, the ants swarmed out and went first toward the center where the fire was; then turned back and ran toward the end. When there were enough on the end they fell off into the fire. Some got out, their bodies burnt and flattened, and went off not knowing where they were going. But most of them went toward the fire and then back toward the end and swarmed on the cool ends and finally fell off into the fire. I remember thinking at the time that it was the end of the world and a splendid chance to be a messiah and lift the log off the fire and throw it out where the ants could get off onto the ground. But I did not do anything but throw a tin cup of water on the log, so that I would have the cup empty to put whisky in before I added water to it. I think the cup of water on the burning log only steamed the ants" (New York: Charles Scribner's Sons, 1929), 327–28. The religious overtones are vastly different in "Big Two-Hearted River" when Nick turns over a log and discovers there a grasshoppers' lodging house. Nick carefully selects fifty, leaving the others unharmed. He rolls the log back, knowing he can get hoppers there every morning. The difference between the log of *A Farewell to Arms* and this is on one level the difference between a fallen and unfallen world. The novel is clearly after the fall, whereas the story creates the edenic world. In "Big Two-Hearted River" the creatures of the world are placed under man's dominion and are to be used (not misused, obviously) for his good. A part of the glory of "Big Two-Hearted River" is that Nick—who has been in Frederic Henry's war and at his front—could touch so much of that unblemished world. Henry's verdict on God and creation tells us more about Henry's state of mind as he tries to adjust to his loss than it does about the world. Powerful as the passage is, we cannot take it as the novel's meaning.

Since Nick knows that he should eat breakfast, he does so with heart. Although the narrator does not tell us so, except through the detailed presentation of what Nick does, we know that Nick has all the old feeling as he makes his buckwheat pancakes. The reader sees it all—so that when the cakes begin "to firm, then brown, then crisp" (*IOT*, 197; *NAS*, 189), he is ready to enjoy the fare with Nick. We are reminded, too, of the deliberation of Nick's actions in Part I—of his program of measuring and evaluating circumstances through the validity of the experience, the sensuous experience. Again, it is measured action. Nick plans for a future time. He prepares a third cake for later eating, along with the onion sandwiches that he next prepares. Nick is ready to confirm yesterday's evaluation: "It was a nice little camp" (*IOT*, 198; *NAS*, 189).

Nick next inspects and readies his fishing gear. The reader is given a precise accounting of this process too, and Hemingway uses many sense words to make the experience also physically real. Nick uses a "heavy double tapered fly line," one "made heavy to lift back in the air and come forward flat and heavy and straight to make it possible to cast a fly which has no weight" (*IOT*, 198; *NAS*, 189–90). Nick removes the coilers from the damp-flannel pads, dampened so that the leaders will be soft. The hook is "springy." Nick pulls the line "taut" to test the knot and the spring of the rod. He is "careful not to let the hook bite into his finger." Nick is ready for the stream: "It was a good feeling" (*IOT*, 199; *NAS*, 190). Without a doubt, feeling is foremost in "Big Two-Hearted River."

Nick appears as the man fully prepared. He is "professionally" happy, ready for the adventure of fishing. But action is always different from the anticipation of action, and Hemingway's simplicity in describing the moment of Nick's entry into the stream is powerfully suggestive: "He stepped into the stream. It was a shock. His trousers clung tight to his legs. His shoes felt the gravel. The water was a rising cold shock" (*IOT*, 199; *NAS*, 190). The big trout who kept themselves steady in the current challenged Nick's imagination at the bridge in Seney. Now Nick is in the destructive element with the fish. He cannot control events in the way he could on the journey to the good camp; he has to wade "with the current." How destructive the element can be, Nick at once *sees* as a grasshopper jumps out of the bottle to be sucked under in a whirl. The hopper surfaces, then floats "rapidly, kicking" until he disappears when a trout takes him. A part of Nick is feeling with the hopper.

The second hopper goes on Nick's hook. What might have been merely a precise detail is surely more than that to the reader who knows "Now I Lay Me": "The grasshopper took hold of the hook with his front feet, spitting tobacco juice on it" (*IOT*, 200; *NAS*, 191). Even though "Now I Lay Me" was written after "Big Two-Hearted River," it is clear that by establishing Nick's faith in the sacred in nature, by showing similarities between Nick and the hoppers, Hemingway meant us to see Nick's action with the second hopper as affirmative, an important gain. Nick not only feels professionally, he now can act professionally. Although he is killing the hopper, he respects the hopper's life. Nick has a sense of communion with the creatures different only in degrees, not kind, from what Santiago will later demonstrate in *The Old Man and the Sea* when he kills the marlin. Nick in looking at the first hopper has seen the rhythm of the Big Two-Hearted River—the rhythm of life and death. War is a violation of this sacred rhythm. Here Nick reaches below the conscious levels of his mind and touches the sacredness of the intended order. By dropping his line into the river, Nick finds that order good.

Hemingway does not let us miss the religious aspects of Nick's fishing, for his first strike is more than an ecological lesson. The first trout is small, but he is the essence of life. Nick sees "the trout in the water jerking with his head and body against the shifting tangent of the line in the stream" (*IOT*, 201; *NAS*, 191). He brings him to the surface, and the trout appears a thing of beauty: "His back was mottled the clear, water-over-gravel color, his side flashing in the sun"

(*IOT*, 201; *NAS*, 191). Nick is careful to wet his hand before he lets the trout—too small to keep—off the hook; thereby Hemingway gives the reader a practical lesson in fishing. If the hand is not wet, a fungus will attack the part where the delicate mucus has been disturbed. To instruct in the art of fishing is not the purpose, however. Nick's consciousness reaches back to previous times when he found many dead trout in the river because of careless fishermen. Moreover, the passage—the only one to make direct reference to other human beings in Part II—is an image of life in our time when the sacredness of life has been wantonly violated. Nick recalls that "again and again" he had come upon dead trout. By keeping the memory general, Hemingway increases the symbolic value of the reference. We may indeed be reminded of World War I and the horrors Nick has witnessed. For Nick, and precisely because of what he has seen in war, life is sacred. He not only sees the beauty of the small trout, he *feels* it, and then his conscious mind works: "As Nick's fingers touched him, touched his smooth, cool, underwater feeling he was gone, gone in a shadow across the bottom of the stream. He's all right, Nick thought. He was only tired" (*IOT*, 201; *NAS*, 192).

There is no disappointment that the trout is too small. Rather, Nick has already proved something to himself: "He was certain he could catch small trout in the shallows, but he did not want them" (*IOT*, 202; *NAS*, 192). He wants the big trout, and he knows that they will not be in the shallows at this time of day. They will be ahead in the "fast, dark water." Like Santiago, Nick prepares, as it were, to launch out into the deep. He must accept the greater challenge. Hemingway marks the decision by presenting another still shot, locating Nick for us in psychological time: "Now the water deepened up his thighs sharply and coldly. Ahead was the smooth dammed-back flood of water above the logs. The water was smooth and dark; on the left, the lower edge of the meadow; on the right the swamp" (*IOT*, 202; *NAS*, 192).

Almost immediately thereafter Nick is caught in intense struggle with the largest trout he has ever seen. The contrast with Nick's fishing in the shallows could hardly be greater. The rod becomes "alive and dangerous." Nick, the rod and line, and the trout seem one thing, as the trout maintains "a heavy, dangerous, steady pull" (*IOT*, 203; *NAS*, 193). Nick lets the line go when he feels "the moment" when the pressure is at its maximum before the leader would break. This marks the peak of the action in "Big Two-Hearted River": "The reel ratcheted into a mechanical shriek as the line went out in a rush. Too fast. Nick could not check it, the line rushing out, the reel note rising as the line ran out" (*IOT*, 203; *NAS*, 193).

From the beginning of the story Nick has carefully tested his emotions, keeping a delicate balance between heart and head knowledge. In the action of the dangerous fishing, all that he has achieved he might suddenly lose. His heart feels "stopped with the excitement." The leader breaks, and Nick's mouth is "dry, his heart down" as he reels in. We are carried back to Nick's initial testing when he saw the ruins of Seney. Nick reels in slowly: "The thrill had been too much" (*IOT*, 204; *NAS*, 193). Feeling vaguely "a little sick" he decides it would be better to sit down, as he had in Seney.

It is significant, however, that even as Nick prepares to depart from the stream, he is feeling with the trout as earlier he felt with the hopper and the little trout. He thinks of the trout "somewhere on the bottom, holding himself steady over the gravel, far down below the light, under the logs, with the hook in his jaw . . . He'd bet the trout was angry. Anything that size would be angry. That was a trout" (*IOT*, 204; *NAS*, 193–94). Nature is filled with determined survivors.

As Nick climbs out into the meadow, he is no longer feeling like Adam experiencing the dew of his first morning. Rather, the water images suggest baptism into experience; Nick stands "water running down his trousers and out of his shoes, his shoes squlchy." He will need to let this baptism come into some kind of focus—and on an emotional rather than an intellectual level. Nick, wisely, does "not want to rush his sensations any" (*IOT*, 204; *NAS*, 194).

Sitting on the log, Nick lights a cigarette—as he has done previously when there has been a lot to take in. Almost immediately we sense the wisdom of Nick's leaving the stream in order to sort things out. A tiny trout rises at the match swimming in the fast current. A big trout would know better, Nick thinks and laughs—taking us back to the moment in Part I when he laughed upon finding the coffee made according to Hopkins' formula bitter. Nick could put his memories of early fishing in an adult perspective—and he will be able to put the incident of the big trout into perspective, too. The scene Nick contemplates as he finishes his cigarette is reassuring. The river never seemed more "two-hearted." Nick's sensuous being takes in the affirmation he needs: "He sat on the logs, smoking, drying in the sun, the sun warm on his back, the river shallow ahead entering the woods, curving into the woods, shallows, light glittering, big water-smooth rocks, cedars along the bank and white birches, the logs warm in the sun, smooth to sit on, without bark, gray to the touch" (*IOT*, 205; *NAS*, 194). The feeling of disappointment leaves Nick. His mind can conceptualize what his senses have confirmed. He thinks, "It was all right now." Recovery and return—that is the pattern of the story, but not return to mere sameness.

The symbols carry darker meaning after the climactic action of the big trout. More seems to be required of Nick after this recovery. As he reenters the river, he does so at a particular spot that reveals more fully than at any previous moment the nature of the river. Nick does not return to the fishing with any unfounded optimism. On the left, where the meadow ends and the woods begin, Nick notices a great elm uprooted. The white birches are true, but so is the elm, "its roots clotted with dirt, grass growing in them, rising a solid bank beside the stream" (*IOT*, 205; *NAS*, 194–95). The elm had gone over in a storm, and there is no escaping the implications of this bank sinister. The river cuts to the edge of the uprooted tree. The currents cut deep channels. Woods, meadow, and stream come together. Nick accepts the condition of the world—and resumes fishing.

The fishing results in another surge of great energy. This time Nick lands a big trout. What is most impressive about the description of Nick's landing of this trout is the emphasis Hemingway places on Nick's new knowledge or acceptance of the river in its relationship to the tree as the key to his success: "Holding the rod far out toward the uprooted tree and sloshing backward in the current, Nick worked the trout, plunging, the rod bending alive, out of the danger of the weeds into the open river" (*IOT*, 206; *NAS*, 195).

Once Nick has the big trout, the pace of the story changes noticeably. The theme of not wanting to rush his sensations becomes even more insistent. Nick has, now, achieved what he set out to achieve on *this* trip. He does "not care about getting many trout" (*IOT*, 197; *NAS*, 195–96). However, his success with the big trout puts his mind on the future— future catches, future challenges—in a noticeable way. Heretofore, the fiber of the story has been decidedly on present action. Memories of the past have been kept in check.

The change in mood is signaled by reference to the sun— in a sentence that is also a paragraph: "It was getting hot, the sun hot on the back of his neck" (*IOT*, 207; *NAS*, 195). The exhilaration of the aubade gives way completely to sober awareness. Even though it is not yet afternoon, Nick is thinking of afternoon and evening. In thinking of future catches and about where the trout would be (always in shadow) Nick thinks of another stream, the one he had fished with Hopkins and others, but he does not think of them. That river was the Black. In Part I, the name seemed only a name. Now it becomes charged with the emotional overtones of the serious awareness that is Nick's after he catches the first big trout:

> The very biggest ones would lie up close to the bank. You could always pick them up there on the Black. When the sun

was down they all moved out into the current. Just when the sun made the water blinding in the glare before it went down, you were liable to strike a big trout anywhere in the current. It was almost impossible to fish then, the surface of the water was blinding as a mirror in the sun. Of course, you could fish upstream, but in a stream like the Black or this, you had to wallow against the current and in a deep place, the water piled up on you. It was no fun to fish upstream with this much current. (*IOT*, 207–208; *NAS*, 196)

Nick continues fishing, but he does so with new caution. He is aware of deep places and deep holes and deepening water. Branches hang down over the water, adding to the somberness. He proves that he can navigate the more treacherous waters of the Big Two-Hearted River. He eventually lands another trout. When he sees the second trout in the sack with the first, he realizes that he has had enough of fishing for one day. It is time to leave the river.

Nick wades through "the deepening water" to a gray log where he can sit in the cool of the shade, with the simple and profound aim of sitting and watching—much as he had done on other occasions in the story. He sits "smoking and watching the river," ready to take another long view; the picture he sees picks up on the suggestions of the evening and coming night that the first successful trout catch aroused: "Ahead the river narrowed and went into a swamp. The river became smooth and deep and the swamp looked solid with cedar trees, their trunks close together, their branches solid. It would not be possible to walk through a swamp like that. The branches grew so low. You would have to keep almost level with the ground to move at all. You could not crash through the branches. That must be why the animals that lived in swamps were built the way they were, Nick thought" (*IOT*, 210–11; *NAS*, 198).

The Big Two-Hearted river is the river of life and death, and each implies the other. In terms of the image of the very first day that Hemingway has built upon, it is the river of both morning and evening. The joy of morning implies the journey to the darker shadows.

There is something enticing about the swamp scene Nick

is watching. It seems to call to him even as he pulls away
from it. It is like the woods in Frost's "Stopping By Woods
on a Snowy Evening." They are lovely, dark and deep. But
the time has not yet come for the speaker of the poem to
enter them. He has promises to keep. Youth, especially,
pulls back from the entry, but it too can feel the pull. Nick
tries to check thoughts of the swamp. He wishes, for the
first time, that he had brought something to read. A book
could challenge him to another view of experience. But he
has no book, and his thoughts revert to the swamp. Nick's
conscious mind has to check the pull the thrice-stated decision that he does not want to go into the swamp partly
belies: "in the fast deep water, in the half light, the fishing
would be tragic. In the swamp fishing was a tragic adventure. Nick did not want it. He did not want to go down the
stream any further today" (*IOT*, 211; *NAS*, 198).

The way to check the call of the deep woods or the dark
swamp is to resort to action. Frost's persona must put his
horse back into motion towards the fulfillment of his obligations. Nick will tend to the fish he has caught. He "whacks"
the necks of the trout, cleans them, tossing the offal ashore
"for the mink to find." He completes the proper care of his
trout, a deed of pleasure that surely confirms the accom-
plishment of this day.

The ending of the story is sober, but convincingly affirmative. Nick gives the "yes" to life that means he will write
truly of war and life. The final paragraph reverses the first
paragraph of the story. There "Nick sat down." Now "Nick
stood up" (*IOT*, 212; *NAS*, 199). He becomes man in motion
as he climbs the bank and cuts into the woods. He is going
back to camp—the good place, to fortify himself for the
challenge of fishing in future days. He looks back: "The river
just showed through the trees." Nick knows about that river
and accepts its two-heartedness. The final sentence is not
whistling in the dark: "There were plenty of days coming
when he could fish the swamp." This is the affirmation that
the artist needs, a belief that the future matters, a belief that

he will have the chance to create work that will have a life beyond life. All of that is implied in the ending of "Big Two-Hearted River." What is most immediately before us is the large sense of miracle, or recovery of the wounded Nick. On that level the title of the story affirms the religious tone that has marked the whole. The river is two-hearted because it creates for Nick the second chance, the miracle of beginning—as it were—all over again.

Chapter Five
Love and Marriage

The basic rhythm of the Nick Adams stories has been a movement from loss or trauma to recovery and fortification ("The Killers" owing some of its force to a departure from this pattern); it is fitting that a story with emphasis on the process of recovery be the turning point of the Nick stories, and that piece is "Big Two-Hearted River." Nick Adams keeps recovering. He has a strong strain of American optimism and vitality.

One fragment published in Young's *The Nick Adams Stories* can serve in an emblematic way for this trait of Nick's. Young's title for the sketch is, appropriately for such an emblematic function, "Crossing the Mississippi." The piece predates the war stories in Nick's chronology and confirms the implication of "Now I Lay Me" that Nick had had apprentice writing experience in Kansas City before the war just as Hemingway had. The time of the story is October, 1917. Nick had previously attended the first game of the World Series, an event that occurred on October 6, 1917, in Chicago, and he can still envision Happy Felsch's home run off Giant pitcher Slim Sallee, whose last name Hemingway renders as Solee. Nick is on the Kansas City train, which has stopped just east of the Mississippi River. He is thinking of the game in New York City, and he feels a "comfortable glow" when he learns from the magazine vendor that the White Sox have won the final game. The White Sox accomplished their World Series triumph in game number six on October 15, 1917.

Nick has realized an ambition that he and Bill had talked about in "The Three Day Blow." He has seen, at last, a World Series game. The Chicago victory in that game and in the series plays against the cynicism that had crept into the earlier conversation. Although Bill's verdict that McGraw could buy all the players he wants had made Nick suggest that McGraw might even "buy" players to lose games, Nick had not given up on baseball. Hemingway, however, points up Nick's essential innocence, for as he wrote of the Chicago victory of 1917 he knew what had happened to the White Sox in the 1919 series. New York gambler Arnold Rothstein had bought off seven Chicago players, including Happy Felsch, to throw the series to Cincinnati. In 1920 Felsch and the six others, now the "Black Sox," were barred from baseball.

The baseball symbolism indicates that Nick is intent on being a man of our time and works effectively with the symbolism implied in Nick's journey across the Mississippi. It is because of the cultural force behind the idea of the Mississippi, essentially mythical for Americans, that the sketch is discussed here in this study rather than in its chronological place. Nick, in the sketch, is the quintessential American. As the train is stopped just east of the river, Nick looks "at the road that was half a foot deep with dust." What is west of the Mississippi? No easy journey, obviously. In the pause before Nick's crossing, Hemingway catches the rhythm of American history. Nick seems to look out with the eye of that history: "There was nothing in sight but the road and a few dust-grayed trees. A wagon lurched through the ruts, the driver slouching with the jolts of his spring seat and letting the reins hang slack on the horses' back" (*NAS*, 133). Nick is not made despondent by the wagon, suggestive as it is of struggle and the necessity for fortitude. Rather it is the link to his thinking of the baseball game. Nick may be a modern man, but he can still experience the challenge that crossing the Mississippi meant to earlier Americans. Significantly for Nick's determination, he learns of the White Sox victory before the moment of crossing. The sports victory whets his appetite for advancing his own frontier: "Crossing the Mississippi would be a big event he thought, and he wanted to enjoy every minute of it" (*NAS*, 134).

He does enjoy it even though the scene on the other side would check the spirit of many a pioneer: "Desolate hills were on the far side that Nick could now see and on the near side of a flat mud bank." However, history and myth merge together to assure Nick that he is capable of facing the challenge: "Mark Twain, Huck Finn, Tom Sawyer, and LaSalle crowded each other in Nick's mind as he looked up the flat, brown, plain of slow-moving water. Anyhow I've seen the Mississippi, he thought happily to himself" (*NAS*, 134). Nick will find his own frontiers. In its chronological place—in the months prior to his going to war—the sketch could serve as a reminder of Nick's essential vitality. To be sure, the darker side of baseball references and the preponderance of images that put the reader in mind of Eliot's *The Waste Land* and Fitzgerald's *The Great Gatsby* make the sketch heavily ironic. The frontier that faces him will be the battle trenches of Europe: Nick will need every bit of his American optimism. As we have seen, his war experiences called all his faith into question. But as we also saw, however dark the Nick war stories are, they all reveal something of his determination to win.

Between the moment of crossing the Mississippi and the fishing of the Big Two-Hearted River, much happened to check Nick's determination. Psychologically the two events are ages apart. "Big Two-Hearted River" builds on the reality of a man with a past and creates the sense that the events Nick recalls were "a long time ago." Nick did not simply leave Milan, return to the States, and take a trip to the Big Two-Hearted River. Nick's trauma in war has been tied up with other traumas in his life—as both "Now I Lay Me" and "In Another Country" have revealed. Both stories raise questions about Nick's future—particularly questions about the possibility of marriage.

The reader of *In Our Time* already knows the answer

to the question later raised so hauntingly in *Men Without Women*. Nick does indeed marry, some time after his return to the States after the war. Moreover, he has married before he takes the trip in "Big Two-Hearted River," even though the memories that creep into his mind in the story have to do primarily with male companionship. Hopkins' fortune is one thing that separates Nick from those days, but it is not the only thing; marriage is another. Those days of fishing on the Black and other Michigan streams are "in another country." Nick's mind chokes off the memories before they get far. The story of *In Our Time* that reveals that Nick has married, "Cross-Country Snow," also indicates that Nick has had to work out for himself many of the implications of his marriage. When that story ends, he still has some ambiguous feelings about the responsibilities facing him.

Chronology was one principle of Hemingway's arrangement of the stories of *In Our Time*. Of course, he might have violated chronology if he had good reason as he jumbled the chronology of Nick's life to good effect in *Men Without Women*. When critics approach "Big Two-Hearted River," they have tended to skip lightly over the fact that "Cross-Country Snow" precedes it. But "Big Two-Hearted River" is not lessened by considering Nick a married man in it—a married man can also feel his way back to Frost's "time made simple by the loss / Of detail." The Adamic imagery can still hold. If we maintain the principle of chronology in *In Our Time*, we already have the refutation to John's conviction in "Now I Lay Me" that marriage would take care of everything. "Big Two-Hearted River" becomes an even more suggestive story.

Although there is no reference to marriage in "Big Two-Hearted River," neither is there any indication that Nick is not married. The discovery of the unpublished Nick material, however, suggests that Hemingway's arrangement of the events of Nick's life in *In Our Time* was indeed chronological. "Big Two-Hearted River" is not only "about" war, but "about" marriage. Young published the part of the story

that Hemingway had cut away under the title "On Writing."
But the cut material deals with more than writing. Consider
the following:

> When he married he lost Bill Smith, Odgar, the Ghee, all the
> old gang. Was it because they were virgins? The Ghee certainly
> was not. No, he lost them because he admitted by marrying that
> something was more important than fishing. . . .
> They [Nick's Michigan comrades] were all married to fishing.
> Ezra thought fishing was a joke. So did most everybody. He'd
> been married to it before he married Helen. Really married to it.
> It wasn't any joke.
> So he lost them all. Helen thought it was because they didn't
> like her. (*NAS*, 234)

The deleted material gives an interesting slant to Nick's
fishing alone on this trip. By deleting the material Hemingway did not necessarily unmarry Nick, and indeed the absence of any reference to the issue of whether Nick should
marry or not—a persistent issue of the stories of the adolescent Nick—would appear to be settled. But obviously marriage has not taken care of everything, and marriage has
meant the end or the alteration of some other relationships—as Bill had warned long ago. The theme of the lost
comrade is, of course, the essence of the Hopkins material.
Comrades can be lost in many ways, sometimes because of
marriage. For the record, the trip that was the basis of "Big
Two-Hearted River" was not one Hemingway took alone; he
made it with two companions.[1] For fictional purposes he
changed many things. Hemingway doubtless meant us to
ponder long about the fact of Nick's fishing alone, particularly since the story follows not only "Cross-Country Snow"
but a quartet of stories in *In Our Time* having to do with
young married people.

Hemingway's critics, usually to good effect, have emphasized the war experience of "Big Two-Hearted River." Hemingway's own comments on the story have strengthened
them in this approach. Now that we have other evidence of

1. Carlos Baker, *Ernest Hemingway: A Life Story* (New York: Charles
Scribner's Sons, 1969), 63–64.

what was going on in Hemingway's mind as he wrote, we should respect anew that the iceberg owes most of its force to what lies beneath the water. And we should consider "Big Two-Hearted River" as also making comment on Nick's relationship with women: like Hopkins, Nick has made some choices, and a major one was a commitment to a woman.

"On Writing," the title later given to the segment of the story Hemingway deleted, is a remarkable vindication of Hemingway's theory of gaining force by leaving out. No one would argue that "Big Two-Hearted River" would gain from the inclusion of Nick's several memories and theories of writing. Although we do think of Nick as a writer in the story and should also think of him as lover, we can be thankful that Hemingway cut the summary of a considerable segment of Nick's experience. The pristine quality of the aubade experience would surely be dimimished by inclusion of the "On Writing" material. Particularly since the material is on writing, we would leave the Nick that we have come to know in the stories. We would think of Hemingway—and the extraordinary good fortune that he had as a young writer, how much had happened to him so quickly, how he had met just the right people in Paris. In the cut segment Nick is too cerebral. Hemingway felt that "talk"—even if presented as memory—could ruin a thing. He wisely curbed the memories and theories and kept feeling and the present foremost. He would *do* a Cézanne rather than talk about doing one.

The Nick materials published after Hemingway's death brought forth one completed story, "Summer People." As Philip Young has indicated, the reasons Hemingway did not or could not publish the story are easy to ascertain. The story presents sexual attitudes and descriptions clearly in advance of what was commercially acceptable. Furthermore, there were many people who would be hurt by the story, who would accept it as fact, no matter how much Hemingway might assert—as Nick does in "On Writing"—"The only writing that was any good was what you made up, what you imagined. . . . Everything good he'd ever written he'd made up. None of it had ever happened. Better things, maybe. That was what the family couldn't understand. They thought it all was experience" (*NAS*, 237–38).

However finished "Summer People" may be, Hemingway might never have wished it published—and certainly not quite as it *was* published. Young indicates that the story is "very likely the first fiction Hemingway wrote about Nick Adams."[2] It is helpful to think of the story from that perspective. Did Hemingway even then regard Nick Adams as "work in progress"? It is likely that he did. He christens Nick completely in the "first" story as Nicholas Adams. The last name does not appear in all of the Nick stories, but it was a part of Hemingway's original conception. The *Nicholas* does not reappear until the late Nick stories. It is noteworthy also that the early Nick story was about Nick's thoughts of himself as a writer and of his determination not to marry.

Although in retrospect we can see it as a fitting enough topic for a first Nick story, nevertheless the tone of the story was not right as a point of departure for future development of Nick. His Adamic side needed to assert itself. Hemingway needed first to portray Nick in his state of innocence before Nick could truly be "work in progress."

Consider the problem this way. If "Summer People" had not been even more *inaccrochable* than "Up in Michigan," where might Hemingway have placed it in *In Our Time*? The difficulty is that the story hardly seems pre-"Big Two-Hearted River." Yet from the standpoint of Nick's chronology, it is. Nick was never more assured of himself than he is in "Summer People." He is confident of himself and his future, and he feels superior to the very people he will miss in "Big Two-Hearted River." There is only the smallest clue that Nick might have been to war, and even that is not a necessary conclusion. We learn that Nick has been swimming in the ocean and that he has studied sea otters. Yet we know that the war has taken place, for the nation is under

2. Phillip Young, Preface, *The Nick Adams Stories* (New York: Charles Scribner's Sons, 1972), vii.

Prohibition. And at least some of the sport of these summer people is dependent upon the automobile. The Michigan stories of *In Our Time* and "Ten Indians" take place in a simpler time. The characters move by wagon or boat or foot or hop a freight. However, in "Summer People" the young people get into a car after the night swim and roar up the roads. Driving is competition. We read: "Big cars from Charlevoix, rich slobs riding behind their chauffeurs, came up and passed, hogging the road and not dimming their lights. They passed like a train" (*NAS*, 224). The narrative tone is at fault in the passage, but the image may be useful for indicating why in "Big Two-Hearted River" Nick travels north of this country. As he drives, Bill helps to inaugurate a twentieth-century adolescent sport: he flashes the spotlight on cars parked along the road, forcing lovers to change their positions. From then on, nobody passes Bill from behind. There is no need for Bill to speed, but that is a part of the modern way.

Summer people in their twenties are often also night people, as they are here. "Summer People" is a night story. As such, its emphasis is not on what Nick *sees*, but on what and how he feels—finally how he feels about himself. The opening image strikes a symbolic note for the rest of the story. It is a hot night, and Nick is at the spring near the lake at Hortons Bay. He puts his hand into the spring but cannot hold it there because of the cold. He thinks, "I wish I could put all of myself in there. I bet that would fix me" (*NAS*, 217). The story will build on contrasting emotions of hot and cold, particularly sexual emotions.

Nick is no sexual innocent in this story. He is rather hard-headed about sex. His friend Odgar is thirty-two, the oldest of these summer people; yet Odgar is an emotional adolescent. He is in love with Kate, but she has no sexual interest in him. She has had other lovers, but this summer she wants Nick. And Nick knows it:

> Now Nick could get it if he wanted it. Odgar would kill himself,
> Nick thought, if he knew it. I wonder how he'd kill himself. He

couldn't think of Odgar dead. He probably wouldn't do it. Still
people did. It wasn't just love. Odgar thought just love would do
it. Odgar loved her enough, God knows. It was liking, and liking
the body, and introducing the body, and persuading, and taking
chances, and never frightening, and assuming about the other
person, and always taking never asking, and gentleness and
liking, and making liking and happiness, and joking and making
people not afraid. And making it right afterwards. (*NAS*, 218)

The passage shows the influence of Gertrude Stein in its
repetition of *it* and in its rhythm. As in the early "Up in
Michigan" Hemingway was trying to suggest the rhythm of
sexual intercourse in words. Also, as in "Up in Michigan,"
he was contrasting sexual experience with love. Nick knows
that the two are not the same. He thinks: "Loving was
frightening." It is a strikingly early admission of a major
Hemingway theme.

But Nick is not, however, frightened about his career, although he knows he has a lot to learn before he can be a
great writer. It even seems probable that he will write about
these summer friends: "What would become of the fellows
like Odgar and Harvey and Mike and all the rest? He didn't
know. He hadn't lived long enough. They were the best
people in the world. What became of them? How the hell
could he know?" (*NAS*, 219). He seems to affirm his commitment to that future knowledge as he kneels and takes a
drink from the spring: "He felt all right. He knew he was
going to be a great writer. He knew things and they couldn't
touch him. Nobody could" (*NAS*, 219).

The chosen one, the called one, Nick is the last one to
arrive at the dock, near where his friends are swimming.
The scene echoes a similar beach scene in Joyce's *A Portrait of
the Artist as a Young Man* just after Stephen Dedalus has
embraced his calling to be a writer. Nick is also greeted by
an unusual name, as was Stephen. "It's Wemedge," Kate
shouts and invites him in. Like a chorus, Odgar, Ghee, and
Bill also call out to Nick with the name that marks him as
one of their circle. Bill's line is in the form of a question that
particularly reminds us of Stephen Dedalus' fear of water

and his keeping himself aloof from the swimmers. Bill's
deep bass comes over the water: "Is this man Wemedge a
nonswimmer?" (*NAS*, 219). Although Stephen does not join
the swimmers, he nevertheless exults in the highly charged
greetings he receives. The calling seems his destiny. And
Nick feels good here, too: "It was fun to have people yell at
you like that."

Hemingway continues to play variations on the Joycean
theme. Nick is quickly out of his clothes and into the water,
"smoothly and deeply, with no consciousness of the dive."
But he does not want to swim, "only to dive and be under
water." The beach experience reenforces the motif of Nick at
the spring, wishing to submerge himself completely.

> He took a deep breath, took hold of his ankles with his hands,
> his knees under his chin, and sank slowly down into the water.
> It was warm at the top but he dropped quickly into cool, then
> cold. As he neared the bottom it was quite cold. Nick floated
> down gently against the bottom. It was marly and his toes hated
> it as he uncurled and shoved hard against it to come up to the
> air. It was strange coming up from underwater into the dark.
> Nick rested in the water, barely paddling and comfortable. (*NAS*,
> 220)

The passage is highly suggestive of the way Nick will
explore all of life. He will go to the marly bottom—but then
push "hard against it to come up to air." The effect on the
reader becomes more Laurentian than Joycean. In terms of
"Big Two-Hearted River," we may well believe that Nick will
one day fish the swamps to good purpose.

The imagery, particularly that of diving, carries sexual implications. It is Kate who asks Nick to do a good dive. He
does, and as he turns to come back to the surface he is
thinking of Kate—wishing he could take her under the
water. And as he lies on the dock next to Kate and Odgar,
he fantasizes about the possibilities of having sexual intercourse under water. He ends by laughing at his imprac-
ticality. Hearing the laughter, Kate, a bold young woman to
be sure, declares that she would like to be Wemedge. When
Odgar naively tells her that maybe she could be Mrs.

Wemedge, Nick retorts that there will never be a Mrs. Wemedge and surfaces his fantasizing by saying he would prefer a mermaid. The joke reveals much about Nick's ideas of women. He is certainly far from being ready for marriage. Indeed, as he says, he is determined that there will not be a wife. A wife appears to be a threat to his career plans, and Nick's first allegiance is to his art. Writing will be his true lover. He will sleep alone—which is the image with which the story ends.

But that ending is delayed until Kate gets what she wants. She is like the Liz of "Up in Michigan" in her desire, but she is definitely wiser and less appealing as a character. Nick has promised nothing. "I'm honest," he had told her on the dock after she had teased him for being immoral (*NAS*, 223).

After the swimming party breaks up, Nick and Kate have their rendezvous. Ghee cautions Nick not to be a fool, and Nick sees the threat as Kate arrives at the appointed place: "He saw Kate coming through the trees in the dark but did not move. She did not see him and stood a moment, holding the two blankets in her arms. In the dark it looked like some enormous pregnancy. Nick was shocked" (*NAS*, 226).

A serious affair with Kate is the last thing Nick wants. He is looking for summer fun, and Kate is not the girl we would wish for the Nick we have come to know in the other stories. It may be that Nick uses a posterior position for sexual intercourse with Kate because he thinks that position has a lower pregnancy risk. There is a cruel joke as the passionate Kate pants: "Oh come, Wemedge. Please come. Come, come. Please Wemedge. Please, please, Wemedge."

"There it is," Nick said (*NAS*, 227). Then his mind is "hard and clear." He sees "everything" very sharp and clear, but the earth has not moved.

The brazen Kate cannot like the treatment that Nick then gives her, although he is not nearly as reprehensible in the manuscript as he is in the printed story, which—of course—Hemingway never saw. Nick does not call Kate "slut" in the manuscript, but by her nickname Stut.[3] Nick and Kate eat together after the sexual intercourse, and Nick gives her a kiss of appreciation before he goes his separate way. Kate would like for them to sleep all night together—which is what married people normally do. Nick is not, however, interested. Alone in his bed he utters a prayer for Kate and another more wholeheartedly for poor Odgar. Nick is happy to be in bed alone—"comfortably, happy, fishing tomorrow" (*NAS*, 228)—and confident that he will be a great writer.

The ending of "Summer People" indicates that Hemingway decidedly had other plans for Nick, that "Work in Progress" would have been an appropriate title. The Joycean overtones are insistent in this portrait of the artist as a young man. Joyce's mode in his novel about Stephen finding a vocation is structured on the pattern of building up to a sense of well-being for the end of each chapter—and then revealing a deflated Stephen at the start of the next chapter. Hemingway has also set Nick up for deflation. It is anticipated in Nick's exchange with Ghee just before Nick leaves to meet Kate. Ghee's parting words are: "Only don't be a damn fool" (*NAS*, 225). And Hemingway undercuts Nick at the end of the story even as Nick lies alone in bed feeling satisfied with his single state and prospects for the future. Hemingway says Nick "prayed as he always prayed, when he remembered it" (*NAS*, 228). Furthermore, there is that touch of guilt that qualifies Nick's sense of well-being. He falls asleep praying for Odgar, who "had been nicer to Nick than anybody ever had." Nick is aware that Odgar might not be able to sleep all night: "Still there wasn't anything you could do, not a thing."

If Hemingway's treatment of Nick were to be comic, the neatest trick to play on him would be to marry him off immediately. That is apparently what Hemingway set out to do; he could not, however, finish the story of Nick's wed-

3. See Peter M. Griffin's "A Substantive Error in the Text of Ernest Hemingway's 'Summer People,'" *American Literature*, L (November, 1978), 471–73.

ding, published as "Wedding Day" in *The Nick Adams Stories*, perhaps because he realized the Joycean approach to his artist was the wrong one for him. Besides, Hemingway had some strong reservations about Joyce's characterization of Stephen; the rejected material of "Big Two-Hearted River" provides a rare instance of Hemingway's expressing a negative view of Joyce: "Daedalus in *Ulysses* was Joyce himself, so he was terrible. Joyce was so damn romantic and intellectual about him. He'd made Bloom up, Bloom was wonderful. He'd made Mrs. Bloom up. She was the greatest in the world" (*NAS*, 238). The deleted material may also instruct us about the method Hemingway had to employ before Nick ever "went" as a character for him: "Of course he'd never seen an Indian woman having a baby. That was what made it good. Nobody knew that. He'd seen a woman have a baby on the road to Karagatch and tried to help her. That was what it was" (*NAS*, 238). It may be, however, that Hemingway found Joyce's presentation of Stephen in *A Portrait* more satisfactory than the presentation in *Ulysses*.[4] He first approached Nick using techniques that show Joyce's influence.

When considered next to "Summer People," the first part of "Wedding Day" takes on a comic flavor. It obviously follows the completed story closely in time, for some of the summer people are participants in the wedding. Bill and the Ghee are a part of the groom's party, and the use of nicknames is an obvious part of both pieces. Furthermore, the opening clause harks back to "Summer People." Nick has been in swimming. In "Summer People" Nick felt superior to the swimmers: "Swimmers, hell, swimmers were slobs, nobody knew about the water but him" (*NAS*, 222). He has taken his place with the norm of society by accepting swimming and marriage. The day is hot, as it was in "Summer People." There is the normal nervousness of the groom's party as they dress for the ceremony. While the ushers and Nick drink, the ushers appear more nervous than Nick

4. According to Hemingway's youngest son, *A Portrait of the Artist* was one of Hemingway's favorite books. Gregory H. Hemingway, *Papa: A Personal Memoir* (Boston: Houghton, Mifflin, 1976), 104.

does. Even though Nick sees the comedy, his thoughts reveal his awareness of how decisive the step is: "He wondered if it would be this way if he were going to be hanged" (*NAS*, 231). We have no description of the ceremony in "Wedding Day"—and perhaps Hemingway planned to give none as a kind of joke in itself. Do not portray the turning point. The comedy disappears as Nick and Helen make their getaway to the lake where Nick will row Helen across to the family cottage.

Carlos Baker's description of Hemingway's wedding to Hadley Richardson is indeed close to events as described in "Wedding Day"—although one of his sources was the then-unpublished fragment under discussion here.[5] In "Wedding Day" Hemingway was probably too close to his own life. He had yet to discover Nick as a fictional character and to move away from the Joycean model of Stephen Dedalus.

But marriage and, indeed, marriage at a quite young age was in Nick's future from the beginning of Hemingway's first experiments with him. Nick was the first of his crowd to marry. (Hemingway was a married man when he wrote "Summer People.") During his Paris years Hemingway heard a great deal of talk about marriage and the artist: could the artist marry and maintain a serious commitment to his art? Should he marry? The word from Gertrude Stein would suggest "no." Artists had considered the question before the twentieth century, of course. A classic fictional statement is to be found in Henry James's short story "The Lesson of the Master." James was, characteristically, ambiguous about the answer—although his own life seemed to give his opinion on the matter.

As we have seen, the issue of whether he should marry or not is a major one in the Nick stories, and he received conflicting advice about it. Although Nick is not Hemingway, he reflects more of Hemingway than any other Hemingway hero. In *Green Hills of Africa* marriage is one of the things Hemingway talks about (in his own voice, of course) when

5. Carlos Baker, *Ernest Hemingway: A Life Story*, 80–81.

the early conversation of the book turns to the subject of writers. Talking about American writers, Hemingway posits that American writers have greater problems than writers of other countries, and certainly on the issue of women. For him, the mature writer should have a meaningful relationship with a woman:

> Writers should work alone. They should see each other after their work is done, and not too often. Otherwise they become like writers in New York. All angleworms in a bottle, trying to derive knowledge and nourishment from their own contact from the bottle. Sometimes the bottle is shaped art, sometimes economics, sometimes economic-religion. But once they are in the bottle they stay there. They are lonesome outside of the bottle. They do not want to be lonesome. They are afraid to be alone in their beliefs and no woman would love one of them enough so that they could kill their lonesomeness in that woman, or pool it with hers, or make something with her that makes the rest unimportant.[6]

At least part of Hemingway believed that he had that something with Pauline Pfeiffer when he wrote *Green Hills of Africa*—as he had had something precious with Hadley Richardson before her. Nick Adams would share, or work to share, this basic faith in what a marriage should do.

There is, however, something haunting about the fact that Hemingway never wrote a story showing Nick "pooling" his loneliness with that of a woman, making something important together. Hemingway preferred the method of indirection with Nick, particularly as regards his relationship with women. He would be specific with the heroes of his novels and show them (at least sometimes) combating their loneliness with a woman. But Hemingway's short stories are decidedly stories of men without women. There are exceptions, most notably "The Snows of Kilimanjaro" and "The Short Happy Life of Francis Macomber," where the marriages are symbolic of failure. In the three short stories of *In Our Time* where we see young married people together, the tone is wry or satirical.

6. Ernest Hemingway, *Green Hills of Africa* (New York: Charles Scribner's Sons, 1935), 21–22.

It is in that wry or satirical context that Hemingway virtually springs the fact of Nick's marriage on us. The story in which this happens is "Cross-Country Snow." Only belatedly in that story does the reader comprehend that it is a part of the marriage group section of *In Our Time*. At first the story appears to be only different from the marriage stories. "Cross-Country Snow" starts with an image of motion, speed, exhiliration—hardly aspects of "Mr. and Mrs. Elliot," "Cat in the Rain," or "Out of Season." Nick is skiing with his friend George in the Swiss Alps, almost as if he had indeed decided that Bill was right in warning him about marriage. The adventure of skiing seems to give Nick, who has been troubled by many things, just what he has needed: "The rush and the sudden swoop as he dropped down a steep undulation in the mountain side plucked Nick's mind out and left him only the wonderful flying, dropping sensation in his body. He rose to a slight up-run and then the snow seemed to drop out from under him as he went down, down, faster in a rush down the last, long steep slope" (*IOT*, 139; *NAS*, 249).

Nothing could be finer, but even as we relish the exhilaration with Nick, we realize that the symbol of the skiing will serve Hemingway in a complex way. Skiing is a tremendous challenge. There is speed, and yet the skier has some control—indeed must have the necessary control. Nick is determined he will "not let go and spill." But he does—going "over and over in a clashing of skis, feeling like a shot rabbit, then stuck, his legs crossed, his skis sticking straight up and his nose and ears jammed full of snow" (*IOT*, 140; *NAS*, 249). Symbolically, that is the story—save for the answer to the question it raises: what does the fallen skier do?

Nick's friend immediately calls over to him, using a nickname and thereby recalling the tight little world of the carefree life present in many stories and exaggerated in "Summer People": "You took a beauty, Mike" (*IOT*, 140; *NAS*, 250). Nick rights himself—and then the reader is allowed to get through the snow and motion to see what Nick looks like, a privilege largely denied the reader in other stories. We learn that he has a big back and blond hair. In this locale he appears almost to be some Nordic hero—but something is clearly amiss. The point is shortly emphasized as Nick watches George come down the hill, and George's skiing is obviously more beautiful than Nick's. This is what Nick sees: "George was coming down in a telemark position, kneeling; one leg forward and bent, the other trailing; his sticks hanging like some insect's thin legs, kicking up puffs of snow as they touched the surface and finally the whole kneeling, trailing figure coming around in a beautiful right curve, crouching, the legs shot forward and back, the body leaning out against the swing, the sticks accenting the curve like points of light, all in a wild cloud of snow" (*IOT*, 141; *NAS*, 250). What is unsaid about George's telemark is as important as what is said. George is at pains to praise Nick's achievements. Nick does not praise George, not because he is mean-minded, but because he is so taken aback by the difference in their proficiency and because it touches old memories. Explaining the difference to himself as much as to George (who knows anyway), Nick says, "I can't telemark with my leg" (*IOT*, 141; *NAS*, 250). The machines in Milan have not, after all, performed any miracle for Nick. Nick enjoys skiing, but clearly not as much as he might have— a fact that should be kept in mind as the reader listens to George and Nick in the final dialogue of the story.

"Cross-Country Snow" moves from action to dialogue, from outdoors to indoors. Nick and George proceed to an inn, ready to enjoy the pleasures of wine and conversation. But those pleasures will be qualified, even as the skiing was qualified. A young girl wearing a blue apron comes to take the skiers' orders. As the superiority in the skiing goes to George, inside the inn he is eager to grant Nick's proficiency in other matters of pleasure. Nick orders the bottle of Sion, politely checking with George, using an affectionate *Gidge* for his direct address. George replies: "You know more about it than I do. I like any of it" (*IOT*, 142; *NAS*, 251). We sense a sophistication in these matters that Nick did not have in "The Three Day Blow." Nevertheless, Hemingway

views Nick in the same wry way in this story. It is a deft
touch that the only time he uses a collective noun for Nick
and George it is *boys*.

After the waitress brings the wine, they have trouble
opening it, perhaps because the room is nearly dark. But
that is not the whole reason, we later discover. Nick does
not want the pleasure of the wine lessened, and he explains
to George that the specks of cork do not matter. George,
ever desirous of keeping things smooth, suggests that cake
will add to the celebration. When the girl returns, Nick understands why there was trouble with the cork: he was dis-
concerted by the girl who is fairly well along in a term of
pregnancy. Hemingway presents Nick's reaction in such a
way as to reveal the quality of mind that is as appropriate to
a writer as to a psychiatrist. Nick thinks, "I wonder why I
didn't see that when she first came in?" (*IOT*, 143; *NAS*,
252). Hemingway can legitimately delay sharing the answer
with the reader because Nick needs to speak to the waitress
about the cake.

The waitress had been singing in the adjoining room, both
when Nick and George first entered the inn and after she
delivered the wine. Her music is significantly always at a
remove from them. They are attuned to different things. The
girl emphasizes the distance of their worlds by answering
abruptly Nick's query about her song. As George says, "She
isn't so cordial" (*IOT*, 143; *NAS*, 252). Inside Nick is the
expert, and he explains to George the reason for the waitress's brusque behavior: "She's from up where they speak
German probably and she's touchy about being here and
then she's got that baby coming without being married and
she's touchy" (*IOT*, 143; *NAS*, 252).

George naturally wonders how Nick knows that the girl is
unmarried. With the novelist's eye, Nick has observed that
the girl wears no ring. Furthermore, he has learned some
things about local customs. He explains that "no girls get
married around here until they're knocked up."

Nick and George are truly in another country, and Hemingway makes us pay attention to this fact, for no sooner has

Nick made this statement than a gang of woodcutters enters, and the waitress serves them. The group sits at two tables "smoking and quiet with their hats off, leaning back against the wall or forward on the table" (*IOT*, 144; *NAS*, 252). There is something solid and reassuring about this group of men. The fellowship of the woodcutters is a counterpart to the celebration of Nick and George. The arrival of the Swiss helps the skiers overlook the unpleasantness of the incident with the waitress. However, Hemingway plays on the contrast between the Swiss and the skiers even as the sight of the woodcutters gives Nick and George a new pleasure: "George and Nick were happy. They were fond of each other" (*IOT*, 144; *NAS*, 252). Their bond is different from that of the woodcutters.

But what about Nick's statement of the local peasant custom of having pregnancy precede marriage? To typical American ears of the 1920s, to Mrs. Krebs of "Soldier's Home," say, the statement would bespeak mainly low morals and gross insensitivity. Still, the woodcutters seem pleasant enough folks. And the singing German girl seems to be happy in her condition rather than not. Nick's words are not just bluff: the story has established him as the knowing, instructing voice in his relationship with George. The reason behind the pattern of the peasant marriages is that the culture puts a major value on fertility, on having children. The peasant man does not want to marry a woman who will not give him children: the waitress may also know that her marriage will soon take place.

The surprise of the story is not just that Nick is married, but that his wife, named Helen just as she was in the fragment "Wedding Day," is pregnant. Furthermore, Nick has not welcomed the pregnancy. We recall his startled view of Kate when she appears with two blankets "like some enormous pregnancy." He has reversed the values of the culture where he now finds himself. He has wanted marriage, but without parenthood. We get strong indication of how much adjustment Nick has had to make. George, who has done an admirable job of reading Nick's moods during the skiing and during the celebration in the inn, finally asks Nick the question Hemingway has carefully prepared us for: "Is Helen going to have a baby?" More crucially, he asks, "Are you glad?" Nick's answer shows no hesitation, but it reflects the conflict: "Yes. Now" (*IOT*, 145; *NAS*, 253). The presence of the woodcutters may even help to confirm Nick in his hard won resolution.[7]

George has waited, of course, for the right moment to ask Nick these significant questions. As in "The Three Day Blow" certain preliminaries must precede the serious talking, and surely "Cross-Country Snow" plays against the themes of that story. Nick and George are bidding adieu to the period of youth and irresponsibility that skiing partly symbolizes, and both of them know it. In fact, they are very suddenly about to leave that freedom, for that very night George has to catch the train from Montreux to leave for school. It is surprising that Nick has to ask the question about when George will leave. We may take it as a sign that it is a question he has not wanted to ask. The delay is certainly effective for adding a note of suddenness to the sto-

7. Hemingway went through a struggle over fatherhood very similar to Nick's. Fatherhood seemed a threat to Nick's plans for a writing career in the early story "Summer People." Gertrude Stein accounted for Hemingway's anguish over Hadley's pregnancy in terms of his fears for his career. As Alice B. Toklas, Stein wrote: "He and Gertrude Stein used to walk together and talk together a great deal. One day she said to him, look here, you say you and your wife have a little money between you. Is it enough to live on if you live quietly. Yes, he said. Well, she said, then do it. If you keep on doing newspaper work you will never see things, you will only see words and that will not do, that is of course if you intend to be a writer. Hemingway said he undoubtedly intended to be a writer. He and his wife went away on a trip and shortly after Hemingway turned up alone. He came to the house about ten o'clock in the morning and he stayed, he stayed for lunch, he stayed all afternoon, he stayed for dinner and he stayed until about ten o'clock at night and then all of a sudden he announced that his wife was enceinte and then with great bitterness, and I, I am too young to be a father. We consoled him as best we could and sent him on his way." *The Autobiography of Alice B. Toklas* in *Selected Writings of Gertrude Stein*, ed. Carl Van Vechten. (New York: Random House, 1962), 201. A little later in the *Autobiography* Stein, with some bitterness, lamented that Hemingway would never write "the confessions of the real Ernest Hemingway." She says, "After all, as he himself once murmured, there is the career, the career" (204). The *Autobiography* was first published in 1933.

ry—like the realization that must have hit Nick when he
first learned of Helen's pregnancy. But time is moving to
bring an end to the companionship that has meant so much
to Nick and George. Their celebration is an attempt to hold
on to it as long as possible. Their use of code names (Mike
and Gidge) and the use by both of the essentially adolescent
"Gee" suggest the nature of the camaraderie about to end.
George catches the mood best: " 'Gee, Mike, don't you wish
we could just bum together? Take our skis and go on to the
train to where there was good running and then go on and
put up at pubs and go right across the Oberland and up the
Valais and all through the Engadine and just take the repair
kit and extra sweaters and pyjamas in our rucksacks and not
give a damn about school or anything'" (*IOT*, 144; *NAS*,
253).

Not giving a damn about school or anything is an appealing program for Nick. Memories of past "swell places" begin
to kindle. In the glow of such memories the two eat strudel
and finish the wine. The glow is all they need; George votes
against another bottle. There will be no drinking competition, as there was in "The Three Day Blow." And the time
has come for George to ask the questions he wants to ask
Nick. Hemingway subtly marks the transition by describing
the two in terms of his description of the woodcutters, reminding us of their values: "They sat there, Nick leaning his
elbows on the table, George slumped back against the wall"
(*IOT*, 145; *NAS*, 253).

From that moment on, the conversation is all high seriousness. George learns that Nick's future is unsettled, that he
will probably go back to the States, but neither he nor Helen
wants to. It is an encouraging sign, however, that Nick will
not agree with George that returning is "hell." Nick says,
"No. Not exactly" (*IOT*, 146; *NAS*, 254).

Appropriately, the conversation returns to skiing—and it
allows us to see further evidence of Nick's growth. When
George wonders if Nick will go skiing in the States, Nick
answers, "I don't know." He is learning to accept the uncer-
tainties. George does not think skiing in America could be

as good as it is here, for the mountains there "aren't much."
Nick agrees: "They're too rocky. There's too much timber
and they're too far away." Although George is thinking of
California, Nick's comment on life is all-embracing: "that's
the way it is everywhere I've ever been" (*IOT*, 146; *NAS*,
254). Nick and George agree that "that's the way it is," and
some of the skiing earlier in the day supports their view.
That skiing had not been perfect; the snow was too deep,
and there had been a wire fence that complicated their
movements. The inn itself was no picture-book establish-
ment. This is the way that Hemingway describes it:
"Through the woods they could see a long, low-eaved,
weatherbeaten building. Through the trees it was a faded
yellow. Closer the window frames were painted green. The
paint was peeling" (*IOT*, 141; *NAS*, 251). We have observed
other checks on romanticizing of the present during the
scene inside the inn.

It would be sentimental for Nick and George to feel sorry
for themselves just because the world seems always to dis-
appoint. The solid Swiss woodcutters are again useful to
Hemingway. They seem to know a better way. Immediately
after George's cynical agreement with Nick, the Swiss get
up, pay, and go out. George is the great wisher of the piece.
"I wish we were the Swiss" (*IOT*, 146; *NAS*, 254), he says.
When Nick quips about their having goiter, Nick and
George can laugh over the joke. Nick's laughter is inevitably
a positive sign, as it is here. Nick will pull away from the
threatening self-pity.

The Swiss have left because of their awareness of time,
because of the necessity of work and their responsibilities.
George sets the signal: "Maybe we'll never go skiing again,
Nick." Nick momentarily panics: "We've got to. . . . It isn't
worth while if you can't." But when George says that he
wishes they "could make a promise about it," Nick draws
back. He has outgrown the too easy optimism about the
future that had ended "The Three Day Blow." Action again
punctuates conversation. Because the sentence is an oft-
repeated one in the Nick stories, we pay special attention to

it. Hemingway reports: "Nick stood up." His judgment
checks the boyish impulse decisively: "There isn't any good
in promising" (*IOT*, 146–47; *NAS*, 254–55). Nick's line, the
last bit of dialogue in the story, highlights the story's portrayal of Nick's new maturity. At that point the story moves
not only outdoors but upwards in its emotional pitch.

Nick and George may never again ski together, but they
intend to relish the skiing in the coming minutes until it is
time for George to leave. Significantly, it promises to be better skiing, for it is colder outdoors (nothing stays the same),
and the snow has crusted hard. A patch of soft snow had
earlier felled Nick. The last line of the story suggests growth
in Nick's perception of the role of time in human life and
how the good of the present should be experienced: "Now
they would have the run home together" (*IOT*, 147; *NAS*,
255).

"Big Two-Hearted River" is partly a testing of Nick's going it alone as well as a confirmation that skiing times—at
least as Nick has known them—have ended. The story has
additional force when we consider that its action occurs
after "Cross-Country Snow," because that story raised the
strong feeling of ambiguity both Nick and Helen had about
returning to the States. Since Nick is succeeding in "Big
Two-Hearted River," he will likely succeed elsewhere. Furthermore, "Big Two-Hearted River" becomes even more affirmative if we consider Nick's married state and the ambiguous feelings toward fatherhood that precede that story. In
going to the Big Two-Hearted River, Nick wanted to leave
"everything behind, the need for thinking, the need to
write, other needs." As we have seen, he wanted to leave
them behind so that he might better confront them. "Cross-
Country Snow" suggests a great deal about some of those
"other needs."

In *The Nick Adams Stories* "Cross-Country Snow" is the
penultimate story, immediately preceding "Fathers and
Sons." Just before "Cross-Country Snow" Young put "An
Alpine Idyll," an inclusion that some readers would object
to. There is, after all, no use of Nick's name in the story.

Critics, when they discuss the story at all, have done so in
terms of an unnamed narrator. Generally, they pass over the
story. Sheridan Baker finds it "unattractive but able," and
that is how most critics have judged the story. Furthermore,
Hemingway had some difficulty in finding magazine publication for it. Carlos Baker's estimation was something of a
minority report as he emphasized its Chekov-like qualities.
However, the story seemed to many too anecdotal, merely a
study in the bizarre.[8]

Long before the appearance of *The Nick Adams Stories*,
however, Young had argued that the story gained considerably in impact if viewed as a Nick story. On this point, he
has been largely ignored, and that is unfortunate. It should
be recalled that there are other first-person Nick stories and
that the story is a part of *Men Without Women*, a volume in
which there are several Nick stories, two others in the first
person. Moreover, from the start Hemingway had thought
of his Nick stories as "Work in Progress." *Men Without
Women* demonstrates his expectation that his readers would
know his earlier work. To his mind—and to the dedicated
Hemingway reader—"An Alpine Idyll" would suggest the
earlier "Cross-Country Snow." The motifs that are common
to the stories are so many that consideration of the two as
companions seems inevitable. And the "I" who tells the
story bears most of the traits we have associated with Nick.
Who is the narrator if not Nick?

To my mind, however, the story works better in the Nick
chronology after "Cross-Country Snow," for dialogue and
other elements of the story suggest an older, more Euro-
peanized Nick. George has left "to get educated," and Nick
is with another friend, John; while time is unspecified, it is
probable that Nick and Helen have been to the States and

8. Sheridan Baker, *Ernest Hemingway: An Introduction and Interpretation*
(New York: Holt, Rinehart and Winston), 58; Carlos Baker, *Ernest Heming-
way: The Writer as Artist* (4th ed.; Princeton: Princeton University Press,
1972), 119–21. For consideration of the story as a Tyrolean "tall tale" see
Edward Hattam, "Hemingway's 'An Alpine Idyll,'" *Modern Fiction Studies*,
XII (Summer, 1962), 261–65.

are once again in Europe. John does not have the same close relationship with Nick that George had with him. There not only are no nicknames in the story, but Nick does not even use John's name in direct address, nor does John use Nick's. These two have been together too long; they have over-stayed the season of good skiing—in marked contrast to the action of the earlier story.

In the Michigan stories, a hot day is the right kind of day. But in the mountains at skiing time, the sun can ruin the pleasure of skiing. As we saw, the freezing over at the end of "Cross-Country Snow" coalesced with other positive signals. In "An Alpine Idyll" we start with a hot day—even though it is early in the morning. The time is May. Nick has pushed the skiing season as far as he could—delaying various duties as long as he could. It is time for him to be coming down from the mountains.

"Cross-Country Snow" dealt with the end of something. "An Alpine Idyll" does so crushingly from the start and immediately casts the title into an ironic vein. First there is the mention of the heat and the end to the skiing. Still in the first paragraph, Hemingway connects these facts with another ending, for as Nick and John, who have just arrived in the town of Galtur, pass a graveyard a burial is conclud-ing. If we are taking the story in *Men Without Women*, the burial may have an even more ominous ring, for the story there follows "Canary for One," which ends with a surprise revelation: the unnamed narrator and his wife are returning to Paris to establish separate residences.

As Nick and John pass the priest who has officiated at the funeral, Nick says to him, "Grüss Gott" (*MWW*, 187; *NAS*, 242), establishing himself as somewhat at home with the language and the local customs. The priest bows, but does not speak. Hemingway calls attention to the silence of the priest, which for the time being is explained by local cus-toms. We discover later the reason for his silence. Although he is a priest and accustomed to hearing of human failings, he has learned something to make him puzzle again over the nature of man.

Nick and John stop to watch the sexton shovel in the dirt.
Only a peasant remains at the graveside. When the sexton
pauses to rest, the peasant takes the spade from him and
proceeds to fill in the grave "spreading the earth evenly as a
man spreading manure in a garden" (*MWW*, 187; *NAS*, 242).
For Nick, anyone's death on this bright May morning seems
particularly unreal: "I could not imagine any one being
dead" (*MWW*, 188; *NAS*, 243). John's sentiments are the
same. It is the first lightening of the story—the first indication that the two are glad to be out of the mountains and in
the valley. The funeral at first serves mainly as contrast to
make us aware of their own sense of renewal. In part, the
burial symbolizes the end of the skiing.

One of the themes of the Nick Adams stories is the proper
pursuit of pleasure. Nick had decided long ago that his father had missed out on a lot of things and that he meant his
own life to be different. This story emphasizes and works with
"Cross-Country Snow" to say that meaningful pleasure requires a very delicate balance. Pleasure must be measured
against other things. Nick and John have been skiing for a
month—no wonder we detect no exuberance in their conversation about it. The sun, basic symbol of reality, has insisted on its right and made them tired:

> We were both tired of the sun. You could not get away from the
> sun. The only shadows were made by the rocks or by the hut
> that was built under the protection of a rock beside a glacier, and
> in the shade the sweat froze in your underclothing. You could
> not sit outside the hut without your glasses. It was pleasant to be
> burned black but the sun had been very tiring. You could not
> rest in it. I was glad to be down away from the snow. It was too
> late in the spring to be up in the Silvretta. I was a little tired of
> skiing. We had stayed too long. I could taste the snow water we
> had been drinking melted off the tin roof of the hut. The taste
> was a part of the way I felt about skiing. I was glad there were
> other things besides skiing, and I was glad to be down, away
> from the unnatural high mountain spring, into this May morn-
> ing in the valley. (*MWW*, 188–89; *NAS*, 243)

The rhythm and repetition of the passage help to convince
us of the tiredness—a fact to be confirmed shortly in John's

quick surrender to sleep once he and Nick are inside the inn. This passage especially suggests that the Nick of "An Alpine Idyll" is older than the Nick of "Cross-Country Snow." He is not wavering here between youthful enthusiasms and adult perspective; he has a more considered view of the nature of pleasure: "I was glad there were other things besides skiing." It has been good to go up to the mountains, but it is also good and necessary for Nick to return to the valley of human involvement.

The citizens of Galtur also appear to know something about how life should be lived. When Nick and John arrive at the inn, the innkeeper greets them in a friendly way and then goes into his office to get them their mail. The world has gone about its business while the two men have been skiing; it will be their responsibility to catch up with the world, and the letters indicate that the two have promises to keep. The cook, meanwhile, has remained sitting on his chair, symbolizing that it is best, after all, not to panic about these demands. There is a time not to work. The cook's passiveness confirms the validity of the impetus behind the whole skiing trip.

Although John and Nick are making their reentry into the world of work, they do so only gradually. They do not abandon their pursuit of pleasure abruptly and decide to go inside for beer. They will be better received in this inn than Nick and George were in "Cross-Country Snow." Drinking the two bottles the proprietor has served them while they read their letters, they at first rush the pleasure of the beer. A smiling waitress lightens the mood further and makes the two men more aware of the pleasure they are having now. When Nick says, "I'd forgotten what beer tasted like" (*MWW*, 190; *NAS*, 244), John makes tight the story's emphasis on right pleasure, declaring that he had not forgotten, that he used to think a lot about it up in the hut. Nick and John are in agreement that they were up in the mountains too long, but Nick has an important line for the story's theme: "Well . . we've got it now" (*MWW*, 190; *NAS*, 244).

Hemingway—and Nick—then give us the essence of pleasure at the right moment. Much as Nick periodically paused in "Big Two-Hearted River," there is a pause for a pictorial view that emphasizes true value:

> The sun came through the open window and shone through the beer bottles on the table. The bottles were half full. There was a little froth on the beer in the bottles, not much because it was very cold. It collared up when you poured it into the tall glasses. I looked out of the window at the white road. The trees beside the road were dusty. Beyond was a green field and a stream. There were trees along the stream and a mill with a water wheel. Through the open side of the mill I saw a long log and a saw in it rising and falling. No one seemed to be tending it. There were four crows walking in the green field. One crow sat in a tree watching. Outside on the porch the cook got off his chair and passed into the hall that led back into the kitchen. Inside, the sunlight shone through the empty glasses on the table. John was leaning forward with his head on his arm.
> (*MWW*, 190–91; *NAS*, 244)

It is a magnificent and pivotal paragraph, distilling the essence of pleasure in the moment. It begins and ends with the symbol of the sun, made fully positive here because Nick has accepted it in its relationship to all life. At first the paragraph seems a still life painting as it focuses on the beer bottles. Then Nick looks out the window at the world of nature and of men—and the two are not in conflict. Nick is taking keen pleasure in what he sees, and his reporting aims at precision. There are four crows walking in the field, a fifth is in a tree watching. Nick is like the fifth crow. The movement of the cook from the porch into the hall that leads to the kitchen calls further attention to the work-leisure theme and leads us back into the inn where the sunlight shines through the empty glasses. John is leaning forward with his head on his arms, asleep.

The point is not just that Nick sees and John does not or that John is more tired than Nick. Rather, the paragraph indicates the importance of the story as an example of the artist's temperament—really the artist at work. Nick has

been skiing, getting away from life's perplexities, and now
he is back in the valley, not just accepting it but looking for
what is significant in it. The pause at the churchyard was
instinctive.

And that pause at the churchyard now becomes Hemingway's means of showing the artist at work. Through the
window Nick sees two men come up the front steps. The
window has just framed a lovely picture for us, but ultimately the writer is concerned with the human drama. The
two men are the sexton and the bearded peasant, and they
enter the drinking room. Nick has picked out the bearded
peasant as the more important of the two. Nick tells us
nothing now about the sexton, but for the third time he
reports that the peasant wears high boots. When the girl
goes to their table, the peasant does not seem to see her.
Nick knows the physical details all say something. He reports that the peasant sits with his hands on the table, that
he wears his old army clothes, that there were patches on
his elbows.

Whereas John can sleep, Nick is too caught up in the
scene before him. He seems to sense "story." Nick cannot
comprehend everything, but he does not want to *miss*
anything: "The girl brought the drinks and the peasant
drank the schnapps. He looked out of the window. . . . The
innkeeper came in and went over to the table. He spoke in
dialect and the sexton answered him. The peasant looked
out of the window. The innkeeper went out of the room. The
peasant stood up. He took a folded ten-thousand kronen
note out of a leather pocketbook and unfolded it. The girl
came up" (*MWW*, 191–92; *NAS*, 245). It is as if a camera
were trying to film these events.

Somewhere in those events, there is a meaning. We may
suspect that the peasant is the bereaved, maybe even that he
lost a wife. He is probably close in age to Nick and John: his
beard is black. More important, he wears an old army uniform. How does a man respond to his wife's death? We perhaps recall the major of "In Another Country." Certainly the
peasant evokes some sympathy from Nick and the reader.

Although poor, he insists on paying for the sexton's wine. Paying a bill can carry heavy weight in Hemingway, and it does here. The peasant makes a pathetic picture as he goes out the door.

Nick's interest shifts from the peasant to the innkeeper and the sexton. Only now do we learn that the sexton is "a little man with a mustache" (*MWW*, 192; *NAS*, 245). A little later we are told that the innkeeper is "a tall man and old" (*MWW*, 193; *NAS*, 246). The reactions of the sexton and the innkeeper highlight the problem that has been teasing Nick: "The sexton was amused. The innkeeper was disgusted" (*MWW*, 192; *NAS*, 245). They have been speaking in dialect; so Nick has missed the explanations. The reader is, of course, curious about the reasons for the interest in the peasant, and delay is good for suspense. But the delay is also useful for keeping the story focused on the artist's search for the significant. Obviously, the writer could make various things of the peasant—depending upon the window from which he looks.

The innkeeper, after some further conversation with the sexton, obviously about the peasant, comes to see if Nick and John are ready to order food. Nick, the writer at work, seizes the opportunity to invite the innkeeper to have a drink with them; he wants to know the mystery behind the peasant. Nick gets immediate confirmation that he rightly read the innkeeper's sense of disgust. The innkeeper's first words as he sits down with Nick are: "Those peasants are beasts" (*MWW*, 193; *NAS*, 246). The innkeeper cannot get over what he has heard about the peasant, and Nick does not need to ask many questions. He needs mainly to be a good listener, and to encourage the innkeeper, which he does. "Tell me" (*MWW*, 194; *NAS*, 246), he says.

Because Hemingway is interested in reaction as well as fact, it is appropriate that the sexton be brought back into the story. The innkeeper calls him over. Nick is willing to pay his dues; so he asks Franz what he would like to drink —insisting until Franz agrees to another quarter litre of wine. The sexton will give Nick a more immediate source than the innkeeper—but his immediacy to the event does not necessarily imply that his response is the correct one.

John is sufficiently awakened by now to ask what is going on. But he will be of no help in coming to terms with the mystery. That will need the sense of the artist—Nick—to write a story like "An Alpine Idyll" before he can find the importance of what has been happening. Even though the innkeeper and sexton do not use dialect, John protests that he will not be able to understand their report: "It goes too fast for me" (*MWW*, 194; *NAS*, 247).

But Nick is a good listener—and from what he reports to us of the conversation, we again feel his interest in accuracy even as he is aware how an event changes as soon as someone begins to tell it. Fact inevitably merges into fiction. The innkeeper starts by confirming for us that it was the peasant's wife who has just been buried. He says, "She died last November" (*MWW*, 194; *NAS*, 247). Since we know that it is now May, the news is a jolt. However, Hemingway is interested in more than the jolt. The sexton corrects the innkeeper, reporting that the wife died in December. The innkeeper is slightly annoyed, but admits to December. When the sexton comes back with a precise date, December 18, the innkeeper says that the important thing for Nick and John to know is that the husband could not bring her in for burial until the snow was gone.

In that Swiss region, a delayed winter burial was not unusual. The innkeeper lets Franz report what is unusual about the present case, the reason that the priest did not wish to bury the wife. The shocking truth is that the woman's face was grossly disfigured, for the husband in the nights of the winter months has used his wife's open mouth as a convenient place to hang his lantern. It is worth emphasizing that Franz does not merely give Nick the facts; he creates the story. One recent Hemingway critic appears to have accepted Franz's amused view as the correct one. Jackson J. Benson presents the story as an example of the sick joke and finds the punch lines at the end of the story when Nick and John turn their attention to the menu and dinner akin to the challenge of goldfish-eating. The more common reaction has probably been closer to that of the innkeeper: Sheridan Baker's "able but unpleasant."[9]

Reactions of humor or disgust are not, however, the only possible responses to the story Nick has heard. Those are undoubtedly the common first reactions—and a reader might experience both. Certainly there is something horrific in Olz's admission (he is named in the sexton's story) that he did what he did "every time" he went to the shed in the night. Franz ends his story on other than a horrific detail. Somewhere in his mind he realizes that the priest asked a very appropriate question, and Franz ends *his* story with the question and Olz's answer:

> "'It was very wrong,' said the priest, 'Did you love your wife?'
> 'Ja, I loved her,' Olz said. 'I loved her fine.'" (*MWW*, 196;
> *NAS*, 248)

As we have seen, there have been moments in "An Alpine Idyll" when Olz has appeared to invite more sympathy than curiosity—as he sits with his hands on the table, or looking out the window as he drinks his schnapps, or when he pays the bill and takes his lonely exit. The scene at the graveyard repays another look. Why does Olz take the spade from the sexton and fill in the grave so carefully, as if "spreading manure in a garden?" Olz can elicit sympathy from us here, too, as we view a man coming to terms with his loss. Who is to say how another man might deal with grief? And it is partly true that Olz's grief has been frozen until now—its significance only made real to him as he returns to the valley

9. Jackson J. Benson, *Hemingway: The Writer's Art of Self-Defense* (Minneapolis: University of Minnesota Press, 1969), 55. The uneasiness of Hemingway's critics in dealing with the story is accented in a recent critique. Note Myra Armistead's hesitation as she concludes: "Since the story deals with a skiiing trip that lasted too long as well as with a tall tale about a corpse, one naturally looks for a connection between the two parts. Hemingway's point may be that, just as the Americans have been skiing too long, the valley people have been telling and hearing the tales too long and have been insensitive to the feelings of their fellow men." See her "Hemingway's 'An Alpine Idyll,'" *Studies in Short Fiction*, XIV (Summer, 1977), 255–58.

and the church. Other figures in literature have acted similarly. Edwin Arlington Robinson's Reuben Bright, a butcher whose wife has died, does all the proper things and then tears down his slaughterhouse. Faulkner's Rider from *Go Down, Moses* seizes the shovel at the graveyard when his wife is being buried and in a wild burst of energy fills in the grave. It is a part of the texture of Faulkner's work that the white community does not know how to judge properly Rider's action. He, also, seems a beast. And there is Faulkner's Cash Burden, who carefully labors outside the window of his dying mother to make her a coffin. We know the theme too from Frost's "Home Burial." There a wife is unable to grasp the deliberate way in which her husband can bury their dead child and then remark to her "Three foggy mornings and one rainy day / Will rot the best birch fence a man can build." And as the poem ends she is intent on sharing that "beastly" behavior with her neighbors. In each of these works, the narrator knows better than to accept conventional interpretation.

In "An Alpine Idyll" it is so with Nick. There seems to be no reason to doubt that Olz loved his wife. The title is ironic not only because there is finally nothing idyllic about the piece. It is not just an idyll, an incident, but becomes much more—particularly when we view it as a Nick story. Surely the incident Nick hears is odd, even horrifying. So was the incident upon which Hawthorne based "Wakefield." Hawthorne's tale rests on a case he had read about in a newspaper: a man had hid from his wife for twenty years, allowing her to think he was dead; after twenty years, the man returned to her. One could respond to the newspaper story with amusement or disgust or both. It was the kind of bizarre event that would strike Hawthorne, and while "Wakefield" is not one of Hawthorne's best tales, it has its force. Hawthorne felt that the odd little event touched the human dilemma. Wakefield was just an average sort of person—yet he was capable of the cruelest kind of behavior toward Mrs. Wakefield. Did he love her? We need not doubt it. Hawthorne found great significance—for himself most of all—in the story of an average man who acted so strangely. He ends his tale with a stark warning: "Amid the seeming confusion of our mysterious world, individuals are so nicely adjusted to a system, and systems to one another and to a whole, that, by stepping aside for a moment, a man exposes himself to a fearful risk of losing his place forever. Like Wakefield, he may become, as it were, the Outcast of the Universe." [10]

Hemingway, of course, would not end his story with so obviously stated a moral, although the repetition of the innkeeper that the peasants are beasts and the sexton's comment that Olz has gone to drink where people do not know about his wife indicate that Olz is well-nigh an outcast of the universe. "An Alpine Idyll" is the story of the coming into being of a story. No sooner has Franz finished his account than the innkeeper asks, "Did you understand it all?" Nick replies, "I heard it" (*MWW*, 197; *NAS*, 248). Indeed he has, or there would be no "An Alpine Idyll." But Nick will have to think further on what he has heard. Nick and John may be about to eat as the story ends, but we may be certain that Nick is going to think abut Olz and his love for his wife. In the larger framework of the story, we see the artist who has returned from the mountains and skiing to the puzzling arena of human beings. That is its inevitable subject.

And not just in an abstract sense. It becomes a haunting thing that Nick and John appear to be so completely men without women—away for a whole month, no reference at all to women in either life. And since the smiling waitress here contrasts inevitably with the pregnant waitress of "Cross-Country Snow," it seems certain that Hemingway would expect us to see that there has been this deliberate exclusion of women from the spring skiing (because Helen is pregnant or caring for an infant?) Nick and John need to return to the world of men with women. There is nothing wrong with Philip Young's suggestion that "An Alpine Idyll" reveals the extent to which Nick has matured. He compares

10. Nathaniel Hawthorne, "Wakefield," in *Nathaniel Hawthorne: Selected Tales and Sketches*, ed. Hyatt Wagoner (3rd ed.; New York: Holt, Rinehart and Winston, 1970), 173.

the story to Nick's reactions in "The Killers." Nick has hardened some; he is able to eat with John.[11]

But that is not the whole of it. Nick needs to let the story
of Olz work on him. It is too easy to dismiss Olz as a beast,
as the innkeeper does, or to say that he is drinking at the
Löwen because his story is not yet known there. Nick is
confronted with paradox—how could a man love his wife
and yet be so insensitive about her corpse? (A Wakefield's
behavior is worse, of course.) By extension, the story asks
how people can treat those they love in the frightful ways
they sometimes do. In marriage, particularly, the possibility
for such mistreatment is almost constant, but whenever men
and women love each other the same phenomenon seems to
operate. Two other stories of *Men Without Women* treat the
theme—"Hills Like White Elephants" and "A Canary for
One." Four stories of *Winner Take Nothing* also depend importantly on the theme—"The Sea Change," "One Reader
Writes," "Homage to Switzerland," and "Wine of Wyoming."
It is fair to say that it is a major theme of the short stories. In
the novels Hemingway gave more emphasis to what men
and women would do for each other, save for *The Sun Also
Rises* and *Islands in the Stream*. The issue is not new for Nick.
It is a part of the fiber of the relationship between Dr. and
Mrs. Adams and was an important factor in what Nick
learned of Ad Francis in "The Battler." It is fitting that Hemingway have a story that would make the theme apply more
directly to Nick's mature life. The best evidence for considering "An Alpine Idyll" as a Nick story is its many parallels
with "Cross-Country Snow." When we observe those parallels, we may decide that one obvious conclusion to make at
the end of "An Alpine Idyll" is that it is high time for Nick to
return home to Helen.

If "An Alpine Idyll" is indeed a Nick story, Nick is like Olz
in at least seeming to keep a low profile. He bears a measure
of guilt—in aesthetic terms if no other. The stale quality of
the exchanges with John speak to the point. But as the con-

11. Philip Young, *Ernest Hemingway: A Reconsideration* (University Park:
Pennsylvania State University Press, 1966), 60.

trast between John and Nick comes again into important play at the end of the story, we sense that Nick has other guilts. John feels nothing but only wants to eat. The ending serves to bring the story back to the creative process, and finally to the question of what to do with a story. We can just forget it—although that is not the effect Hemingway wanted. Clearly Nick will not forget this one.

But even though the relationship of the writer to his story is vital, the point of a story is never simply that the writer is the character in the story. His personality is veiled for artistic reasons. The story is more important than the writer, and once it is finished, it exists apart. "An Alpine Idyll" gains as a story about perceiving stories by keeping Nick unnamed, which is not to say that Hemingway did not mean for his reader to recognize Nick Adams, or to relate the events of the story to Nick's life. The pursuit of the artist's personality may be a part of the challenge for the reader, especially of an artist like Nick who believed that he could get rid of an experience by writing about it.

The title of this chapter, "Love and Marriage," underscores a major theme of the Nick stories—and of other Hemingway writing: one may think immediately of the collection *Men Without Women* (and probably other titles) and then recall that Nick is an important character in that book, too. Hemingway treated love and marriage for Nick much as he treated Nick at war—obliquely. There are no stories showing Nick courting or romancing—no scenes to match the love scenes of *A Farewell to Arms*. "Summer People" shows him in sexual congress, but the point of that story— never published in Hemingway's lifetime—is that the affair was not one of the heart. The great Nick love story remains "The End of Something," and that shows Nick breaking away from Marjorie. Thereafter Hemingway chose to portray Nick in a doubtful frame of mind about the advisability of marriage—as "Summer People" reveals, in part because of his career objective, but more importantly because of the great risk. The early Nick stories indicate how circumstances made Nick aware of all that could be lost.

Nevertheless, Nick was a man destined to marry, was destined to be a writer who would seek a woman to help him kill his loneliness. Hemingway gave Nick's wife the evocative name *Helen*, and perhaps the very selection of that name (a name that was also close to Hadley) dictated his desire to keep her in the stories as a shining, distant object of beauty. His attempt to write of Helen and Nick's wedding day did not work; what he had written had showed Nick, not Helen. However lovely Helen might be, Nick's attitudes also pull him towards both isolation and the male camaraderie of his Michigan days. Two stories, "Cross-Country Snow" and "An Alpine Idyll," show Nick married but in retreat from the responsibilities of adulthood. The story of Olz emerges as Nick's own confession of his failure to give enough of himself in marriage. Still it is a mark of his increased maturity that in "Cross-Country Snow" he has come to accept, even welcome the fact of Helen's pregnancy. In "An Alpine Idyll" we see him returning to artistic involvement. The progressions go together, and both are as well a part of the current of "Big Two-Hearted River."

Chapter Six
Father and Son

In "Out of Season," a story that appeared in Hemingway's first book, *Three Stories and Ten Poems*, Hemingway does not reveal to the reader the name of a major character in the story, although we do get the wife's nickname, Tiny. Hemingway calls the husband " the young gentleman," and he later abbreviates the designation to "the y. g." Not naming the man adds to the comedy of the story, inviting the reader to be amused at the off-season fishing and the embarrassment of the quarreling couple and their drunken guide. With some modification, Hemingway took this story into *In Our Time*. In that collection there are two other stories wherein the reader never learns the names of major characters, "A Very Short Story" and "The Revolutionist"—both of which had earlier appeared as chapters of *in our time*, a work in which precise identification of characters was often not important.

During this apprenticeship fiction, Hemingway learned that he could withhold the names of characters for various effects, and he found the device useful throughout his career as a short story writer. In *Men Without Women*, the collection that followed *In Our Time*, the device of not naming major characters is important in several stories; it is used in eight of the fourteen. "Hills Like White Elephants" concentrates on dialogue between an unnamed American man and his unnamed girl about an abortion that he wants and she does not. In "A Canary for One" there are three characters, an American husband (the unnamed narrator of the story), his American wife (also unnamed), and an unnamed American mother. The narrator and his wife are on the verge of divorce—although this fact is withheld from the reader until the end of the story. The situation is close to events in Hemingway's own break-up with Hadley, and even though events from Hemingway's life frequently found their way into Nick's life, Hemingway always drew back from an exact duplication of himself in Nick. Perhaps Nick was too meaningful a character to Hemingway for Hemingway to connect him with the end of that something other than obliquely. In *Men Without Women* Hemingway seems not yet to have thought of Nick as a mature adult beyond the advent of impending fatherhood. I find no internal evidence that would lead me to conclude that Hemingway intended us to conceive of "A Canary for One" as a Nick story—as there is internal evidence in "In Another Country." Still, Hemingway placed "A Canary for One" directly after "Ten Indians," a story showing Nick in his first disappointment over love. The husband's feelings are underplayed in "A Canary for One," but we realize at the end of the story that they are strong. The loss Nick feels at the end of "Ten Indians" is nothing to the loss the husband feels *throughout* "A Canary for One." It becomes even more significant that the story in *Men Without Women* after "A Canary for One" is "An Alpine Idyll," a story that is Nick's. Hemingway would seem to imply that divorce awaits Nick or at least to emphasize the seriousness of Nick's too long separation from his wife and responsibilities.

Of the stories in *Men Without Women* whose major characters are not named, it is appropriate that Hemingway not name the "he" of the satiric "Banal Story" and that he leave the soldiers unnamed in "Today is Friday" (the only time Jesus' name is used in the story, it is taken in vain). In "A Simple Enquiry" "the major" is the only designation for the homosexual major, and the anonymity fits the kind of loneliness Hemingway treats in the story. "Che Ti Dice La Patria" is another story with an unnamed narrator. He might be Nick, but there is little reason to think that he is necessarily so. The narrator is a sharp observer who is tough in his thinking and has a sense of humor. The story provides an interesting example of keen intelligence at work in analyzing a Fascist state. The narrator is traveling with a friend, Guy. The narrator uses Guy's name, but Guy never uses the narrator's. We admire the skill of the narrator, but the point of the story—as the title suggests—has to do more with what is perceived than with the relationship between that and the perceiver. The emphasis is fundamentally different, then, from that of "An Alpine Idyll."

Hemingway's third major collection, *Winner Take Nothing,* also uses the device of withholding from the reader the names of important characters. Six stories are told in the first person, narrator unnamed ("After the Storm," "The Light of the World," "The Mother of a Queen," "A Day's Wait," "A Natural History of the Dead," "Wine of Wyoming"). Possibly the number should be seven. Doc Fischer in "God Rest Ye Merry, Gentlemen" calls the narrator Horace, and he makes quite a point of doing so. Dr. Wilcox never uses the name Horace. Dr. Fischer has something of a literary bent, and he may be addressing the newspaper reporter-narrator by the name of the Roman satirist as a joke. It fits the mood of the grim tale with the ironic title. But although anonymity adds to the effect of some stories, the fact that Hemingway does not mention the name of a character does not *always* mean that he did not mean for us to realize the character's name. Among the first person stories, we have already noted the almost universal acceptance of "The Light of the World" as a Nick story.

In *Winner Take Nothing* third person narratives also feature unnamed major characters. One of Hemingway's most widely acclaimed stories, "A Clean, Well-Lighted Place," is one of these stories. He pushed the device of not identifying his characters so far in that story that critics now argue about who speaks which lines. "The Sea Change" corresponds to "Hills Like White Elephants" in treating discussion between an unnamed man and an unnamed woman whose life together is at a crisis. We do not learn the name of the reader who writes the pathetic letter in "One Reader Writes."

No other successful writer of short stories so frequently refrained from naming major characters—or only partially named them. Sometimes the device gives a satiric or comic effect. Frequently it helps mirror the modern world's loss of faith and value. But, as we have seen, Hemingway achieves other subtle effects from the technique.

We have also seen that it has given Hemingway's critics problems—particularly when they come to the career of Nick Adams. One approach is to admit into the Nick Adams canon only those stories in which Nick is named. But if one takes that approach, what does one do if Nick's last name is not used, as it is not, for but one example, in "Ten Indians"? His father is not even identified as a doctor in that story. The later "Fathers and Sons" connects the two stories, but to use "Fathers and Sons" to help identify the protagonist of "Ten Indians" is to admit complex critical premises. That is precisely the point. Hemingway has always been more complex than he seems, and the principle of the Nick stories as "work in progress" is constant. The reader must supply contexts. In "Ten Indians" Nick's boyish quality is emphasized by Hemingway's not using his last name. The reader who elects not to let story comment on story will miss a great deal. Furthermore, Hemingway arranges stories in all three of his major collections in significant order. "Fathers and Sons" is last in *Winner Take Nothing* for good purpose. Nor would we expect "A Way You'll Never Be" immediately to precede it. We have repeatedly seen that Hemingway has a sense of Nick's career—and he intends that the careful reader should too.

"An Alpine Idyll" afforded us an interesting illustration. So does "A Day's Wait," a generally underprized story. Many critics simply ignore it. Sheridan Baker says it "seems almost straight journalism." Not even Philip Young has taken seriously Carlos Baker's designation of "A Day's Wait" as a Nick story. He does not include it in *The Nick Adams Stories*, arguing that it is mainly about the boy. Yet Carlos Baker is

not even tentative about naming it a Nick story.[1] I think he is
on solid ground, for the story comments so pointedly on
earlier Nick stories that it would be difficult to conclude that
Hemingway was not thinking of Nick. If the narrator should
not be seen as Nick, it is likely that Hemingway would have
identified him otherwise. The same is probably true of "The
Light of the World," also included in the third volume of
short stories.

"A Day's Wait" had no publication prior to its appearance
in *Winner Take Nothing*. The book gains a great deal from its
presence. It is a warm story to follow "Homage to Switzerland," a study of three men without women and men without family. "A Day's Wait" becomes especially evocative after
the final segment of "Homage to Switzerland" with its revelation of the suicide of Mr. Harris's father. It is surely a
useful story to have before "Fathers and Sons"—especially
when we accept it as a Nick Adams story.

Until "A Day's Wait," the tenth story of the book, the
warm, the normal, the familial has been virtually absent
from *Winner Take Nothing*. We pay tribute to these values in
"Homage to Switzerland"; we experience them in "A Day's
Wait." In the context of *Winner Take Nothing* the opening
sentence of "A Day's Wait" is astonishing: "He came into the
room to shut the windows while we were still in bed and I
saw he looked ill" (*WTN*, 91). Before focusing on the boy
and his illness, we need to take in the whole scene. A boy
(nine years old, we learn shortly) has come into his parents'
bedroom where the *two* are still in bed. There is no further
reference to the wife in this brief story, and the fact heightens the simplicity and meaning of the opening image. If
there is much of the atypical in stories like "The Light of the
World" or "The Sea Change," the opening of "A Day's Wait" is
an age-old situation. It evokes the completely wholesome as

1. Sheridan Baker, *Ernest Hemingway: An Introduction and Interpretation*
(New York: Holt, Rinehart and Winston, 1967), 88; Philip Young, "Big World
Out There': *The Nick Adams Stories*," in Jackson J. Benson (ed.) *The Short
Stories of Ernest Hemingway* (Durham: Duke University Press, 1975), 43; Car-
los Baker, *Hemingway: The Writer as Artist* (4th ed.; Princeton: Princeton
University Press, 1972), 134.

a child in need seeks out his parents. But some readers might be troubled by Hemingway's not mentioning the sleeping partner after the first reference. The counterpart in Hemingway's own life to this event involved a stepmother for his first son—John Hadley, or Bumby as his father called him. Pauline Pfeiffer had come between Hemingway and Hadley, the Helen of "Wedding Day" and "Cross-Country Snow." Hemingway's reticence about the sleeping wife in "A Day's Wait" becomes significant in the context of the late stories of *Winner Take Nothing*—especially "Wine of Wyoming" and "Fathers and Sons." Hemingway chose not to emphasize any sense of parental separation in "A Day's Wait."

From the opening image of family security, "A Day's Wait" narrows to the relationship between the father and his son. Because the story comes down so precisely to this relationship, it is fitting that the narrator's name is never used. The boy would not use it in addressing his father, and no one else is allowed to get close to the story's forestage. The narrator, in this story, is not interested in the boy's relationship to anyone other than to himself. Hemingway chose to tell the story in first person because he wanted to put emphasis on that relationship. If the point were merely about the lad's brave wait for death, third person would have done just as well.

As it is, we are made to recognize Nick for ourselves. The situation of "A Day's Wait" would lead us to think of Nick since it focuses on a father-son relationship. Nick's relationship with his own father had long haunted him. There was much that was good about his associations with his father, but as he grew up he questioned Dr. Adams' ways increasingly. In "The Three Day Blow" while discussing his father with Bill, Nick grieved that his father had missed a lot, and he was envious of Bill's more easy going father. Later, the role of fatherhood is one that Nick fears—one that for a time at least he did not want. Since Nick's ambiguity about the matter was so pronounced, and since as early as "Cross-Country Snow" it is clear that fatherhood awaited him, attention to Nick in the role seems a destined way of measuring Nick's adult life.

There is something gratifying in considering "A Day's Wait" as a part of the fulfillment of this theme. The narrator of "A Day's Wait" is responsive to his son who has just disturbed his sleep. He recognizes that there is need. "What's the matter, Schatz" (*WTN*, 91), he asks, using an affectionate nickname—a practice we might well expect Nick as father to use. The German nickname is also in keeping with the cosmopolitan orientation that Nick's son has had—an experience important to "Fathers and Sons."

The narrator does the proper things: sends the boy back to bed, dresses, checks the boy's temperature (102 degrees), and calls the doctor. (Although the narrator misses some important signals in the story, it is nevertheless an impressive piece for demonstrating his gentleness as a father. He is not afraid of his softer, or feminine, side—it does not conflict with his more traditionally masculine role as hunter.) The doctor comes and prescribes the proper medicine. He assures the narrator that there will be no danger if they avoid pneumonia and if the fever does not go above 104.

It does not occur to the narrator that the doctor has given him information that it would be useful for his son to have. So he does not share it, assuming rather that his son will accept his own confidence that all is well now that the doctor has come. No person knows fully the experience of another, and people commonly make wrong assumptions, often about those very dear to them. The father does here.

He knows that his son feels miserable even if he does not know that he has information that could make the boy feel much better. The father asks Schatz if he would like to be read to. We recognize Nick in the question, for Nick has always found reading a great pleasure. Reading to one's offspring is a healthy and warm activity—and one that seems here a family tradition. The boy agrees, but his heart is not in it. The narrator reports his son's response: "He lay still in the bed and seemed very detached from what was going on" (*WTN*, 92). The word *detached*, in this context, is a verbal echo of another Nick story and relates the boy's experience to his father's. In "In Another Country" Nick—also an unnamed narrator there—told us of one of his Milan companions who "had lived a very long time with death and was a little detached. We were all a little detached" (*MWW*, 62; *NAS*, 170).

The narrator reads aloud for a while from Howard Pyle's *Book of Pirates*, but he must finally admit that the exercise is pointless. So he talks to the boy. He asks the right question, but he does not know what the answer means:

> "How do you feel, Schatz?" I asked him.
> "Just the same, so far," he said. (*WTN*, 92)

"Fathers and Sons" will also treat the problem of communication. Missing the signal his son has given, the narrator reads to himself and waits until it is time to give the boy another capsule. He expects that the boy will go to sleep. Instead, he finds the boy "looking at the foot of the bed, looking very strangely." The father suggests that the boy "try to go to sleep." Again, the father hears but does not hear: "I'd rather stay awake" (*WTN*, 92). We are taken back to Nick's determination not to sleep in "Now I Lay Me" lest his soul leave his body. It is ironical here that the father should miss it himself.

"A Day's Wait" is far from being mere journalism. It powerfully contrasts the emotions of its two principles, highlighting the failure of the father to sense what the son is experiencing, his failure to realize what his son is expecting to die at any moment. The boy tells his father: "You don't have to stay in here with me, Papa, if it bothers you" (*WTN*, 92). It is a brave line, enunciating the Hemingway theme of the privacy of death. Each one must do it alone.

Almost shockingly, the father has missed the meaning of his son's statement, and after giving him his eleven o'clock capsule (he has been with the boy a long while), he goes out to hunt. The hunting serves to identify the story more firmly as a Nick story—to remind us of the bond that hunting was between Nick and his father, even as we sense it as a tie between the narrator and Schatz. As the story moves out of doors, the contrast between the boy's psyche and the father's is overwhelming. It is obvious that the father does not think his son is going to die. The indoor-outdoor contrast also affirms the father's exultation in life even as the son fears his death:

> It was a bright, cold day, the ground covered with a sleet that had frozen so that it seemed as if all the bare trees, the bushes, the cut brush and all the grass and the bare ground had been varnished with ice. I took the young Irish setter for a little walk up the road and along a frozen creek, but it was difficult to stand or walk on the glassy surface and the red dog slipped and slithered and I fell twice, hard, once dropping my gun and having it slide away over the ice.
>
> We flushed a covey of quail under a high clay bank with overhanging brush and I killed two as they went out of sight over the top of the bank. Some of the covey lit in trees, but most of them scattered into brush piles and it was necessary to jump on the ice-coated mounds of brush several times before they would flush. Coming out while you were poised unsteadily on the icy, springy brush they made difficult shooting and I killed two, missed five, and started back pleased to have found a covey close to the house and happy there were so many left to find on another day. (*WTN*, 92–93)

But a shock awaits the narrator, with his confidence about "another day," as he returns to the house. The irony that he has missed what his son has been feeling is overwhelming as we learn in a sentence that is also a single paragraph that the boy has refused to let anyone into his room. The boy explains that he does not want to let anyone get what he has, but the real impact comes from the sense of the force of death, which now seems more allegorical than ever. The narrator finds the boy "in exactly the position I had left him . . . staring still, as he had stared, at the foot of the bed" (*WTN*, 93). The image is strikingly like Elizabeth I's death scene, like her determination not to go to sleep but to meet the grim reaper awake.

The father can see that the fever is worse. It has risen four-tenths of a degree, probably heightened by the boy's conviction that death will come at any moment. The father, understandably but wrongly, does not tell the truth when his son asks what his temperature is: "Something like a hundred," he tells Schatz. But the boy knows better. The dialogue over the temperature again makes clear that Hemingway is thinking not only of Schatz but of Nick's past. "I don't worry," the boy explains, "but I can't keep from thinking" (*WTN*, 93). Who more than Nick Adams should respond deeply to that line? But the narrator is here in a dramatic situation. He passes along some famous advice that he once received: "Don't think." Schatz says that he is "taking it easy" and he looks "straight ahead." Nick the narrator, but not Nick at the time, knows what the boy was going through: "He was holding tight onto himself about something" (*WTN*, 93). The verbal echoes to stories like "Big Two-Hearted River," "The Killers," and "Now I Lay Me" are pronounced. And the courageous little boy takes us all the way back to the haunting question of "Indian Camp": "Is dying hard, Daddy?"

Only Schatz does not need to ask the question. He thinks he has the answer to that one. His father meanwhile has taken up the pirate book and commenced reading, but stops when he sees the boy is not listening. Schatz asks what time he is likely to die. Then the mystery between centigrade and Fahrenheit thermometers can be explained. A little information can help a lot. The boy slowly relaxes, as he realizes that he is not going to die now. But he has had his day's wait. It should be no surprise to us that the next day the boy cries "very easily at little things that were of no importance" (*WTN*, 93).

"A Day's Wait" portrays a warm, loving relationship, but it also shows how even in that context it is easy to miss big issues. Even in warmth and security the fact of life is always colored by the reality of death. Although the narrator does not tell us how he evaluated this experience, we feel that he had to have seen more in it than the anecdotal. We are told how the boy responded to the revelation. We are left to consider how the narrator dealt with it. Again, the use of first person narrative for a story about a writer suggests that

the writer knows what is significant in it—for the boy and
for himself.

One other story told by an unnamed narrator deserves
consideration as a Nick story.[2] That story, "Wine of Wyoming," has also been ignored more often than not. Sheridan
Baker says that it "has little to recommend it beyond the
curiosity of American prohibition in rural form, and the fact
that it seems to be almost straight Hemingway autobiography." In their silence, most Hemingway critics appear to
agree. Hemingway himself had been very confident of its
merits when he sent it off to Maxwell Perkins in 1930, although that feeling was not unusual for him after he had
finished a story. Perkins immediately accepted the story for
publication in the August issue of *Scribner's Magazine*.[3] It
was Hemingway's first short story since publication of *A
Farewell to Arms* and the first story of *Winner Take Nothing* to
be written. Yet it appears near the end in Hemingway's arrangement of that collection. Was Hemingway burying inferior work or emphasizing the brilliance of "The Gambler,
The Nun, and The Radio"? Those answers would be too
facile. It is time to give more careful attention to the artistic
choices Hemingway made in writing and placing "Wine of
Wyoming."

The story does not have the verbal or exact situational
echoes of earlier Nick stories. Yet the narrator is like Nick
(and like Hemingway, we must grant Sheridan Baker). He is
a writer who likes to hunt and fish. In fact, he knows what it
is to be a serious fisherman. An American, he has nevertheless spent a great deal of time in Europe and has frequently
compared the values of European culture and American culture—as Nick was well on his way to doing even as a young

2. The essentially comic purpose of "Out of Season" prevents me from
considering it as a Nick story, and of course the name of the wife is wrong.
At the time Hemingway wrote that early story Nick had not yet taken on a
definite outline. Carlos Baker suggests that it might "easily be associated
with Nick's life on the continent." But he found the real interest in the story
in the character of Peduzzi. *Hemingway: The Writer as Artist*, 130.
3. Sheridan Baker, *Ernest Hemingway*, 84; Carlos Baker, *Ernest Hemingway: A Life Story* (New York: Charles Scribner's Sons, 1969), 210.

soldier. Note, too, the persistent question of what he would do after the war. For most soldiers, returning to the States would be so obvious a course as to hardly merit mentioning, but in "Cross-Country Snow" returning to America seemed some sort of doom to Nick now that Helen was pregnant. The narrator of "Wine of Wyoming" prefers the values of Madame and Monsieur Fontan to the values of American life. He is also Catholic, opting in that regard for the values of tradition and the Old World. "Wine of Wyoming" is Hemingway's international short story: juxtaposing the values of two cultures, it is his most Jamesian. The body of the Nick stories might well lead us to anticipate that there might be a Nick story eventually on the theme. "A Day's Wait," seen as a Nick story, would also seem to anticipate such a theme, for the boy's emotional struggle is the result of his use of the European thermometer rather than the American thermometer.

Although *Winner Take Nothing* is generally a darker collection than *In Our Time* or *Men Without Women*, "Wine of Wyoming" is in many ways a very comic story, but mainly in the first two of its four parts. During half of the story it appears that it is the narrator's function to portray vividly for us the colorful Fontans, a French couple who have settled in Wyoming. One loves beer and one loves wine, but their loves (various loves we come to realize) are severely threatened by the Puritan culture of the New World which has outlawed all spiritous drink.

As the story begins, the narrator is visiting the Fontans to share in some of the fine beer they make. He is immediately established as "one of them." When two men drive up and ask to buy some beer, Madame Fontan, recognizing that the men are already drunk and are only interested in getting drunker, decides not to sell. The narrator has tried to assist her by putting the bottles on the floor, but she does not really need his help and quickly sends the intruders on their way.

Even before the narrator describes Madame Fontan, we like her because of her efficiency. When the narrator describes her, there can be no doubt of his feeling for her. She is a "plump old woman with lovely ruddy complexion and white hair. She was very clean and the house was very clean and neat" (*WTN*, 110). She represents value in every way, and she is concerned for the right people. Having served the narrator beer, she wonders where he has eaten and insists that he should eat at her house. We quickly realize that it will be great fun listening to this assured woman, for she frequently falls into French with often hilarious effect. "Mangez ici," she insists. She cannot believe that any American hotel would serve quality food. She *once* ate in an American restaurant—and was served raw pork!

Madame Fontan is dismayed with most Americans not only because their ways are foreign to her but because their ways threaten her ways. At first we do not take the threat overseriously. Her son is married to an American, she laments, who serves him "beans en can" (a tasty meal in its place, we recall from "Big Two-Hearted River"). But Madame Fontan has other complaints about her daughter-in-law. She is lazy and does nothing all day except to read books. In the evenings she goes to the movies. She is too fat and so cannot have any more babies. Everything Madame Fontan has ever believed about marriage and its purpose is undermined by her son's Indian (true American is the joke) wife.

The narrator has a suggestion: "Why doesn't he get a divorce?" (*WTN*, 111). How easily it trips from this tongue! It certainly fits the darker mood of *Winner Take Nothing*, which repeatedly treats the mysteriousness of sex and love. His suggestion epitomizes the modern temperament that the Fontans find so distasteful. In fact, it is a shocking question for the Catholic narrator to ask this Catholic woman. In a first reading, we might well pass over its significance, but we are less likely to do so if we are paying attention to the narrative point of view.

One of the things we slowly come to realize about the narrator is that he is married. Hemingway never actually states this or lets any of the characters do so, but the narrator's wife eventually appears and speaks in the story, without any label for her status, however. Hemingway is again experimenting with point of view. What he leaves out comes to play against what he is so deliberately putting in.

When we take the information that Hemingway delays giving us back to the beginning of the story, we find something strange about Madame Fontan's invitation to the narrator to have dinner with the Fontans. "You come and eat with us tonight" (*WTN*, 111), she says. *You* can be singular or plural, to be sure. But there is no doubt about the opening sentence of the second movement of the story: "That night I had dinner at Fontan's" (*WTN*, 111). No one accompanies the narrator to that dinner, and there are no explanations. The narrator resorts to conspicuous silence.

The dinner at the Fontans' is one to remember. On only a couple of instances do the darker tones intervene, most noticeably at the end of the dinner. Fontan, appropriately, enters the story in this section. The narrator describes him warmly, as he had earlier described Madame. With his "bright eyes" Fontan seems in every way a suitable mate for his wife; they go together most attractively. We get some amusing dialogue because Madame does not understand that the narrator is a writer. She thinks that he prints books—she can understand that kind of labor. Her not understanding that the narrator is a writer adds to the glow of the section, for the narrator enjoys these people who are obviously liking him for himself, because they share beliefs in certain values. They care nothing about his fame or critical reputation. And because of the Fontans' interest in him, the narrator assumes more importance for us in the second movement than he had in the first. It becomes clear that the purpose of this story is not just to display the Fontans.

In the second section of "Wine of Wyoming" we get our happiest view of the Fontans and their family life. The food—its abundance and quality—is both the source of good humor and symbolic of shared joy. The narrator cannot eat enough to please Madame. He has had two helpings of chicken and potatoes, two helpings of salad, three ears of sweet corn, and cucumbers—all served with a new wine "very light and clear and good." Madame encourages: "Mangez! Vous n'avez rien mangé. Eat it all. We don't save anything. Eat it all up" (*WTN*, 112). Such hospitality pleases and entertains the narrator.

He is further entertained with the Fontans' younger son, André, who obviously on the way to becoming Americanized, creates an aura of a normal family life. André wants to go to the movies. Although his voice is breaking, he can still get in for a child's price if he gives the ticket seller fifteen cents. But he wants the adult fare from his parents so that he can get the quarter changed and have a dime left for his own pleasure. As André leaves, his mother reminds him to return immediately after the show.

André is a useful character in the story not only because he enhances the sense of the Fontans as a family; he also helps to emphasize the very good time that the narrator is having. When André returns from the movie, he finds his parents and their guest still sitting at the kitchen table, talking about hunting. Madame is recalling a splendid Labor Day the Fontans had had at Clear Creek. The recollection is a moveable feast; talking about the past family pleasures is itself another kind of great pleasure. "My God, nous avons chanté" (*WTN*, 113), says Madame Fontan.

The emphasis on the quality of the Fontans' lives—they are people who know how to live—makes us curious about the quality of the life of the narrator. Especially on a rereading, one is likely to ask why the narrator is still with the Fontans so late. And Fontan gives a voice to our concern when he asks the narrator: "How do you like America?" (*WTN*, 114). The narrator's answer is not very cheering. He is in essential agreement with Madame Fontan: "It's my country, you see. So I like it, because it's my country. Mais on ne mange pas très bien. D'antan, oui, Mais maintenant, no" (*WTN*, 114). Although the cultural aspect of the statement is at first most arresting, the direction of the story makes the statement a highly personal one. The narrator does not eat as well as he used to—and maybe being in America is just a part of the decline.

Even Madame's reservations about books point towards the narrator's problems. André wants to go hunting alone, but he (like his sister-in-law) also reads a lot. The best that his mother can say for the habit is that it is better than getting into trouble. The comedy results from the fact that the narrator writes books—and presumably as a boy also read a lot of them. But Madame is insistent that too many books are bad. "Ici, c'est une maladie, les books" (*WTN*, 115). It is a good joke, but more than that. When all is over, we have to take the Fontans seriously. The Fontans raise the issue not only about the relationship between reading and living, but between writing and living.[4] Can the writing of books also take one away from the feasts that life affords? Obviously. The more the narrator reveals about himself, the more we sense that this *is* an issue for him.

And we keep getting more information about the narrator. Madame Fontan sees the plethora of books in America as symbolic of another American failure—there are too many churches in America. A comic leap, to be sure. But madame does not feel that being a Catholic is very acceptable in America—rather there is pressure to change one's religion if one happens to be a Catholic. Particularly in a sparsely populated area like Wyoming, the Fontans feel rather alone in their Catholicism. The narrator moves to check that sense of isolation. He says, "We are catholique" (*WTN*, 116). There it is—the first *we* of the story. The Fontans are not puzzled by the reference, but the reader should be.

The third section of the story commences with *I* rather than *we*: "The next afternoon I drove out to Fontan's" (*WTN*,

4. "Books are for the scholar's idle time," said Emerson. "Wine of Wyoming," while building on the contrasts between Europe and America to Europe's advantage, further demonstrated Hemingway's place in the American aesthetic that stems from transcendentalism. See C. Hugh Holman, "Hemingway and Emerson: Notes on the Continuity of an Aesthetic Tradition," *Modern Fiction Studies*, I (August, 1955), 12–16.

117). The narrator has returned to the Fontans to inform
them that he will be going away tomorrow. He explains: "To
the Crow Reservation. We go there for the opening of the
prairie-chicken season" (*WTN*, 120). He promises to come
back to visit them after the hunting before going away, for
summer is ending. There is one ambiguity of pronoun in the
invitation from the Fontans: "You come back here all right?"
(*WTN*, 120). Hemingway will delay the reader's harder delib-
erations on the pronouns until the final section of the story.

In the third section the comic is replaced with the unmistakably serious, the narrator's declaration that he did not
think Al Smith would be elected president serving as a somber transition sentence to the second half of the story. It had
taken some effort for Madame Fontan to grasp that "Schmidt
est catholique" (*WTN*, 117). Acceptance of that fact has given
her a straw of hope, for she would like to think that Smith's
election would mean an end to Prohibition and a check on
American barbarities.

There is a sharp contrast between the hard revelations of
the third section and the pleasures of the second section.
Since we are now so immensely fond of the French couple,
we are appalled to learn just how much they have suffered
because of Prohibition. They have paid $755 in fines, and
Fontan has been in jail. The fines took all of the money
Fontan had made in the mines, and Madame has had to take
in washings. Their earlier cheerfulness seems nothing short
of amazing. And still the Fontans persist in their dedication
to the good; they never sell their beer before it meets their
standards. Even as the narrator arrives, Fontan is not at
home but with the wine. "He has to watch it now to catch it
just right" (*WTN*, 118). The Fontans charge modest prices for
their products; making a lot of money is not important to
them. From their point of view, Smith's election would mean
the vindication of good sense and good health. Madame
relates some disgusting scenes that she has witnessed—
Americans who come and put whiskey in their beer, vomit
in their food, and the like. The narrator explains that they

"want to get sick, so they'll know they're drunk" (*WTN*, 119). The 1920s in America are rendered as ugly and disgusting.

Fontan arrives home "looking very old and tired from the heat" (*WTN*, 120) to hear some of his wife's lament. He cannot deny what she reports although he would rather think of the nice people who come, men who had been in France and learned there the meaning of wine. His wife has a story to tell the narrator about such a man and about his struggles with his emasculating American wife. He sneaks his beer while she is at the movies and is in bed when she returns. The story links to the life of the Fontans' married son, of course.

"We count on you" (*WTN*, 121), Fontan says as the narrator takes his leave. The reader senses as never before what the visits of this writer who has lived in France have meant to the Fontans.

In the fourth section, the story's emphasis shifts dramatically from the Fontans. In this section the narrator lets us see more of his own life than of theirs. The first word of the final section of the story is *We*. As *I* gives way to *we* in this movement there should be no doubt that the real subject of "Wine of Wyoming" is not the Fontans, but the narrator and how he perceives the Fontans, his country, and his life. The *we* remains unspecified, although the context of the story and Hemingway's placement of it in *Winner Take Nothing* indicate the *we* means the narrator and his wife. The opening paragraph is a study in fatigue and disappointment. The narrator and his wife have returned from hunting, tired and empty. They had not even seen a prairie-chicken, much less shot at one. The day is hot, and they find only a patch of shade for their noon meal. The lunch at the side of the road is a joyless affair, and they do not have any of Fontan's beer or wine to quench their thirst. Instead of the pleasure of the hunt, there had been only the meanest sort of shooting: "We came up behind a prairie-dog town and stopped the car to shoot at the prairie-dogs with the pistol. We shot two, but then stopped, because the bullets that missed glanced

off the rocks and the dirt, and sung off across the fields,
and beyond the fields there were some trees along a water
course, with a house, and we did not want to get in trouble
from stray bullets going toward the house" (*WTN*, 121).
Against this context, the narrator takes our view to the
mountains of Wyoming, as he had done in the opening
sentence of the story. But we now begin to see more than
Wyoming scenery in them. They look blue this day: "there
was only the old sun-melted snow and the ice, and from a
long way away it shone very brightly" (*WTN*, 121). The summer is ending, but it seems here that many things are ending with the summer.

Seeking "something cool and some shade" the couple
make their way to the Fontans'. It is cool there inside the
dining room, but the good Madame is alone, and she has
only two bottles of beer. The visit is brief and reflects the
tiredness of the hunters. They promise to return in the evening when Fontan will be there, informing Madame that
their summer ends in the morning. Since they will be leaving Wyoming, Madame promises a fête.

There is no fête, but through no fault of the Fontans. The
narrator is occupied with hum-drum details of preparation
for travel that afternoon. He half-excuses himself: "When it
was supper-time I was too tired to go out" (*WTN*, 121). He
goes to bed early, feeling a little guilty, but he is soon asleep.
The next morning he and his wife are again busy, "packing
and ending the summer." By two in the afternoon they are
ready to depart. Then the narrator remembers the Fontans.
Hemingway's use of dialogue at this point is arresting. The
wife speaks for the first time in the story, but Hemingway
does not here, or later, identify her in any way.

> "We must go and say good-bye to the Fontans," I said.
> "Yes, we must."
> "I'm afraid they expected us last night."
> "I suppose we could have gone."
> "I wish we'd gone." (*WTN*, 122)

We might briefly wonder about Pauline Hemingway's re-
flections on her husband's handling of point-of-view as she

typed the final version of the story before it was sent to
Maxwell Perkins. The events she could recognize as stem-
ming from her and Ernest's experiences, but she may also
have realized that the fiction was different from the events;
the events in the story had happened two years earlier, at
the time Hemingway was finishing *A Farewell to Arms*. The
ending of "Wine of Wyoming" catches much of the darkness
of the ending of that novel. Psychologically that was a dark
time for Hemingway. Pauline might have died in childbirth,
as Catherine Barkley had; and Hemingway was still close to
the guilt he felt over the divorce from Hadley. It would never
do to make Nick Adams' married life as complicated as
Hemingway's had become. The suggestive had repeatedly
served Hemingway as the right approach to Nick. His noticeable silence on the narrator's wife in "Wine of Wyoming"
may have seemed to him the proper device for suggesting to
us what Nick's marriage had become, not necessarily Hemingway's and Pauline's.

Obviously, the writer and his wife do not function together in the way that Fontan and his wife do. But there is a
shared assumption between them about the significance
of the Fontans. And so they do go to say goodbye to the
Fontans as they end their summer. This time Fontan is at
home. He looks old and tired, the narrator again notices.
Ironically, the narrator's attempt to do the right thing only
causes Fontan frustration and a sense of failure. In his disappointment of the previous evening, Fontan had drunk the
three bottles of wine he had. When his friends arrive after
all, he is determined to get some more wine so that there
can be some semblance of the fête. The narrator drives him
to the house of the married son, but they find it locked. The
locked house fits the ultimate mood of the story in its emphasis on denial. We have been inside the Fontans' house
and know the pleasure that is provided. The locked house
of the son symbolizes the future and its denial of the wine of
the good life. Hemingway renders it with a distressing final-
ity: "We stopped in front of a frame house. Fontan knocked
on the door. There was no answer. We went around to the

back. The back door was locked too. There were empty tin cans around the back door. We looked in the window. There was nobody inside. The kitchen was dirty and sloppy, but all the doors and windows were tight shut" (*WTN*, 123).

Fontan's son is at work, and the blame for the locked door is placed on the daughter-in-law. Save for Madame Fontan, there are no positive images of women in the story. American women appear basically threatening. Fontan laments: "We couldn't get the wine. My own wine that I made" (*WTN*, 124). He feels disgraced and Madame feels sad. And so the two couples say their goodbyes, with the promise that the writer and his wife might return in two years.

The story ends with the focus on the writer and his wife as they drive away from the Fontans and away from Wyoming. The tone is subdued. The narrator again notices the mountains. "It looked like Spain, but it was Wyoming" (*WTN*, 125). Kenneth G. Johnston says that the mountains symbolize lost illusions, the failure of the American dream.[5] The narrator is sure that the Fontans will not have a lot of luck and that "Schmidt won't be President either" (*WTN*, 125). Unlike Nick at the end of "The Three Day Blow" he holds nothing in reserve.

Potentially one of Hemingway's most topical, most political of stories, "Wine of Wyoming" is more than that. It does, as Johnston says, have one eye on history—and in a very large sense. Wyoming, one of the last frontier states, seems engulfed by the twentieth century. The narrator feels that the good hunting of Wyoming will last at least until the Fontans are dead, but the incident with the prairie dogs suggests that already the good hunting is doomed. For the narrator, America seems wrong, and his final line is hardly cheerful as he thinks again of his failed promise to the Fontans: "Oh, yes. . . . we ought to have gone" (*WTN*, 126).

5. Kenneth G. Johnston, "Hemingway's 'Wine of Wyoming,'" *Western American Literature*, IX (November, 1974), 159–67. Johnston belabors Madame's attitudes toward other nationalities. Hemingway is a good observer here of peasant attitudes; furthermore, Polish jokes are old, and Madame's use of them is aesthetically justified as reenforcement of her belief in quality.

Ultimately, Hemingway puts the emphasis not on America, or the Fontans, but on the narrator. The future for the narrator seems as qualified as is that of the Fontans. We might well be reminded of the Nick Adams stories in which he expressed hesitation or neutrality about prospects of returning to the States. More specifically, we might remember Nick's reservations in "Cross-Country Snow" about the American mountains: "They're too rocky. There's too much timber and they're too far away." "Wine of Wyoming" seems to be the realization of Nick's somber judgment. The story becomes even darker when we pay attention to the parallels between hunting and sexual fulfillment, a parallel that Hemingway had found useful in his early "The Doctor and the Doctor's Wife." He made the motif dominant in several stories written in the 1930s—most noticeably in "The Snows of Kilimanjaro," "The Short Happy Life of Francis Macomber," and one Nick story, "Fathers and Sons."

"Fathers and Sons," the final story of *Winner Take Nothing*, seems to clinch the case for identifying the narrator of "Wine of Wyoming" as Nick Adams. "A Day's Wait," "Wine of Wyoming," and "Fathers and Sons" form a Nick trilogy in the second half of the collection. Hemingway's arrangement of the stories in that sequence is purposeful beyond merely ending with a Nick story that would have the broadest philosophical and personal time perspective. It is worth remembering, too, that "A Day's Wait" and "Fathers and Sons" had not had previous publication. Hemingway seemed to be inviting his readers to consider the oldest story of the collection, "Wine of Wyoming," in a new light, to see it as a part of a late Nick trilogy.

In each of the stories there is a context of the familial base, although there is eroding of it in the course of the three stories. The wife is in bed with Nick at the start of "A Day's Wait." In "Wine of Wyoming" the familial model is the Fontans (whose way of life is doomed in America). The narrator's wife, although present in the second half of the story, is cast in a curious, even alarming, nebulousness. While she also feels sad for the Fontans, the story provides no evidence that she understands them. The narrator, never letting his own name into the narrative, never lets his wife's name or substitutes for it into the narrative either. He never even uses the word *wife* in connection with her. The Fontans do not appear interested in the wife, either; their care is all for Monsieur.

In "Fathers and Sons" there is no mention of wives or mothers. The story's focus is defined in the title. But surely the silence is again conspicuous. Nicholas Adams is driving through the southern countryside, with his son as his sole companion. We know—and the story emphasizes—that this is not Nick's country. Where is he going and why? This is not a short jaunt, but a long trip. Nick and his son will not even be at their destination when the day's driving is over. Nick has been driving for a long time, and the boy has fallen asleep. Sheridan Baker sensed the problem, but came up with the wrong solution. He says that Nick is a "traveling salesman."[6] But although Hemingway may have aged Nick more rapidly than we might have expected, he did not change Nick's occupation. (Nick is now thirty-eight; in "A Way You'll Never Be" he is given Hemingway's birth year, 1899. Strictly speaking, "Fathers and Sons" would be set in 1937 then, four years after its publication.) Nick, in fact, thinks about a future time when he would write about his father. The story presents Nick with a firmly held theory of writing: "If he wrote it he could get rid of it. He had gotten rid of many things by writing them" (*WTN*, 154; *NAS*, 259). Nick Adams is a writer, and the Nick Adams stories have insistently played upon this aspect of his being. Nick from his youngest years was interested in the reading and making of books. And this forms a link with both "A Day's Wait" and, very obviously, "Wine of Wyoming."

The fact remains that Hemingway tells us nothing about Nick's destination. We can, of course, carry over *Hemingway's* biography, for the germ of this story came from a trip Hemingway made with his oldest son, John Hadley. But we

6. Sheridan Baker, *Ernest Hemingway*, 39.

need not be so precise. What should concern us more is how the story works. Had Hemingway wanted to invent something, something as simple as Nick's taking his son to see an aunt or to a scout camp, he might easily have done so. But he sensed that not being precise would enhance the story— and he knew that the Nick stories and *Winner Take Nothing* had provided enough context for the reader to understand Nick's present situation. The story conveys a modern image by emphasizing motion, even uprootedness—linking it even more tightly with "Wine of Wyoming." All of the story takes place in the moving automobile. The boyhood of Nick's son is and has been very different from his own. That although there may have been some gain, there is surely also some loss—the story leaves no doubt. The son appears a shuttlecock, but a modern one. Great distances appear to separate his parents. In any event, extended travel is a big fact of his life—and of his father's.

We will recognize Nick's son as the little boy of "A Day's Wait." He is not much older, not yet twelve we learn. He addresses Nick with the same "Papa," and he obviously trusts his father. His father is a hunter (hunting is another major link between "A Day's Wait," "Wine of Wyoming," and "Fathers and Sons"). Schatz looks forward to the time when he can get a shotgun and go hunting by himself. We recall the narrator's interest in André Fontan, who is also dreaming of the time he can go hunting by himself. Nick knew exactly what that excitement is like, even as he feared that André would not have the opportunities for as much good hunting as he has had. Nick's son in "Fathers and Sons" also takes us back to "A Day's Wait" when he talks about their life in France. In "Wine of Wyoming" the narrator was a writer who had lived in France. The parallels are too many and too concentrated for us not to think that Hemingway intended the reader to recognize "A Day's Wait" and "Wine of Wyoming" as Nick stories.

Set in an automobile, "Fathers and Sons" has a subtle rhythm as the movement of the journey counterpoints the action, which occurs mainly inside Nick's head. In *Winner*

Take Nothing it contrasts with the chaos of Nick's thinking
revealed in "A Way You'll Never Be." In the context of Nick's
entire progress (which the specificity about his age would
call to our attention), the mood of the story contrasts with
"Big Two-Hearted River." There Nick wanted to avoid thinking. Here thinking is all right, even a solace—although it is
still in many ways carefully controlled thinking, not threatening because it coincides with the rhythm of the car on this
trafficless Sunday, with the rhythm of the fall season and the
late afternoon hour, and the rhythm of the son's sleeping on
the seat beside Nick. The driving and the thinking are in
every way superior to the last day's hunting in "Wine of
Wyoming." Nick's senses and his thinking here go together
perfectly. Nick may have lost many things (some that scarcely bear thinking of in the story), but he still has some treasured possessions, and—as in "Cross-Country Snow"—he
is aware that he has them at the moment. The detail that
heightens Nick's sense of pleasure and well-being is the fact
that his son is asleep at his side. The man of thirty-eight can
feel the paternal tug to the very fibers of his being that the
young man in his early twenties in "Cross-Country Snow"
could only faintly imagine.

Hemingway does not need to tell us this; he makes it
the essence of the brilliant opening paragraph. It is a long
paragraph for a Hemingway story, but it has only three sentences—two long sentences on either side of a short one.
The short sentence pronounces good what Nick is seeing.
It is autumn—we have left the distressing heat of "Wine
of Wyoming." Autumn is a time for remembering; this
place (somewhere in the South) makes Nick think of another place. Somebody's home always makes us think of our
own. There is a sense of past in the paragraph, of future
(the sleeping boy), and a satisfying present. Nick hunts the
country in his mind as he drives by. Those perspectives will
play on each other throughout the story—as they do in "Big
Two-Hearted River." Here, however, Nick is not worried
about choking off memories.

Hunting, inevitably, makes Nick think of his father, who

had taught him the art and sport. Hunting is the given of
the first story of the Nick chronology, "Indian Camp." And
it will be a link between Nick and his sleeping son. Dr.
Adams' great advantage as a hunter came from his eyesight.
"His father saw as a big-horn ram or as an eagle sees, literally" (*WTN*, 152; *NAS*, 257). Nick's memory soon provides
him with very precise, very revealing moments of his boyhood with his father. Driving through the South, he is suddenly back in northern Michigan.

Nick not only remembers episodes, but he also evaluates
his father. He shows at thirty-eight a great deal more understanding of his father than he had demonstrated in "The
Three Day Blow." Then, with great sadness, he had mainly
felt that his father had missed a lot. Now Nick sees more:
"Like all men with a faculty that surpasses human requirements, his father was very nervous. Then, too, he was sentimental, and, like most sentimental people, he was both
cruel and abused. Also, he had much bad luck, and it was
not all of it his own. He had died in a trap that he had
helped only a little to set, and they had all betrayed him in
their various ways before he died. All sentimental people
are betrayed so many times" (*WTN*, 152–53; *NAS*, 258). The
story reveals that the great hunter died by shooting himself,
although Hemingway cannot quite bring himself to state
that fact bluntly. It is an event Nick is still working through
in his thinking, something he will yet write about, but it is
noteworthy that Nick takes some of the responsibility for
the betrayal of his father. And the very context of the story
implies that Nick's sleeping son will one day judge Nick,
too—that such is the fiber of life. Hauntingly, Nick is much
like his father. Nick believes that "all men with a faculty that
surpasses human requirement" are nervous, and Nick is also
such a man. He does not have his father's eyesight, but he
has an unusually keen sense of smell, and other stories have
revealed to us Nick's nervousness.

Nick can now accept many of his father's limitations and
even view some of these limitations with humor. He is grateful to his father for excellent instruction in two things, fish-

ing and hunting. About sex, the fact that he was a medical doctor notwithstanding, his father was reticent and totally Victorian. "His father had summed up the whole matter by stating that masturbation caused blindness, insanity, and death, while a man who went with prostitutes would contract hideous venereal diseases and the thing to do was to keep your hands off people" (*WTN*, 154; *NAS*, 259). When Nick asks his father questions about sex, the brief answers reflect the doctor's discomfort about even discussing such matters. Nick learns, for instance, that mashing is "one of the most heinous of crimes" (*WTN*, 154; *NAS*, 259). But it is a crime about which Nick gets very little precise information from his father.

As the middle-aged Nick drives along, he remembers how he received his true education in sexual matters. "Fathers and Sons" is a story in which Nick deliberately seeks to let early memory enter. The story had presented three memories of events in Nick's boyhood before Nick decides to recall in detail his first sexual experiences. The experience he now deliberately seeks to recreate becomes the longest and most sustained as dramatic episode of the story's several memories. Hemingway's use of a fragment marks the deliberation and emphasizes how different the kind of experience Nick seeks here is from that he sought in "Big Two-Hearted River": "Now if he could still feel all of that trail with bare feet" (*WTN*, 155; *NAS*, 260).[7]

He can, and Nick's memory or feeling almost removes us with him from the consciousness of the present in the South. "Fathers and Sons" becomes a Michigan story. Nick's northern summers are one of the things for which he is grateful in this tribute to his father. For there had to be not only instruction in fishing and hunting, but one had to live in a place where one could do these things. There is also a satisfying completeness about the specificity of the vivid rendering of the Michigan experience, for in this last of the Nick stories we are brought close to the first Nick story.

7. *The Nick Adams Stories* fails to print the deliberate *if* of Hemingway's sentence.

Nick's remembrance is set "in the hemlock woods behind the Indian camp" (*WTN*, 155; *NAS*, 260) in which Nick's initiation into the realities of death and birth took place. Nick does not now think of these things. The reader, however, has been reminded of them, for Nick has *just* been reflecting on his father's death and his thinking has made clear that it was by suicide. "Is dying hard, Daddy?" Nick had asked in the first story. He has been learning the answer for many years.

In "Fathers and Sons" Hemingway recounts that Nick's sexual education had its foundation in the context of the Indian camp. In Nick's long memory of an afternoon's hunting and sexual adventures, the tenth Indian of "Ten Indians" ceases to be the missing Indian. The amorality exemplified by the Indian girl Trudy (earlier known as Prudie) is in sharp contrast to Dr. Adams' strict Victorian codes. Trudy does not mind how often she has sex and is as likely to initiate the act as not. Nor does she mind that her brother Billy is present. He is, after all, her brother. Furthermore, it would be just fine with Trudy if she and Nick "make a baby"—never one of Nick's desires in his adventures in the hemlock woods.

The amorality of Trudy and Nick's cavorting and Nick's disregard of his father's teaching are important aspects of Nick's long memory, but they are not all of it. Trudy's ways could never be Nick's finally. Nick becomes comically traditional when Trudy reports that another of her brothers (actually a half-brother) planned to sleep some night with Nick's sister Dorothy. He is at once outraged honor and describes to Trudy how he would kill Eddie. Trudy makes a good audience. Nick, the writer to be, seizes on the situation life has offered to him; he sees a good story. "'I'd scalp him,' he says happily." Then he betters it: "I'd scalp him and send it to his mother." When Trudy reports that Eddie's mother is dead, Nick comes up with another solution: "After I scalped him I'd throw him to the dogs" (*WTN*, 156–57; *NAS*, 263). Using his imagination to create a story is obviously a great pleasure for Nick—like sexual experience itself. Trudy, terrified for Eddie, entices Nick back to her

body, and Billy is sent to do a little hunting by himself. It is
an amusing account, but we may well sense that Nick's
memory is also partly story. Nick was in his early teens
while he sported with Trudy (obviously younger than Eddie,
who is seventeen). What fun to make him a sexual athlete!
The intercourse that Trudy and Nick have is at least their
third of the afternoon.[8]

The Indian connection is yet another link between "Fathers and Sons" and "Wine of Wyoming." The Fontans cannot approve of their son's marriage to the lazy, fat "indi-
enne." The hard working son is "crazy pour elle." When
the narrator goes to her house with Monsieur Fontan, he
reports: "Close to the window you could smell the inside
of the house. It smelled sweet and sickish like an Indian
house" (*WTN*, 123). He knows something about Indians,
and we may imagine how he reacts to Madame's indictments
of her daughter-in-law. In "Fathers and Sons" what Nick
knows about Indians is closely aligned with his especially
keen sense of smell: "So that when you go in a place where
Indians have lived you smell them gone and all the empty
pain killer bottles and the flies that buzz do not kill the
sweetgrass smell, the smoke smell and that other like a
fresh cased marten skin. Nor any jokes about them nor old
squaws take that away. Nor the sick sweet smell they get to
have. Nor what they did finally. It wasn't how they ended.
They all ended the same. Long time ago good. Now no
good" (*WTN*, 160–61; *NAS*, 266–67). "Wine of Wyoming" is
in agreement with Nick's memory and judgment. Furthermore, the "sick sweet smell" of "Fathers and Sons" quoted
above is a close echo of the "sweet and sickish smell" of
"Wine of Wyoming" and even more revealingly the review
of Nick's thought includes a translation of the words of the
narrator of "Wine of Wyoming" when he explains to Madame Fontan his ambiguous feelings towards America:
"D'antan, oui. Mais maintenant, no."

8. Jackson J. Benson underscores the parallels between hunting and sexual experience in Nick's education in *Hemingway: The Writer's Art of Self
Defense* (Minneapolis: University of Minnesota Press, 1969), 10–11.

Nick is amused with himself as he relives (and reshapes?) his adventures with Trudy. But his memory is surely accurate as it catches his postcoital sensations. Trudy's question about a baby makes Nick realize that his father's ways are not totally wrong. Sexuality cannot be lived *just* as it was with Trudy. Trudy wants Nick to stay, but Nick wants to return home for supper. Trudy then invites Nick to come back to her after supper, but he tells her flatly "No" and makes no excuses.

Evening and supper—that is the end of Nick's memory. And his thoughts go back naturally to his father, for it is now evening and supper-time as Nick drives along. He generalizes about the relationship between evening and not thinking about his father, contradicting the general principle even as he formulates it, for he has by no means finished thinking of his father. Evening has made him cease thinking of Trudy—and put his concentration right back on his father.

> Nick was all through thinking about his father. The end of the day never made him think of him. The end of the day had always belonged to Nick alone and he never felt right unless he was alone at it. His father came back to him in the fall of the year, or in the early spring when there had been jacksnipe on the prairie, or when he saw shocks of corn, or when he saw a lake, or if he ever saw a horse and buggy, or when he saw, or heard, wild geese, or in a duck blind; remembering the time an eagle dropped through the whirling snow to strike a canvas-covered decoy, rising, his wings beating, the talons caught in the canvas. His father was with him, suddenly, in deserted orchards and in new-plowed fields, in thickets, on small hills, or when going through dead grass, whenever spliting wood or hauling water, by grist mills, cider mills and dams and always with open fires. (*WTN*, 159; *NAS*, 264–65)

The lyrical tone has recaptured the rhythm of the moving automobile. What the intensely moving passage convinces us of is that Nick's father is not only *suddenly* in his mind, but continually, and that Nick loved his father very much. Although Jackson J. Benson's analysis of "Fathers and Sons" is provocative, it surely distorts when it emphasizes the story as a revelation of the mature Nick's "rancor" towards his father, as a revelation of "the bitterness and shame" that Nick still feels toward his father for not resisting Victorian sentimentality.[9]

Nor does Hemingway here become guilty of the same sentimentality that Nick faulted his father for displaying. He ends the paragraph that contains the extended passage above with a blunt sentence on Nick's relationship with his father, perhaps the saddest in the story: "After he was fifteen he had shared nothing with him" (*WTN*, 159; *NAS*, 265).

Nick has one more memory to run through his mind in this twilight zone. It is the truly shocking memory in the story, and there is no embroidery in it. It is, if anything, in the vein of confession. Nick recalls the time that he was in the woodshed, with the door open, his shotgun aimed at his father who sat on the porch reading the paper. Nick thought: "I can blow him to hell. I can kill him" (*WTN*, 159; *NAS*, 265). Nick was angry after receiving a whipping for lying about a suit of hand-me-down underwear he had refused to wear because, with his sharp sense of smell, he could still detect his father's odor in it. Nick had put the underwear in the creek and then reported that he had lost it.

This final memory of the story had nothing to do with Dr. Adams' too easy accession to his wife's demands, to his surrendering to Victorian sensibility and femininity. Rather, we see the stern, domineering father figure in the episode. Although it is extreme for anyone to draw a bead on a parent, it is not unusual for a child to wish a parent dead—particularly for the male child to wish the father dead. The thirty-eight-year-old Nick recognizes in admitting to the murderous instinct of his childhood that the buried wish is now fulfilled, ironically and sadly.

We need to pay attention to the details of that final memory. What would have been lost if Nick had received a hand-me-down shirt from his father? A great deal. The underwear

9. *Ibid.*, 13.

is a particularly horrifying object for a male just coming into his manhood—although probably on an unconscious level. Underwear becomes unspeakably intimate in this context— to have the son's sex where the father's used to be is a violation of an ancient taboo. Anthropologists and psychologists have taught us how deep-seated the concept of fathers and sons as sexual rivals is, how sons throughout the animal kingdom come to challenge the sexual dominance of the parent or are sent away before this can happen. Dr. Adams and the boy Nick are completely unaware of this level of their conflict. The writer who remembers this incident (and his reader) is another matter.

The underwear functions symbolically to force the young Nick into some awareness of his father as a sexual being. And that is typically a knowledge that comes late in a child's experience—certainly in such homes as Nick's. (Recall what a shock it is for Biff Loman in *Death of a Salesman* when as a high school senior he—for the first time really—has to consider his father as a sexual creature. And Biff's family has not been as genteel as that of Dr. and Mrs. Adams.) Death might be less traumatic.

The affinity between sex and hunting or violence has been a constant in "Fathers and Sons." Nick is out hunting at the time he is learning the way of a man with a maid. Nick's father had given him his first bit of sexual knowledge while they were hunting—and after a squirrel had bitten Nick. In Nick's imagination "mashing" is a violent concept. The ultimate result of putting your hands on yourself or other people is death, the doctor teaches. And Nick plans a violent end for Eddie Gilby as a result of the report of his sexual intentions toward Nick's sister Dorothy.

At the same time, we should not neglect the tone of many of those associations. There is a good bit of humor involved. Nick as a boy does not strike us as a monster, any more than does Nick the man. It seems to me that the key to the associations between sex and violence—and especially to Nick's confessional final memory—is to be found in Hemingway's title, "Fathers and Sons." He borrowed it from Ivan Turge-

nev's novel *Fathers and Sons*. Hemingway's concern with father-son relationships has been a constant in the Nick stories. Had he never written "Fathers and Sons," it would still
not be difficult to imagine Hemingway's being deeply moved
by Turgenev's study of the conflict between generations, a
conflict set at a time of great philosophical questioning about
the ultimate meaning of life and the shape living should
take. Hemingway was convinced that life in his time could
hardly be lived as it has been in his father's. And his fiction
leaves no doubt that he could not feel that all the changes
were gain. As "Wine of Wyoming," to take one example,
suggests, Hemingway's sympathies were often with an earlier America, an earlier Europe. Turgenev's novel is balanced
in its sympathies. The generations may not understand each
other often, but the tug of love operates powerfully in the
young and the old. At thirty-eight, Nick can look at both
generations. The emphasis of "Fathers and Sons" is not on
rancor, but on understanding and the normal (even as the
story admits how complex the normal is by presenting
Nick's memory of the underwear incident).

The structure of the story insists on the point. The black-
est of Nick's memories of his father is sharply contrasted
with the concluding dialogue of the story, a dialogue that
Nick will prize for the values it embodies—ease of conversation between father and son and a considered cherishing of
the past and family bonds. Nick has just been frankly ac-
knowledging his animality, his sense of smell that has not
done him much good: "It was good for a bird dog but it did
not help a man" (*WTN*, 160; *NAS*, 266). In this story, sex is
closely associated with the sense of smell, essential to the
primitive hunter. The juxtaposition of events underscores
the aspects of sexuality that Nick only intuits at the end of
the afternoon with Trudy. He is not a bird dog. Human
sexuality carries with it profound implications. It would be a
mark of gross sentimentality (or worse) to think of living
adult life on the level of Nick and Trudy in the summer
woods.

The twilight memory had brought Nick to this admission.

Hemingway picks up on the incitation of the memory he
had so movingly presented, describing for us how "suddenly" Nick's father would be present. Nick's reverie is
ended because suddenly Nick's son speaks. Nick cannot
help wondering how long the boy has been awake. The
story insists on the reality of the dead, the presence of the
past: "What was it like, Papa, when you were a little boy and
used to hunt with the Indians?" (*WTN*, 160; *NAS*, 266). Nick
is "startled." For the rest of the story we will be able to
evaluate, once again, Nick in the role of father.

Although Nick is startled, the son's question is a classical
one. It is the absolutely normal request—tell me about the
old days. It is also a hard question, for in talking about one's
own early past one usually goes back to what is most crucial
in the forming of the person who now is. (No other part of
Hemingway's work stresses this aspect of life in the intense
way that the Nick Adams stories do—although it is a muted
motif in *A Farewell to Arms* and *For Whom the Bell Tolls*.) Only
through frequent and patient questioning does the child
usually get any insight into this realm. Nick's son makes a
good beginning here, for he is persistent and thoughtful.

The question is dramatically forceful because Nick has
been thinking of precisely those things the boy wants to
know about. The question is also amusing, for we know
how vividly Nick remembers life with the Indians. Here, in
fact, is Nick's opportunity to talk to his son about sex. He is
truthful to his son, but he is aware that he is omitting important things: "Could you say she did first what no one
has ever done better and mention plump brown legs, flat
belly, hard little breasts, well holding arms, quick searching
tongue, the flat eyes, the good taste of mouth, then uncom-
fortably, tightly sweetly, moistly, lovely, tightly, achingly,
fully, finally, unendingly, never-endingly, never-to-endingly,
suddenly ended, the great bird flown like an owl in twilight,
only it daylight in the woods and hemlock needles stuck
against your belly" (*WTN*, 160; *NAS*, 266). Nick's son is not
yet twelve, but could many parents (even one who has lived

adult life in much freer circles than that of the doctor and
the doctor's wife) ever talk to a son on quite this level?
Would the parent then cease to be playing a parent's role?
Would he be flaunting his sexuality? Hemingway's conviction seems to be that the subject is forever a difficult one for
father and son to discuss—and maybe the lesson of the
underwear is as forceful an explanation for the reticence as
we need seek. Sons who have been awakened to their own
sexuality (a stage Nick's son is nearing) usually seek information they wish from sources other than a parent, even in
more liberal circles. It may not be amiss to recall the embarrassment in Turgenev's novel between Nikolai Kirsanov and
his liberal son Arcady when the father explains that he has
taken a mistress since the son's last visit and has a child by
her. Intellectual recognition is not the same as emotional
understanding. If Nick *had* told his son about his experience
with Trudy, we would have been shocked. Perhaps no other
aspect of life than human sexuality so powerfully symbolizes
the realization brought home to Nick on this trip—the immense difficulty of being a good father.

The son's challenge to the father seems an inevitability.
Hemingway reminds us of the pattern not only by his title,
but by having Nick tell his son that he had also asked his
father what the Indians were like. Even though we respond
warmly to the degree of communication that takes place
between father and son, we cannot really be assured that
Nick is being a better father to his son than his own was to
him. The uprootedness implied in the given of the long
automobile trip and made explicit in the final dialogue and
the absence of home as a destination caution us against that.
Nick's son is already looking forward to his own majority, to
the time when he can get a shotgun and hunt by himself.

We may doubt that Nick and his son will ever visit the
tomb of the grandfather (the grandfather whom the boy can
scarcely remember because he has grown up in France, but
whom he values as being in his family); nevertheless the
promise is there, and it leaves us with a more mellow note

than the bitter repentance in the final sentence of "Wind of Wyoming": "'Oh, yes,' I said. 'We ought to have gone.'" In "Fathers and Sons" there has been a psychic visit to that tomb. The ending of the story is edged in love and forgiveness. When asked what his father was like, Nick tells his son, "He was a great hunter and fisherman and he had wonderful eyes." And he admits to his father's superiority to himself as a hunter: "He shot very quickly and beautifully. I'd rather see him shoot than any man I ever knew" (*WTN*, 161; *NAS*, 267–68).

Nick explains to his son, not entirely convincingly, that they have not visited his grandfather's tomb because it is a long way from here, that they live in another part of the country. The explanation touches quickly on the family still in the North, on the tight delineation of the story that would exclude any consideration of wives or mothers. The boy is convinced that life holds more steadily in France and hopes that they can all be buried there. (His acceptance of death, his willingness to talk of it, deepens our conviction that this is the Schatz who faced his own death in "A Day's Wait.") But Nick will not agree. He says simply, without hesitation, "I don't want to be buried in France" (*WTN*, 122; *NAS*, 268). The line reveals his new acceptance of all of his life, of what he is and how he is—and of his father. A country is also its past. Nick knows where he belongs.

The story ends on a light touch. The boy, wanting family cohesion, suggests that they all ought to be buried in Wyoming. He thinks that he could then stop and pray at the tomb of his grandfather. Amused, Nick replies, "You're awfully practical" (*WTN*, 162; *NAS*, 268), reminding us of his own young manhood in "The Three Day Blow" when he was impressed with his own practicality. "Fathers and Sons" is the evensong to the Nick Adams stories, as "Big Two-Hearted River" was its aubade. It gives a moving conclusion to Hemingway's portrayal of his first major and most important character.

In the previous chapter we noted Hemingway's extreme

reluctance to portray Nick in romantic situations or to show him with his wife. Nick married is also Nick in retreat from what he had sought—although he comes to accept his impending fatherhood, even look forward to it. For the student of Nick's life the prospect of Nick's own fatherhood ultimately recalls the earlier stories that touches insistently on Nick's relationship with his own father, and eventually Hemingway brought that theme home full cycle.

Whereas Hemingway hesitated about showing Nick in married life, he indeed did so—but belatedly and in a very veiled way—in a group of stories near the end of his third major collection, *Winner Take Nothing*. In two of these stories, "A Day's Wait" and "Wine of Wyoming," Nick is unnamed. The first of these stories has previously been considered a Nick story, but neglected as such. However, context, verbal echoes, and Hemingway's placement of "Wine of Wyoming" near the end of *Winner Take Nothing* all suggest that it also belongs in the Nick canon. In "Wine of Wyoming" the narrator shares a brief scene with his wife (the only scene in any story portraying Nick talking with a wife), and it is loveless and flat. The trilogy of Nick stories in *Winner Take Nothing* intimates that Nick has not been as successful in marriage as he would have liked, and, given his long-standing ambiguous attitudes towards marriage, failure may have been inevitable. But even as the stories imply this failure, they also reveal that Nick has found meaning and love in marriage. Although the sleeping wife in "A Day's Wait" is probably a second wife, there is an aura of a warm family bond. Nick is still a hunter (reminding us of those values and skills that his father had given him), but he also demonstrates amply a tender, affectionate side as he deals with his sick son. In "Wine of Wyoming" we sense Nick's appreciation for the traditional and the familial—but largely through his appreciation of the French Fontans. Finally, in "Fathers and Sons," Hemingway defines Nick in a situation that reenforces the conviction that Nick's own marriage was not as solid as that of the Fontans. He is traveling with a son,

probably between Nick's current home base and the boy's
mother's base. But Nick loves the boy profoundly and
through him senses what he himself has missed because of
some of his choices. Nick was wrong in "The Three Day
Blow" when he observed that everything evens up. And
Nick is still learning that lesson. Midlife, through his own
fatherhood, he comes to greater understanding of his youth
and his parents. His love reaches forward and backwards.

Chapter Seven
Epilogue: "The Last Good Country"

In 1938 Hemingway's short stories were gathered and published with his only full-length play as *The Fifth Column and the First Forty-Nine Stories*. The first four stories in the volume were his most recent, all written after *Winner Take Nothing*. Hemingway wrote a short introduction for the collection, his only introduction for a collection of his own. He ended by saying: "I would like to live long enough to write three more novels and twenty-five more stories. I know some pretty good ones."[1] After he wrote that in 1938, Hemingway saw publication of three more novels, if we count *The Old Man and the Sea,* and he wrote a great deal more besides in the novel genre. But even as he wrote the introduction to *The Fifth Column and the First Forty-Nine Stories,* his career as a short story writer was virtually over.

His last burst of energy as a short story writer produced a group of stories from his experience in the Spanish Civil War. "Old Man at the Bridge" was one of the first forty-nine. Three stories using Chicote's bar in Madrid as a background were published in *Esquire* within four months in late 1938 and early 1939. Two other stories with the Spanish conflict as background, although one of them is set in Havana, appeared in *Cosmopolitan* in 1939. The four set in Spain were collected posthumously and published with the Spanish play as *The Fifth Column and Four Stories of the Spanish Civil War* in 1969. The fact is that with Hemingway's immersion

1. Ernest Hemingway, Preface, *The Fifth Column and the First Forty-Nine Stories* (New York: Charles Scribner's Sons, 1939), vii.

into the writing of *For Whom the Bell Tolls* his short story writing had all but ended. His readers—not doubting that he knew some more good ones—have regretted that he had not been able to write many of the final twenty-five stories he had envisioned in 1938.[2]

Some of those stories would surely have been Nick stories. Nick had been an almost constant angle of vision for Hemingway throughout his story-writing career—obviously meaning more to him than, for example, George Willard meant to Sherwood Anderson. George Willard had never spilled beyond *Winesburg, Ohio*. In *Winner Take Nothing*, by my count, five of thirteen stories are Nick stories. It is a large percentage. And if Hemingway's interest in Nick flagged after "Fathers and Sons," so did his involvement with the short story. The two famous African stories were to follow, but, in a broad sense, Hemingway's career as a short story writer parallels his interest in treating Nick.

It is a commonplace of Hemingway criticism that his heroes aged as their creator aged. Nick is in part an exception. Hemingway took him to age thirty-eight in "Fathers and Sons" to give him that poignant two-way look that forms the backbone of the story. And although Hemingway speeded Nick's age up a bit from his own to do that, he never took Nick beyond thirty-eight, and a good bit of the story is concerned with a much younger Nick. Furthermore, two stories of *Winner Take Nothing* view Nick at much earlier years—"A Way You'll Never Be" is a war story and "The Light of the World" shows Nick at seventeen, not yet on his own. Perhaps Hemingway felt that thirty-eight was as far as his picture of Nick needed to go.

Hemingway would probe the difference between youth

2. Hemingway spent the summer of 1956 working on short stories, four unfinished stories of World War II and "Get Yourself a Seeing-Eye Dog." The latter was published along with "A Man of the World," written the next year, in the centenary number of the *Atlantic Monthly* (November, 1957) under the heading "Two Tales of Darkness." The Hawthorne-like designation of these two is arresting. I call attention also to Hemingway's ordering of the tales, not in the order of composition. From first to last, Hemingway used placement of his stories to emphasize meanings.

and age on other fronts. He does so in *Across the River and Into the Trees* by giving the fifty-one year old Colonel Cantwell a very young mistress. The contrast in age in *The Old Man and the Sea* is pronounced with the friendship of Santiago and the boy Manolin. In *Islands in the Stream* Thomas Hudson is a battered artist who not only loses the women he loves, but he also loses his three sons to death before he himself is killed.

Starting with *To Have and Have Not* (1937), death becomes the fictional end for the Hemingway hero—literally for all of them except Santiago (and his is implied). At about the same time, death became the inevitable ending in the short stories. Of the four new stories of the first forty-nine, three end in the death of the major character: "The Short Happy Life of Francis Macomber," "The Capital of the World," "The Snows of Kilimanjaro." The old man of "Old Man at the Bridge" is like Santiago; his death is imminent. In each of the five short stories that came from the Spanish Civil War, death figures importantly. Death is an important factor, certainly in many of the earlier stories, but it was not the necessary end, nor was it often portrayed. And we have repeatedly seen Nick's pulling away from surrender to darkness—hard as that might sometimes be. Nick was a character whom Hemingway would never kill off.

It is not, finally, surprising that Hemingway returned to Nick after "Fathers and Sons" or that when he did so he would again be writing about a young Nick. That did not happen until 1952, and the genre that the material found expression in was novel rather than short story. The basis of the Nick story was a boyhood incident of Michigan days when Hemingway, aged sixteen, had illegally shot a blue heron and as a result was pursued by the law. It was probably one of the good stories Hemingway someday meant to tell. Returning to Nick in 1952 must have had special significance for Hemingway. The specter of wearing out had long been a frightening one, the more so since his friend Scott Fitzgerald's career had become a haunting reality for him. Hemingway's last success in public and critical estimation had been *For Whom the Bell Tolls* (1940). The disappointment over the 1950 *Across the River and Into the Trees* was well-nigh universal. Hemingway might protest critical stupidity, but he also hated to think that the best might be over. The events of his own life often found him looking backward (Pauline's death in late 1951 had been especially disturbing), and he was not always pleased with the vistas. Probably it seemed to Hemingway in 1952 that he might reverse the trend. The critical acclaim for *The Old Man and the Sea* that year was reassuring and exhilarating. But if Darrel Mansell is anywhere near the truth, the praise for the work would also have profoundly troubled Hemingway. Mansell argues from internal and external evidence that Hemingway probably wrote *The Old Man and the Sea* some fifteen years before it was published. We have no conclusive proof that Mansell is correct, and we may never have any. We do know, however, that Hemingway was disturbed by his son Gregory's reaction to the book. He wrote his father that the work was "sentimental slop."[3] No mere critic could have said anything so unsettling. Maybe the thing for the champion to do was to go back to Nick Adams, to write that Nick novel after all. He might find new vitality by making a young hero the center of his book.

Other writers in their later careers have found youthful protagonists an antidote to their own dark corners. To be sure, the blackness might win after all—as it did for Mark Twain in *The Mysterious Stranger*. That work gains much of its power from Twain's use of the two innocent boys who confront a black world. Melville's late return to fiction with *Billy Budd* and its young innocent also give us one of the major works of Melville's canon. Its posthumous publication, in fact, prepared the way for the high critical evaluation now placed on Melville's work. In the twentieth century

3. Darrel Mansell, "When Did Ernest Hemingway Write *The Old Man and the Sea?*" in Matthew S. Bruccoli and C. E. Frazer Clark, Jr. (eds.) *Fitzgerald/Hemingway Annual 1975* (Englewood, Colo.: Information Handling Services, 1975), 273–80; Carlos Baker, *Ernest Hemingway: A Life Story* (New York: Charles Scribner's Sons, 1969), 506.

the best example of the phenomenon of the late use of a young protagonist is William Faulkner. Faulkner—like Hemingway—had learned from Sherwood Anderson that the vantage point of the youthful innocent could be immensely powerful for creating great ranges of emotion. We think of Quentin Compson, Isaac McCaslin, Bayard Sartoris, Chick Mallison, and finally Lucius Priest. The variations Faulkner achieved were many, but early and late fictional focus on a young man was useful to Faulkner for keeping a broad perspective on his Yoknapatawpha County. It could not be given over entirely to the likes of a middle-aged Gavin Stevens nor even to so comfortable a figure as V. K. Ratliff. There was something renewing to be achieved through the recognition of a boy's will and a boy's way. Hemingway may have been attempting to recapture that vitality when he returned to Nick Adams at a crucial time in his own career.

The result was, however, a torso of a novel—not the final gracious gift to the public that *The Reivers* was for Faulkner. Hemingway wrote more words on Nick for that start than he had on any other piece, but he abandoned the novel, although he apparently returned to it as late as 1958.[4] The temptation as he wrote seemed to be to put too much of the blackness appropriate to an older Nick into the young Nick's mind. Faulkner bridged the distance between youth and age in *The Reivers* by having Lucius Priest narrate his experience of initiation into the world of good and evil as reminiscence to his grandchildren. Faulkner's subtitle, *A Reminiscence*, colors the meaning that we put on the tale. It is worth recalling, too, that *The Reivers* was dedicated to Faulkner's grandsons. For him, as well as for Lucius Priest, the novel was a reaching across the generations.

The point here is not to suggest that Hemingway should also have told his story in first person as reminiscence. His method with Nick had always been to present him vividly in present circumstances, although he had juxtaposed dif-

4. Philip Young and Charles W. Mann, *The Hemingway Manuscripts: An Inventory* (University Park: Pennsylvania State University Press, 1969), 47.

ferent periods of time in telling Nick stories. "Fathers and
Sons" depends on the method. "Now I Lay Me" had also
achieved force through this device. Rather, the comparison
with Faulkner serves to underscore a base of experience in
Faulkner's world that gave a coherence to his last work of
fiction that Hemingway could not find, although the Nick
Adams stories suggest how much he had desired this base.
It is as if Nick in that novel fragment had to start all over to
find his direction. Hemingway may have stopped writing
the novel because there was really no place to take Nick. He
might have solved the plot requirements of the story more
or less satisfactorily, but what was he going to do with Nick
philosophically, emotionally, spiritually? Faulkner knew
where his hero was going and what he was affirming because the hero was telling the story a lifetime later.

There seemed no good direction to take Nick. Indeed the
risk was rather that Hemingway might undo the balanced
vision of "Fathers and Sons." Perhaps he felt that when he
quit writing. He was probably also concerned about the
course of a work so unlike any other Nick piece—a work in
which plot, as opposed to situation, would be the means of
revealing Nick. The novel that Hemingway had undertaken
was in many ways like the fiction that Nick and his sister are
reading or refer to— *Swiss Family Robinson, Lorna Doone, Kid-
napped, Wuthering Heights*—almost as if Hemingway were attempting his own hand at Romance. The Nick Adams
stories had been rooted in their vivid sense of life in our
time. The direction of the 1952 work was altogether otherwise. Hemingway had reached back to a genre that has universal appeal for young readers—stories in which the young
hero escapes from the adult world and survives by his own
wits. Examples are legion. The wish to escape and survive
on one's own resources partly accounts for the appeal of
such characters as Tom Sawyer and Huck Finn—and the
Nick of stories like "The Battler" and "The Light of the
World."

The story that Hemingway set out to tell owed something
to one of his boyhood experiences, as we have observed, but

he was taking great liberties with the events. His story was tending toward either a melodramatic or an anticlimactic direction. And what he could do was hampered by the outline that he had already given Nick's career. Could the Nick who was to confront or had just confronted in stunned horror the brutality of calculated murder in "The Killers" intend to shoot a game warden's son because the son knew Nick had shot a buck out of season? How would the critics like it then? Hemingway would also, by 1952, even have to ask himself how might his son Gregory, the harsh critic of *The Old Man and the Sea*, like it. For his readers now, the personal suffering of Hemingway's last years is profoundly underscored by the fact that even as he was making a last attempt at a Nick novel, he would have no more books published in the remaining nine years of his life.

From a biographical viewpoint, the late Nick work tells us more about the Hemingway in his fifties than about Hemingway's youth. As we consider the work critically, we need always bear in mind that it was not completed and that Hemingway had not turned it over to us. If there are flaws, Hemingway critically was aware of them. Although Philip Young concluded after examining the manuscripts of Hemingway's posthumous work that Hemingway "was not a very good judge of how well or ill he was writing, day to day, over some long periods of time," it is worth emphasizing that the abandonment of wrting was also critical judgment. Hemingway never thought that the Nick novel was ready for publication. The work that was eventually published as "The Last Good Country" is the only posthumous Nick piece that received a great deal of editing. The editing was done at Scribner's, and Young testifies that the several cuts were necessary because of wordiness, too slow a pace, poor continuity, and dubious taste. He pronounced the editing skillful.[5] The title came from Mary Hemingway, who

5. Philip Young, "Posthumous Hemingway, and Nicholas Adams," in Richard Astro and Jackson J. Benson (eds.) *Hemingway in Our Time* (Corvallis: Oregon State University Press, 1974), 14; Philip Young, " 'Big World Out There': *The Nick Adams Stories*," in Jackson J. Benson (ed.), *The Short*

picked it up from her husband's narrative, and it serves splendidly. When Nick and his sister Littless (the nickname suggests a special bond) have arrived at the secret wooded place that he had found away from all corrupting civilization, Nick tells her, "This is the way forests were in the olden days. This is about the last good country there is left" (*NAS*, 89). Although the theme has other significance, the lines also suggest that for Hemingway, Nick's youth and his own might now also seem "the last good country."

Incomplete and edited as it is, there is nevertheless much to interest us in the work. There are many fine moments. We are reminded of several events in Nick's past and in Hemingway's fiction. The work touches on some of Nick's most profound hungers in evocative ways. It is a fascinating experience to consider Hemingway returning to Nick in the novel form almost two decades after the last Nick story.

In the last completed Nick story, "Fathers and Sons," there had been an implicit promise of more about Nick. Nick could not at the time recounted in the story yet write about his father, although the flow of Nick's thought and the nature of his experience with his son in the car indicate that he now seems ready to write about the doctor. The implicit promise is that there would be more for Nick to write about his family, how the family had betrayed Dr. Adams, along with the admission that Nick could not write of these things now because "there were still too many people alive" (*WTN*, 154; *NAS*, 260). "The Last Good Country" emerges as the beginning at least of the fictional exposure of the Adamses.

In the final unit of the Nick stories as we have considered

Stories of Ernest Hemingway: Critical Essays (Durham: Duke University Press, 1975), 30. On the other hand, Delbert E. Wylder argues that in his late "Two Tales of Darkness" Hemingway "managed to blend perfectly his use of naturalistic detail with his romantic sensibility in order to explore the greater depth of human experience." See his "Internal Treachery in the Last Published Short Stories of Ernest Hemingway," in *Hemingway in Our Time*, 53–65. Julian Smith also calls attention to the merit of these last stories. See his "Eyeless in Wyoming, Blind in Venice: Hemingway's Last Stories," *Connecticut Review*, IV (April, 1971), 9–15.

them—and in the second half of *Winner Take Nothing* starting with "Homage to Switzerland"—a major theme is a celebration of and a longing for the security of family tradition
and support, even while the stories indicate the stresses
placed on those very things in modern life. It again is instructive to place Hemingway's last work concerning Nick
next to Faulkner's *The Reivers*. Whereas Hemingway's attention to the theme was not as apparent as Faulkner's, both
writers had dealt with the pressures of modern life that
disrupted the old patterns and old sensibilities. They could
not always approve the changes. From one point of view, we
might say that the impetus behind both "The Last Good
Country" and *The Reivers* is nostalgia. Both works return to
the early years of the century, to the time before mechaniza-
tion was present in virtually every aspect of life. The automobile is a toy in *The Reivers*; horse flesh is still the more
interesting reality. In "The Last Good Country," when Suzy
gets a ride into the village and Packard's store with Mr.
Evans and the down-state man, they travel as everyone in
the area traveled—by horse and buggy. Both stories are
summer stories. Their young protagonists are freer than
they know. They are not burdened with school or duties.
Both plots involve deceptions to insure successful runaway
adventures. Lucius and Nick are both in potentially dangerous circumstances, but the work would not lead readers
to anticipate seriously that either hero would come to much
harm. Besides, we know Nick in later stories—and Lucius is
telling his story to his grandchildren in 1961. The difference
on this final point is more than a matter of technique. Hemingway, although he had long been challenged by the concept of the dignified old man (and created some for us),
could never define Nick as one of them—very likely because
Nick was too close to himself. Put another way, while Nick
did not remain forever young in Hemingway's eyes, he
could not take him past that emotional divide marked in
"Fathers and Sons." Nick was never to know fully in his
adult life, any more than he had in his childhood, the family

base found in the likes of the Garners and the Fontans. Nick
has tastes of it and longs for it. But, to borrow the metaphor
of "Wine of Wyoming," Schmidt was not elected president.

In *Islands in the Stream* there is the same longing for family
solidarity, but Thomas Hudson has already recognized that
his best hopes there have been far from realized. He has
lived much of his life away from his three sons. When Hudson comes to die, he dies for himself, defining himself to
himself. *Islands in the Stream* is the most family conscious of
all Hemingway's novels; indeed, most of his novels imply a
fleeing from family. But the Nick Adams stories have always
been a counterpoint to that movement—although, of course,
there are very honest tensions showing. The Nick stories
help us to understand better the meaning of the fleeing that
characterizes the novels. Although Nick had had a strongly
marked reluctance to assume the role of fatherhood, we discover the adult Nick finding great fulfillment in this role.
Nick has always pondered his own destiny in relationship to
his family, longing for what was only partly there, even as
he was also fleeing.

With Faulkner, the pattern was quite otherwise. More
rooted, once he had settled on his province of Yoknapatawpha County, Faulkner was engaged in revealing several
family lineages. Meanings were most frequently found in
the family context. The fire on the hearth burns throughout
Faulkner, giving a direction in even the worst of times. It is
the value of the hearth that makes its celebration in *The
Reivers* strike so appropriate a final note for most of Faulkner's commentators. It has been observed that for the South
the family was destiny, and Faulkner's work and career
would illustrate the point.

Paradoxically, Hemingway both fled and sought the family. The intensity of that action is behind many of the Nick
stories, and it emphasizes what the concept meant to Hemingway. It was undoubtedly one of the things that Allen Tate
as early as 1929 had sensed in Hemingway. He makes a
spirited defense of Hemingway in a letter to Donald Davidson. Tate wrote Davidson that Hemingway "is a Yankee

whom we would do well to capture." He praises Hemingway's style and his sense of immediacy. But "fugitive" Tate was impressed with Hemingway on other grounds, too. He told Davidson that Hemingway "is one of the most irreconcilable reactionaries I have ever met; he hates everything that we hate, although of course he has no historical sense to fall back on; and amusingly enough, he told me recently that when the South lost the Civil War it was a great calamity for all men, for it made the ordinary pleasures of life cost money! The man has an astonishing, if untutored insight into all these things."[6]

On the other hand, it must be admitted that Hemingway's treatment of the theme of family has increasingly seemed the microcosm for life in our time. We may well doubt if any southern writer after Faulkner will ever be able to give family the centrality that he and other southern writers before his time gave it. Hemingway's emphasis on disintegration seems to have caught the flow of the age. And Hemingway has not been given enough credit for the power of the understatement in his pictures of the disintegrations, or enough credit for showing stunned participants rather than placing blame. Edmund Wilson credits Hemingway for bringing the battle of the sexes into the open in his later work with such stories as "The Short Happy Life of Francis Macomber" and "The Snows of Kilimanjaro." There is some truth in the position. At the same time there is a great deal of the nonjudgmental in the Hemingway short stories as regards the breakup of a marriage or a relationship. One thinks of works such as "A Canary for One" and "The Sea Change." Portraits of males are not necessarily more positive than portraits of women. In the second of Hemingway's "Two Tales of Darkness," his last short fiction, we focus on a sensitive writer, physically but not spiritually blind, who hopes that his handicap will not be detrimental to the quality of the life of his companion/wife. In the Nick Adams

6. "The Agrarian Symposium: Letter of Allen Tate and Donald Davidson, 1928–1930," ed. John T. Fain and Thomas Daniel Young, *Southern Review*, VIII, new series (October, 1972), 845–82.

stories, the device that Hemingway generally used for Nick as husband is that of conspicuous silence; as we have noted he refuses to tell the reader the why and wherefore of Nick's journey in "Fathers and Sons," and he witholds identification of the wife in "Wine of Wyoming."

But in "The Last Good Country" there is plenty of blame to go around. Nick Adams never had the supportive family base that Lucius Priest had. Nick's father is an absent father, and family affairs have been turned over to an incompetent mother. The fictional presenation is not, of course, to be equated with the Hemingway family, although the fiction mirrors Hemingway's perception of his own family and reflects Hemingway's bitterness over family conflicts that had marred his summer in Michigan when he was age twenty-one. The doctor has to earn a living if his family is to have summers in Michigan and other good things, but emotionally Nick feels abandoned by his father in "The Last Good Country." We feel his absence even as in "Soldier's Home" we are distressed that Kreb's father has turned decisions (or at least their implementation) over to his wife and made thereby a kind of betrayal.

No Nick story brought Nick and his mother together to share a scene. It is as if Hemingway rejected her in "The Doctor and the Doctor's Wife" as a possible character for later stories. In "Now I Lay Me" Nick thinks about his mother and her destructive ways, but the image there is one of nightmare—a visual image of a force. There is only a single line of her speech echoing into eternity: "I've been cleaning out the basement, dear." The rejection of the mother in "The Last Good Country" is brutal. Mrs. Adams is still in that dark bedroom where we found her in "The Doctor and the Doctor's Wife." She has one of her sick headaches—she has withdrawn permanently from the realities of life. Much like Faulkner's Caroline Compson, she is inadequate, full of complaints, and often incapacitated in her room. Nick and his sister make her seem the essence of a Victorian parent who does not know what children are or what to do with them. They refer to her always as "our mother." Although Dr. and

Mrs. Adams have other children besides Nick and Littless, they too are denied embodiment in the story. We know the name of one other sister, Dorothy, from "Fathers and Sons," but never learn the names of the other children. In "The Last Good Country" the other children are off visiting friends or something—their mother is not quite sure where.

Mrs. Adams is governing from her bedroom, but not very well. She writes reports to "our father." She is obviously a pampered woman and has a girl to do the work in the house. Nick and Littless take a slight revenge on their mother when they steal the family food supplies before running off. Mrs. Adams had already made out her grocery list, and Littless seems to take pleasure in observing that Mrs. Adams will have to make a new list when she discovers that the food supply has been depleted.

But Mrs. Adams is worse than incompetent. She is a betrayer, an accomplice of the enemy—giving food and shelter to the authorities who are after Nick. We later discover that she is Nick's arch critic. Littless tells Nick: "Our mother said everything you write is morbid" (*NAS*, 90). The extremely negative portrait of Mrs. Adams touches on one of the key problems of the narrative. Hemingway has strained verisimilitude. It is not just that Grace Hall Hemingway acted very differently from Mrs. Adams when the authorities invaded Windemere, the Hemingway cottage on Walloon Lake in search of Ernest (she vigorously sent them on their way). Rather, it is hard to accept that a game warden would even think of taking over anyone's cottage to catch any boy— much less a son of a respected doctor—who had shot a buck out of season. It is even harder to accept that the deputy summoned from downstate to assist in the pursuit is also a hardened veteran from the raw West. The given will not work. Huck Finn's desire to escape Pap, on the other hand, finds the reader fully ready to accept Huck's urge for flight. And after Huck and Jim have put their lots together, the reader has no trouble in granting that the law will be in pursuit. Two against the community—they are exciting and believable odds.

In "The Last Good Country," however, Nick and Littless seem destined to receive assistance from the community, assistance of a special sort. The story takes one of its more novelistic turns when Nick and Littless begin their serious travel to Nick's last good country in the wilderness. It dips back in time to the Adams' cottage as the warden and the downstate man awaken to discover Nick has outsmarted them. Most of the Nick stories have been exclusively restricted to what Nick himself has been experiencing. Nick is not present to relish the chagrin of the two wardens, but he has an able friend present to do it for him—Suzy, the hired girl. She displays some of the indignation that would have been proper to Mrs. Adams had she been allowed on the scene. But, doubtless, Mrs. Adams needs to stay in her room so that she will not have to admit that people behave as the wardens have. Suzy, however, has a refreshing touch of the ironist about her. "How do you feel this morning?" (*NAS*, 93) she asks the downstate warden. It is obvious to her and to us how he feels after his night of drinking. Moreover, Suzy—unlike Mrs. Adams—knows the best thing to do to help Nick. She gets a ride with the wardens to the village store, not only to replenish the family's food supplies but to inform Mr. and Mrs. Packard of what has happened.

Plot creaks a great deal when Mr. Packard confronts Evans and the downstate man. Mr. Packard had lived in the raw American West for some eighteen years before he returned to northern Michigan, claiming it as his last good country also. Most assuredly, Mr. Packard has been in Wyoming at the time of the Johnson County cattle wars—the era and the setting of Owen Wister's *The Virginian*.[7] Hemingway found himself in this Nick novel merging the idyllic with the tradition of the western. In fact, Mr. Packard is delighted to feel himself again in the drama of those old days. There is some rough and not completely believable dialogue between Pack-

7. Hemingway read and admired Owen Wister, and Wister took a great interest in Hemingway's work. See Carlos Baker, *Hemingway: A Life Story*, and *Ernest Hemingway: Selected Letters, 1917–1961*, ed. Carlos Baker (New York: Charles Scribner's Sons, 1981).

ard and the wardens. Packard remembers that the down-state warden had been in Cheyenne when one Tom Horn had been hanged. He attempts to refresh the warden's memory: "You were one of the ones that framed him with promises from the association. Do you remember now? Who owned the saloon in Medicine Bow when you worked for the people that gave it to Tom? Is that why you ended up doing what you're doing? Haven't you got any memory?" (*NAS*, 102). The reader is set up for the likelihood of Packard's later recollection of the downstate warden's past, thus giving him the knowledge that will convince the warden that it will be in his best interest to call off the pursuit and prosecution of Nick. Hemingway has evoked a tradition in which the shootout is inevitably the end. Even before play against such novels as *The Virginian* becomes obvious in the talk between the wardens and Packard, the reader is set up for such a confrontation. Nick, unlike Huck Finn, will travel with his rifle. It was not, ultimately, Hemingway's kind of novel, and his recognition of this fact may have been one of the reasons he did not finish the work.

Interesting as it is to speculate on the plot developments of "The Last Good Country," that aspect should not keep us from discovering in the Packards an importance beyond their usefulness to plot.[8] The Packards are surrogate parents for Nick, even more so than the Garners are in "Ten Indians." Packard's experience in the West has a symbolic meaning in addition to being important for development of plot.

8. David R. Johnson (comparing "The Last Good Country" to Mark Twain's fragment "Huck and Tom Among the Indians") suggests that Littless' imaginings about service as a whore's assistant may be preparation for the threat of her capture and possible rape. He wonders if Hemingway ceased writing the Nick novel because Nick was in a position similar to Huck's, leaving himself contemplating an end of something not very easy to write about. See "'The Last Good Country' Again the End of Something," in Matthew J. Bruccoli and Richard Layman (eds.) *Fitzgerald / Hemingway Annual 1979*, 363–70. On the other hand, Sandra Whipple Spanier would expect a different sort of development presumably since she finds a major source for Hemingway's work to be J. D. Salinger's *The Catcher in the Rye*. Spanier's article "Hemingway's 'The Last Good Country' and *The Catcher in the Rye*: More Than a Family Resemblance," is forthcoming in *Studies in Short Fiction*, Winter, 1982.

Packard represents the active life, the life of adventure. He has felt and responded to the lure of the frontier. In the story Hemingway was writing, Nick was following Packard's example, seeking his own frontier. One of the great values of Robert O. Stephens' *Hemingway's Nonfiction: The Public Voice* is to correct the tendency to see Hemingway as the archetypal expatriate. His book emphasizes Hemingway's "essential identity as American, with American ideals and assumptions," and Stephens recognizes that Hemingway's fiction mirrors this identity.[9] Certainly the Nick stories do. In "Fathers and Sons," Nick, despite great dissatisfaction with the contemporary American scene, asserts that he wants to be buried in America when he dies. In our discussion of "Crossing the Mississippi" we saw how Nick revealed an essentially American spirit. We find it powerfully present in Nick's whole approach to experience in "Big Two-Hearted River." It is in the fiber of his recurring recoveries. Philip Young's original comparison of Nick to Huck Finn is right, from the point of view of his American representativeness alone.

That aspect of Nick's character came, if in diluted form, from his father. John Packard is its ideal embodiment. A proven man of action, Packard makes fun of the "change-of-lifers" (*NAS*, 99)—as he calls the resorters who stay at his wife's hotel and spend their time sitting on the porch in rocking chairs. He is also a man of words. His anger against the wardens works because it is controlled anger. He does not find himself in an embarrassing situation because of his speech, as Dr. Adams did in "The Doctor and the Doctor's Wife."

After Nick was fifteen, he and his father had shared nothing. Packard fills the void. He seems to understand Nick and can talk with him. Nick is pleased when Packard tells him that he has original sin. Packard had said: "You're going to have things to repent, boy . . . That's one of the best things there is. You can always decide whether to repent

---

9. Robert O. Stephens, *Hemingway's Nonfiction: The Public Voice* (Chapel Hill: The University of North Carolina Press, 1968), 151–79.

them or not. But the thing is to have them" (*NAS*, 100). And even though Nick is a great reader in "The Last Good Country," as in several other stories, he will insist on the active life. That is, of course, what has got him into trouble before this story begins. Nick's later decision to go to war in 1917 needs no further explanation. We note, too, that Packard accepts Nick's desire and destiny to be a writer in a way that Nick's family cannot. Packard advises, "You going to be a writer you ought to get in on it early. [He is referring to interest in culture.] Don't let them get too far ahead of you" (*NAS*, 100). It was probably a mistake for Hemingway to make as much of Nick as a writer as he does in "The Last Good Country." His mother's protests against his morbidity and the darkness of Nick's view tend to speak to us more of a later Nick or Hemingway. The Nick here would not be quite as stunned as he later is by the events of life. For "The Last Good Country" John Packard's understanding of Nick, however, says a great deal about the hungers of Nick's life.

Packard is especially admirable as a man because he understands and lives comfortably with his wife. Their ways are different, but they are not antagonists; no one feels managed. Mrs. Packard is interested in culture (Owen Wister's *The Virginian* is again relevant, with its tension between the hero and Molly Wood), but culture is not allowed to destroy virility. That is a part of the challenge to Nick as a writer. Mrs. Packard does not let the desire for culture destroy her womanliness, either. Like Mrs. Garner, she has a healthy sexuality. In a novelistic passage that fills us in on the background of the Packards (the kind of summary we do not get in the Nick stories), we learn that the Packards share their bedroom and bed—the reverse of the situation in "The Doctor and the Doctor's Wife." Furthermore, Mrs. Packard has a sense of humor: "'I don't mind if you call them change-of-lifers,' she told him one night in bed. 'I had the damn thing but I'm still all the woman you can handle, aren't I?'" (*NAS*, 99).

Far from being Nick's betrayer, as Mrs. Adams is, Mrs. Packard is Nick's ally. She buys illegal trout from him frequently, and he goes to see her, not his mother, before he and Littless leave. Mrs. Packard gives him the kind of advice and encouragement that Mrs. Adams would never give. Note how she allies their fates: "Buying is as bad or worse than selling," she said. "You stay away until things quiet down. Nickie, you're a good boy no matter what anybody says. You see Packard if things get bad. Come here nights if you need anything. I sleep light. Just knock on the window" (*NAS*, 77). Nick calls her "Aunt Halley." Before he leaves, she kisses him. Hemingway reports: "She smelt wonderful when she kissed him. It was the way the kitchen smelled when they were baking. Mrs. Packard smelled like her kitchen and her kitchen always smelled good" (*NAS*, 78). We never associate Mrs. Adams with food; rather Mrs. Adams seems the denial of its preparation and offering. In this regard she is also like Caroline Compson. When Mrs. Compson threatens to make breakfast for the family on that Easter Sunday that ends *The Sound and the Fury*, Dilsey says, "En who gwine eat yo messin?" Knowing the many inadequacies of Mrs. Adams and her desire to manage, we do not wonder for long about what Mrs. Adams wrote to the doctor in the letter to fill him in on developments. It is worth recalling that in "Fathers and Sons" we learn not only about Nick Adams' extraordinary sense of smell but also that there was only one person in his family that Nick liked the smell of, a sister. He avoids contact with all others in the family.

In the Nick stories the concentrated definition of issues and the sharp focus on the immediate have effectively kept the fact all but buried that Nick has siblings. We learn of a sister in "Fathers and Sons," but none is portrayed. Almost the only rendering of a brother-sister relationship in Hemingway's stories comes in "Soldier's Home." Although it is not a Nick story, its family situation is very close to that found in "The Last Good Country." The only support Krebs finds within the family comes from his "best" sister. She can speak to him with affection and elicit responses from him that show ease and pleasure—in sharp contrast to the conversations Krebs has with his mother. Kreb's sister is a tomboy, like Littless of "The Last Good Country." She boasts that she can pitch baseball better than a lot of boys and that none of the other girls is any good. Kreb's sister anticipates Littless in thinking of her brother as her beau and gets him to agree that she is his girl. He admits that he loves her. The dialogue is playful, perhaps slightly embarrassing, but it serves as a useful contrast to the strained dialogue between Krebs and his mother that reaches a crisis when he will tell his mother that he does not love her.

The "best" sister would have a much greater role in "The Last Good Country." She finds a measure of freedom in flight with Nick immensely greater than Harold Kreb's sister would ever find in baseball. She is escaping her sexuality by becoming a boy. She cuts off her hair, thereby symbolizing her close identification with Nick in a special kind of bonding. Hemingway had already seized on the unisex haircut as a motif in his unfinished novel "The Garden of Eden," begun in 1946. It is not that Hemingway has forgotten that his characters are sexual beings—rather the contrary. Littless talks about becoming Nick's common-law wife; there is talk about whores, and there is a great deal of kissing between Nick and Littless. Nick is already sexually initiated. Littless knows about Trudy, the tenth Indian, but she accepts everything about her brother nonjudgmentally. He is her tutor. Hemingway is walking a thin line, but seems intent on keeping Nick's relationship with Littless just on the right side of incest. Nick is smart enough to know the dangers, but he supposes these things would work themselves out. The reader would have the assurance of the other Nick stories that they do.

Pixie-like and spritely in action and word, Littless has the first line of the story. "'Nickie' his sister said to him. 'Listen to me, Nickie'" (*NAS*, 70). The opening line creates suspense, arresting attention for the definition of the circumstances that necessitate flight. The opening line also defines Littless' role. She will serve as Nick's conscience. There is murder in Nick's heart. Littless wants to run away with Nick not for the adventure alone, nor even primarily. She asserts,

"But you're not going to kill people and that's why I'm going with you" (*NAS*, 74). She senses that he needs her. The circumstance is not only that the law is after Nick; it is also the moment of crisis in the family, as all of the evidence points. Some support within that sphere was never more desirable.

Littless reminds us of Maria of *For Whom the Bell Tolls* more than any other of Hemingway's heroines. She cuts her hair and is quick and animal-like. Like Maria, she is the ideal comrade, willing to go wherever her guide will take her. *For Whom the Bell Tolls* ends with Maria's not being able to stay with Jordan. The novel ends, fittingly in its terms, with Robert Jordan's death. In "The Last Good Country" Hemingway plays a variation on the theme. Here Hemingway was committed not only to getting Nick out of a difficult scrape in an honorable way but to sending him into life with more understanding of himself, pointing him towards his goals as a writer with new insights. A companion, particularly one from within the family, would be a useful device for this end since Hemingway wished to explore the theme of family even after Nick's flight was under way.

Because Nick cares for Littless, worries about her comfort and health and her understanding, he gains our sympathy. She helps create the conviction that if Nick is the outsider in the Adams family, it is not because he is not potentially a good member of the family. The trouble has to be with "the others."

In "Soldier's Home" Mrs. Krebs embarrasses Krebs profoundly when she tells him that "God has some work for everyone to do" (*IOT*, 98). Krebs shocks her piety by saying that he is not in God's kingdom. In "The Last Good Country" Littless can ask her brother—partly because they are where they are—if he believes in God. Nick does not know, but he has already confessed that he has religious feelings. In the secret place, he feels strange and the way he "ought to feel in church" (*NAS*, 89). Prayers are not here a bad idea. Using Littless to ask Nick the right questions, Hemingway taps the profound religious sense of "Big Two-Hearted

River," and it is not surprising that Nick in "The Last Good Country" says his prayers before going to sleep.

Although Littless is very useful to Hemingway for plot purposes and for defining the issues of the story, he was well on the way to making her a vibrant character throughout the story. The dialogue between Littless and Nick, once they are in the woods, has an especially appealing, imaginative quality. There is often a desirable humor that checks Nick's black thought. To the extent that "The Last Good Country" is idyllic, it is so in those parts after Nick and Littless have made their hard journey and have arrived in that untainted country that only Nick knows about. There, at least for a while, Nick and his sister can have a lovely time. Curiously, their running away parallels the efforts of Frederic Henry and Catherine Barkley to make a separate peace. Littless might well be Catherine—Brontë's as well as Hemingway's—when she promises, "We'll take good care of each other and have fun. We can have a lovely time" (*NAS*, 86). Nick is, by the way, reading *Wuthering Heights* to his sister when the narrative breaks off. What Nick and Littless are leaving behind is similar to the familial cruelty of Brontë's novel. Nick and Littless promise not to be like the others and fight, agreeing that they have seen enough of fights in families.

The reward for any runaway is the experience of doing on one's own and sometimes relishing the company of someone in like circumstances. When Nick returns from fishing, we get the high point of the anticipated lovely time. Littless is reading, but she has been busy; while her brother was fishing, she had cut her hair. The playful dialogue that ensues is unparalleled in the Nick works. The pleasure of extended dialogue within the family (Nick's own) gets its fullest realization here—the closest equivalent being Nick's conversation with his son in "Fathers and Sons." Because of the dialogue, it is not difficult to understand why Nick agreed to his sister's coming. She pretends to having got Nick knockout drops from the Queen of Whores in a Sheboygan saloon called The Royal Ten Dollar Gold Piece Inn and Emporium where she worked as the whore's assistant. She feels herself "intensely desirable" to the Queen and her circle because she is "the sister or the brother of a morbid writer" and "delicately brought up" (*NAS*, 114). Littless has great fun feeling herself morally ruined—and she charts her downfall from her theft of the whiskey from the wardens. Crime, she tells her brother, comes easy for them. "We're different from the others" (*NAS*, 116). She practices being a boy, much to Nick's delight. Littless' imagination has been fired by her brother's life and their shared habit of reading. In contrast to her mother she actually reads her Bible. And she knows how fierce that book sometimes is. She imagines doing to the wardens and the Evans boy what Jael did to Sisera (Judges 4: 17–22). But Littless is also practical (Hemingway plays on the idea in various ways—linking the story to "The Three Day Blow"). Littless also plays on the amusing edge of impiety. She produces chocolate for them, chocolate she got "from my savior" (*NAS*, 117). Her savior is a box where she saves things.

The presentation and sharing of food have been important motifs in many of the Nick Adams stories. That careful attention be paid to food in "The Last Good Country" seems inevitable. After all, the work begins with Nick and Littless' prudent gathering of a good supply of food and utensils—so that Nick has to carry a pack every bit as heavy as the one that he carries in "Big Two-Hearted River." In the secret part of the forest where Nick and Littless had felt as if they were in a cathedral, Nick had comforted Littless with apples. After they have camp set up and Nick has been fishing, there is both Nick's cooking and the eating of the fish to correspond with the happy dialogue between Nick and Littless. Nick prepares the food, and Littless' chocolate is her contribution to the highly satisfactory meal.

After Nick has cleaned the utensils and Littless is asleep, he has time to savor some of the whiskey—also Littless' contribution. In the silence, alone, the whiskey adds to Nick's mellow mood. He does some serious thinking, but it is a good ending to a satisfactory day. In the morning, his sister will awaken to find another fine meal underway. The reader will remember the good morning at the opening of Part II of "Big Two-Hearted River" and can also experience something of that old feeling:

> He mixed the batter [of prepared buckwheat flour] and put the skillet on the fire, greasing it with the shortening which he spread with the cloth on the stick. First it made the skillet shine darkly, then it sizzled and spat and he greased it again and poured the batter smoothly and watched it bubble and then start to firm around the edges. He watched the rising and the forming of the texture and the gray color of the cake. He loosened it from the pan with a clean chip and flipped it and caught it, the beautiful browned side up, the other sizzling. He could feel its weight but see it growing in buoyancy in the skillet. (*NAS*, 120)

Nick and Littless' appetites increase from what they see and smell. No wonder they find the cakes "delicious with the butter melting on them and running down in the cut places with the syrup" (*NAS*, 121). They finish with prunes (very practically) and tea. Littless has the right word for the whole meal when she says that the prunes taste "like a celebration" (*NAS*, 121).

Writing to John Dos Passos while Dos Passos was at work on his *USA* trilogy, Hemingway advised his friend to be certain to get the weather in. Weather, he said, is very important. Hemingway had found it so for most of his fiction and for virtually all of the Nick Adams stories. A story like "The Last Good Country" has to be set in good weather, else there will be no idyll at all. Hemingway's beginning of the story reached back all the way to the early "Summer People," repeating its opening image. Nick is watching "the bottom of the spring where the sand rose in small spurts with the bubbling water" (*NAS*, 70). Nick watching is familiar enough. The spring is useful for the sense of the young Nick's confronting his destiny in the story, his coming to terms with his place in his family. We note, too, that from the perspective of his personal destiny and measuring, Hemingway quickly has Nick look far beyond the spring to the sources of threat and conflict. He is a man taking the measure of his position, much as we find Robert Jordan in the opening scene of *For Whom the Bell Tolls*. Jordan's life has brought him to the realization that there is a time to kill, as well as to die. His situation bears some similarities to Nick's. Perhaps "The Last Good Country" remained unfinished because Hemingway could not bring Nick to Jordan's realization about living and dying. Hemingway's novel of the Spanish Civil War appears to have been much on his mind as he worked on the Nick novel; he seems to push the similarity between Nick and Robert Jordan by identifying Nick as Nick Adams innumerable times in the first section of the story before settling into the simpler Nick. In many of the Nick stories Hemingway was very spare in using Nick's name, and, as noted, sometimes he did not let Nick's name into the story at all. Thomas Hudson is the only other Hemingway protagonist besides Robert Jordan habitually labeled by his full name. In his first two novels, both first person narratives, Hemingway's approach to his protagonist was more oblique. The heroes tended to reveal themselves only gradually. Indeed, Frederic Henry's name is hardly used at all. With both Robert Jordan and Thomas Hudson, Hemingway was committed to a more direct portrayal of the hero, to creating clear outlines of the whole man. By repeatedly using Nick's full name in "The Last Good Country," Hemingway prepares his reader for a similarly detailed presentation of Nick's young manhood—for the abundance of the novel rather than the suggestiveness of the short stories. But Hemingway's desire for a detailed picture of Nick at sixteen seems to be in conflict with the nostalgia involved in a re-creation of his own lost boyhood days. "The Last Good Country" was destined to be a summer story.

The Nick novel was not only set in the good country, but in the easy season. Even though Nick and Littless take food supplies for their trip to the woods, they will have to replenish those supplies. They can live, because it is summer, like Indians of another day—dependent upon the land. Nick's fishing for their first supper contributes to the idyllic quality of the work. The fishing is a very great pleasure. The next day will find Nick hunting. "The Last Good Country" is the only work about Nick showing him as both hunter and fisher. He is as professional about the one as about the other—showing something of the same reverence for his prey that he showed in "Big Two-Hearted River." Admiring the big trout he has killed, Nick thinks, "I've hurt him and I have to kill him" (*NAS*, 110). The scene contrasts markedly with the adventure over the big trout in "Big Two-Hearted River." But there is nothing like the attention given to the bait in the story of the returned soldier. The fishing in "The Last Good Country" points up the heightened state of Nick's nerves in the other story. As Hemingway worked on the Nick novel, he surely refished some other streams of his fiction.

It is noteworthy, however, that "The Last Good Country" establishes hunting as the more adult and more dangerous activity. The fishing is quieter. Everything goes beautifully while Nick is the fisherman, but tensions arise when he becomes a hunter, and we are reminded of Hemingway's persistent coupling of hunting and sexual maturity. The birds Nick kills are beautiful, and Nick knows they will taste lovely. But they have a kind of life that a fish does not have. For the hunter, there is a keener sense of victim. In "In Another Country" Nick himself seems to have a close identi-fication with the slain animals of the hunt. He tells us, "There was much game hanging outside the shops, and the snow powdered in the fur of the foxes and the wind blew their tails. The deer hung stiff and heavy and empty, and small birds blew in the wind and the wind turned their feathers" (*MWW*, 58; *NAS*, 168). But much has happened to Nick since he left the Michigan of his boyhood. In "The Last Good Country" the change from fishing to hunting signals the end of the idyll. Littless is disturbed by aspects of the hunting, and Nick has to reassure her. As if to check her brother's profligacy, she also asks, "Are they out of season, too?" (*NAS*, 127). And Nick's own pleasure in hunting soon gives way to fears that the Evans boy is near. Has he heard the shots? It should not be forgotten that hunting is the cause of the trouble Nick is in.[10]

It is while he is fishing that Nick reflects that he should have been an Indian. Not an Indian of the present day, of course. The Nick stories have skillfully juxtaposed the life of the Ojibways with Nick's, and there are several references to the Indians in "The Last Good Country." The scene in Mr. Packard's store when Mrs. Tabeshaw comes in to sell her baskets is an authentic touch, and it emphasizes what the present status of the Indians is. When Nick and Littless go into the woods, moccasined to be sure, they are partly playing Indian. No one can follow their trail. And Nick feels himself proficient in reading Indian signs. Both he and Littless take satisfaction in the knowledge that they are in Indian country.

The Indian theme of this late Nick work is another reminder of the Americanness of Hemingway's thought. Nick is a man who might have found greater satisfaction in another time. He would have done better, perhaps, in John Packard's day when the West was still open. (Indeed, Littless asks Nick if they will go out West, *NAS*, 117.) "The Last Good Country" raises some of the issues of Steinbeck's *The Red Pony*, especially in its concluding section, "The Leader of the People." What does the leader do after the land has been conquered, after the people have reached the western ocean? Although Edmund Wilson wrote the words in 1939, his judgment on Hemingway's work takes on a sharp edge in light of "The Last Good Country." Wilson wrote: "Going

10. Doubly so. First there is the inciting incident of the dead buck. Second, although Scribner's cut it from the narrative, Nick had made Trudy pregnant. See Young, "'Big World Out there,'" 33. In "The Last Good Country" killing and sexuality are concepts Nick has to deal with, and on both scores Hemingway reached an impasse. Nick's postcoital turning from Trudy in "Fathers and Sons" becomes more meaningful if Trudy were pregnant. The tension over sexual experience in "The Last Good Country" also cut across the mature Nick's reflection on his father's sexual instruction: "While for the other, that his father was not sound about, all the equipment you will ever have is provided and each man learns all there is for him to know about it without advice; and it makes no difference where you live."

back over Hemingway's books today, we can see clearly what an error of the politicos it was to accuse him of an indifference to society. His whole work is a criticism of society: he has responded to every pressure of the moral atmosphere of the time, as it is felt at the roots of human relations, with a sensitivity almost unrivaled."[11] Hemingway was habitually appalled by life in our time. No wonder Nick looks with longing to a simpler time as he fishes. No wonder that late in his career Hemingway turned with more than a little nostalgia to his Michigan boyhood.

But to deduce simply that Nick wanted an earlier time when he could have adventures and no consequences is to overlook much of the data. "The Last Good Country" is permeated with a longing for familial values. Perhaps these, too, might have been more readily available in an earlier time. Many of Hemingway's contemporaries peopled their fiction with protagonists who welcomed modernity, and attempted to define themselves exclusively in terms of the contemporary. Fitzgerald's Jay Gatsby is one of the most impressive of such modern types. Gatsby changes his name and his past to suit himself. He accepts the arena of his time as he goes out to fulfill his chosen destiny. In Hemingway's fiction, the pull is quite the other way—certainly with Nick Adams. Nick as a boy felt compelled to discover the contemporary world, but it inevitably led to a shudder. One could all too easily become "morbid." By the time Nick became a soldier, he had admitted the burden of his past and had taken to exploring it. Nick as the mature writer in "Fathers and Sons" indicates that such exploration has been the nature of his writing career. Nick Adams is decidedly closer in temperament (and in several circumstances) to Faulkner's Quentin Compson than he is to a character like Gatsby or, to take a character with whom he is more frequently likened, Anderson's George Willard.

Although Nick is finally a character burdened by the past

11. Edmund Wilson, "Hemingway: Gauge of Morale," *The Wound and the Bow: Seven Studies in Literature* (New York: Farrar Straus Giroux, 1980), 195.

while at the same time longing for the past, we never totally discount his capacity for living in the present. But such living was never easy, as we know from "Big Two-Hearted River." The most successful part of "The Last Good Country" is the part that shows Nick and Littless enjoying their experience in the big woods. Their problem is much like that of Robert Jordan and Maria in *For Whom the Bell Tolls*: "Nick was happy with his sister and he thought, no matter how this thing comes out we might as well have a good happy time. He had already learned there was only one day at a time and that it was always the day you were in. It would be today until it was tonight and tomorrow would be today again. This was the main thing he had learned so far" (*NAS*, 124).

Somehow, however, the ability to live in the present is better sustained with Robert and Maria, probably because they have earned their happy time. In "The Last Good Country" Nick is indeed more morbid than we have ever found him before. The glory of Nick's and Littless' excursion is broken by that morbidity. While the two are out seeking berries, a nightmarish feeling that the world pursues even into the last good country interrupts their bucolic scene. Nick is rendered incapable of continuing the berry picking. He has just finished explaining to Littless that the stream he has fished in is "the last really wild stream there is" (*NAS*, 128) save for one other, probably the Big Two-Hearted. By asking if the Evans boy, the warden's son, knows of it, Littless breaks the spell of the moment. The thinking that Nick has more or less successfully choked off takes over, and in this last of the Nick stories, the frightening aspect of the familiar Nick pattern reasserts itself. It catches up the tension between Nick the boy-man who craves experience and Nick the brooder about reality. Nick tells Littless, "I have to think about things now the rest of my life" (*NAS*, 129). With this somber feeling, Nick goes searching to see if the Evans boy is indeed in the area. Plagued by formless little fears, he becomes like some Emperor Jones wandering in the jungle.

Nick's nerves have disrupted the security of the good place he and Littless have made; at that disruption Hemingway took his leave of Nick. Hemingway could no longer believe in the hope that there were plenty of days for Nick to fish the dark swamps. Better, after all, he might have reasoned, to have his last word on Nick be "Fathers and Sons," the story with which he had ended two books— *Winner Take Nothing* and *The First Forty-Nine Stories*. In that story, thought and memory move towards benediction to a degree found in no other Nick story, and in that story Nick shows the greatest measure of understanding and forgiving his father. There, through Nick, Hemingway forgives even as he would be forgiven.

Index